PRISONS OF TH

Andrew Coyle

P

First published in Great Britain in 2022 by

Policy Press, an imprint of
Bristol University Press
University of Bristol
1–9 Old Park Hill
Bristol
BS2 8BB
UK
t: +44 (0)117 954 5940
e: bup-info@bristol.ac.uk

Details of international sales and distribution partners are available at
policy.bristoluniversitypress.co.uk

British Library Cataloguing in Publication Data
A catalogue record for this book is available from the British Library

ISBN 978-1-4473-6246-3 hardcover
ISBN 978-1-4473-6247-0 paperback
ISBN 978-1-4473-6248-7 ePub
ISBN 978-1-4473-6249-4 ePdf

Cover design: River Design
Front cover image: iStock/invizbk
Printed in the United Kingdom by CMP, Poole
Bristol University Press uses environmentally responsible print partners.

Contents

1

Introduction

This book is about the world of prisons and prisons of the world. Its linking thread is a professional journey of almost 50 years which began in Edinburgh Prison in Scotland in 1973 and has continued through the United Kingdom on to hundreds of prisons in over 70 countries. This odyssey has encompassed experiences in Asia, in remote Siberia and regions of northern China, the Himalayas and war-torn Cambodia; in South Africa in the immediate aftermath of apartheid and in prisons throughout the African continent where there were inhuman conditions and drastic shortages of resources; in the Middle East as the second intifada erupted in Israel and Palestine; in Latin America in countries recovering from civil war and dictatorships; in North America where the United States has the highest rate of imprisonment in the world; in Caribbean countries where many prisons reflected the region's brutal colonial past; and in Europe, where countries in the East were coming to terms with the collapse of the Berlin Wall and the break-up of the Soviet Union, while those in the West were struggling with their reduced sphere of influence in the world.

The book describes and analyses the way that imprisonment is used around the world through the lens of my personal experiences both as governor of what at the time were two of the most problematic prisons in the United Kingdom and also as an adviser on prisons to many governments and intergovernmental bodies as well as an expert witness in several high-profile court cases about prison issues in North America and elsewhere. I draw also on the knowledge gained from my academic work and writings as Professor of Prison Studies in King's College London.

There have been a number of occasions during my years of governing prisons when I have had to search deep inside myself, questioning whether I could justify what I was doing or was being asked to do, ostensibly for the greater good of society. At an intellectual level I would ask myself from time to time how it was that I had come to be spending my life locking up fellow human beings. At a situational level in a number of instances I have had to answer more searching questions about the terrible and at times inhuman conditions which

I presided over in prisons such as Peterhead in the north east of Scotland and Brixton in south London. Despite the fact that I continued to work in this environment and came to earn a degree of respect for the manner in which I attempted to bring some humanity into the prisons for which I was responsible, I never felt entirely at ease inside the prison environment and I rationalised that if I ever did come to be totally at ease I would know that it was time to leave.[1]

Some of the key features of introducing positive change in the demanding environments of Peterhead and Brixton are described in the first chapter of this book and these set the foundations for the international work in which I was subsequently involved. My hard-earned frontline service proved to be crucial in establishing my credibility when I later embarked on the challenge of encouraging positive change in some of the most dispiriting and inhuman prison systems in the world and in engaging with prison staff who were often highly sceptical of any suggestion that prisons should be managed decently and humanely in accordance with internationally agreed standards.

During my latter years as a prison governor and then while directing the International Centre for Prison Studies in King's College London I was called on increasingly to assist in prison reform initiatives in a range of countries. The decade of the 1990s was a period of great political and social change in Central and Eastern Europe as newly independent states moved away from the heavy hand of the Soviet years. Most of them wished to be accepted into the wider European community beginning with membership of the Council of Europe, some of them in the hope that they would in due course be able to join the European Union. My work with the Council of Europe and its Committee for the Prevention of Torture (CPT) took me to the majority of these countries, sometimes over a period of many years, as they began to shake off the terrible legacy of the Gulag and in this volume I recount a number of these experiences, notably in respect of the largest country in the region, the Russian Federation, where I was a member of the first international delegation to visit prisons in 1992 and later of the first CPT inspection team to travel to prisons east of the Urals.

Some 93 per cent of all prisoners are male and it is a truism to say that prisons are primarily male institutions, built and designed by men, to hold men, with rules and regulations designed with males in mind. The chapter on women describes a shocking example of how women prisoners in England were shackled while giving birth as a consequence of an order which insisted that all prisoners under escort in hospital should be shackled at all times. The arrangements in prisons take little account of the fact that many of the women who are there will have been subject previously to physical, sexual or emotional abuse, are more likely to suffer some form of mental illness and react to imprisonment quite differently from men. They are indeed the forgotten minority.

Countries in Asia have a wide and varied history in respect of their use of prisons. India has experimented with prisons for those serving very long sentences in what are in effect small villages where prisoners live with their families and go to work each day to support them. This, however, is not the experience of the vast majority of prisoners in India who are crammed into large overcrowded and insanitary prisons. In the prisons of China and Japan there are soul-crushing levels of discipline where every movement is monitored and punishments are harsh. I recount how Cambodia slowly recovered from its atrocious experiences under the Khmer Rouge but is now confronting major problems of overcrowding and shortage of resources. In a number of countries prisons are learning to cope with a rising proportion of elderly prisoners, many of whom require a high level of medical and social care, and I describe the immediacy of this issue in Japanese prisons.

Many of the prisons in Latin America are cesspits of violence, exacerbated by the deadly influence of all-powerful gangs; violence which seeps through the prison walls into the communities of the poor and back again. I offer examples of this from several countries in the region together with one ray of hope from the Dominican Republic. In many countries prisons and poverty go hand in hand, and I provide examples of this from a number of countries in sub-Saharan Africa where the post-colonial legacy is writ large.

In writing this book I have not set out to provide a comprehensive review of all the world's prison systems; rather, I have selected a number of countries and regions which serve to demonstrate particular key issues and dilemmas, both within the prison environment and affecting wider social and political attitudes to justice and related matters. Working in this fashion has inevitably meant that there are a number of obvious omissions. There is little discussion of the situation in south Asia where I might have made reference to the use of prisons, for example, in India, which still merits its description as the world's largest democracy, with one of the lowest rates of imprisonment in the world at 35 per 100,000 of its population yet one of the highest proportions (at almost 70 per cent) of pre-trial prisoners.[2] In a similar vein, much could have been written about the history and current use of imprisonment in Australia and New Zealand, particularly in respect of their indigenous citizens. Across the wider European region there are significant variations both in the level of use of imprisonment as well as in the nature of its delivery in a number of close neighbours, all of which are worthy of investigation and comment. We could go on, but that may be the subject of a future study.

Over the years I have been asked to provide my expertise in a variety of official capacities. I have given evidence in several court actions in North America about the excessive use of solitary confinement in Canada and the United States; one case, for example, concerning men who had spent several decades in solitary confinement in California and another of a 19-year-old woman who died by her own hand in an isolation cell in a Canadian prison while staff watched her on closed-circuit television. Both of these cases are covered in the book. Another case to which I refer concerned prisoners in Barbados where I appeared before the Inter-American Court of Human Rights in Costa Rica. In 2002 I became involved in a Middle East peace initiative when I was asked at very short notice to set up an international monitoring process for Palestinian prisoners who had assassinated an Israeli cabinet minister. This involved face-to-face meetings with Ariel Sharon and Yasser Arafat, and I describe this experience in some detail.

This is not a penal travelogue, nor is it a book of penology (the study of punishment in general and prisons in particular) or of criminology (the study of crime and criminals). It certainly raises many issues which are germane to these two academic disciplines as well as to anthropology, sociology and political science but it goes much further. Through reference to many examples of how imprisonment is used in different continents and cultures it poses questions about how governments and societies use the prison as a means of responding to a variety of underlying and fundamental social issues. The book highlights important and complex social and indeed moral issues which are deserving of considered political and public debate. A useful starting point for this discussion is an examination of why imprisonment has become the default solution for many of these wider issues. Some years ago an American professor of philosophy posed the question in this way:

> Certainly the speed with which imprisonment superseded other traditional forms of legal punishment, and has come to represent a largely unquestioned resource of the criminal justice system, might give us pause and lead us to wonder whether it is not too convenient a device for dealing with the complexities of human failure. (Kleinig, 1998: 277)

In 2020 there were 11 million men, women and children in prisons around the world, many of them detained in conditions which can only be described as inhuman and degrading as is illustrated in the following chapters. However, it is not enough merely to point the finger at these worldwide failings and to suggest that imprisonment is often used as a 19th-century solution to 21st-century problems. It is also necessary to offer an alternative vision, and this is the theme of the book's final chapter. An important conclusion which I have reached after 50 years immersed in the prisons of the world is that, while the efforts of those who seek to reform prisons from inside the system and of academics and others who study and comment on them from outside should continue and indeed be redoubled, radical change is unlikely to be achieved by these means alone. In the short and medium term real change for the wider benefit of society is more likely to come about if many of the resources which are currently invested in the demand-led imprisonment industry are substantially transferred to initiatives such as those which have come to be known as Justice Reinvestment and in the longer term through what is known as the Human Development model. Both of these are discussed in the final chapter. If this were to come about, we might achieve the vision of a former Minister of the Interior in Uganda, speaking at a conference on the subject of penal reform in Africa at the end of the 20th century: 'One day in the distant future, people will probably look back on what happens in most countries today and will wonder how we could do that to our fellow human beings in the name of justice' (Omaria, 1997: 91).

2

The world of prisons

In early 1973 I came across a newspaper advertisement inviting applications for appointment as Assistant Governor in the Scottish Prison Service. The job description caught my attention since it seemed to hold out the prospect of a career which might prove satisfying and worthwhile with the added attraction of moving into a completely new world which I suspected might challenge me on a number of fronts. (Little did I then know how true that was to be.) My application was successful and in September 1973 I reported to the Prison Service Staff Training College in Wakefield, West Yorkshire to begin training as an assistant prison governor. The subsequent stages of my prison service career in Scotland can be briefly listed:

- 1973 Assistant Governor in Edinburgh Prison
- 1976 Assistant Governor in Polmont Borstal
- 1978 Deputy Governor of the newly opened Shotts Prison
- 1981 Scottish Prison Service headquarters, responsible for security and staffing matters
- 1986 Governor of Greenock Prison
- 1988 Governor of Peterhead Prison
- 1990 Governor of Shotts Prison

In 1991 I transferred to HM Prison Service England and Wales, where I had been asked to take over as Governor of Brixton Prison and where I remained until March 1997 when I moved to the University of London.

In an earlier publication I wrote in some detail about a number of my experiences as a prison governor (Coyle, 1994). For present purposes I will limit myself to some reflections on several of the key periods of my time as Governor of Peterhead and Brixton Prisons which undoubtedly influenced my approach to my subsequent academic and international work as described in later chapters.

Peterhead

My first appointment in charge of a prison came in mid-1986 at Greenock in the west of Scotland where the prison held convicted men serving long sentences. I suspect that there are many similarities between a prison governor and the captain of a ship. The sea captain has to operate within broad parameters which have been set at a higher level but once the ship sets sail the captain has overall responsibility for everything that happens on board, and all other members of the ship's company are responsible to him or her. I remember my first morning at Greenock when all the senior staff sat in the boardroom for the traditional daily briefing. Someone raised an issue which needed a decision. There was a pause in the discussion and I realised that everyone was looking expectantly at me; I was the Governor and my decision would be final. That was a style of decision-making which I tried to change to a more collegiate model when I was at Brixton, as I shall describe shortly. In the course of my historical research into how prisons had developed I had been very taken by the work of Frederic Hill who had been the first Inspector of Prisons for Scotland in the 1840s. He regularly commented on the importance of good leadership in prisons and on my office wall I had a framed facsimile of a comment he made in one of his early reports:

> The Governor of a large prison should be a person of a strong native talent, and of great decision of character, yet of kind and affable manner; he should possess a great insight into human character, and into the various causes of crime, and the springs of action; and he should be influenced by a strong desire to promote the permanent welfare of the prisoners committed to his charge and should be possessed of powers of command, and of holding others to responsibility; and in order to maintain these effectually, it is necessary that he should be able to determine what everyone under his authority can reasonably be expected to perform, and to judge of the manner in which every duty is discharged. (General Board of Directors of Prisons in Scotland, 1841)

While making allowances for the language of an earlier age, it seemed to me that was not a bad description of how I should go about my business.

Between November 1986 and October 1987 there was a series of major riots in several large Scottish prisons during which a number of prison officers and prisoners were taken hostage or injured and the fabric of prisons was severely damaged (Scottish Prison Service,

1989). As the disturbances progressed, the Prison Service came under unbearable pressure both operationally and also externally as the media spotlight became ever more intense. In response, two specially trained national Incident Command teams were established to be deployed to manage and defuse major incidents as they sprang up and I was appointed as commander of the first of these teams. I later wrote the story of my experiences as commander of Alpha Team during this period in a book which described and analysed the skills required of a commander of an emergency or other major incident (Flin and Arbuthnot, 2002).

The most serious of the incidents took place in Peterhead Prison in October 1987. Peterhead had been opened in 1888 as the first and only convict prison in Scotland, intended to hold all men sentenced by Scottish courts to penal servitude, that is, imprisonment with hard labour. Set on a headland which jutted out into the North Sea, it had been built in that location so that the convicts could quarry the local granite that was needed to construct the great sea wall which is still in place to protect the town's harbour from the north-east gales. After the convict system was abolished in 1948 Peterhead continued to hold men who were serving long sentences and who had been assessed as not being suitable for 'training'. In effect it still had the former convict prison ethos and was for those prisoners who had been classed as troublemakers or who had an especially high profile. One view from within was that there was the Scottish Prison Service and in a parallel but separate system there was Peterhead Prison. Almost all of the prisoners came from the central belt of Scotland, most of them from Glasgow and its surrounding area, and for them being held so far from home in very harsh conditions was regarded as additional punishment. The vast majority of staff came from north east Aberdeenshire and were of fishing and farming stock, having little in common culturally with the urban prisoners from west central Scotland. I had seen the same arrangement several years previously when I had visited the troubled Attica Penitentiary in upstate New York where almost all the staff were White, recruited from the local farming community, while the vast majority of prisoners were urban young Black men from New York City at the other end of the state.[1]

Peterhead had a long history of violent incidents, including some of those which took place in the late 1980s. In the course of one in October 1987 two prison officers were taken hostage and one of them was paraded across the rooftop of a cell block in the full glare of international television and other media. This happened shortly before the annual Conservative Party conference and was front-page news for several days. The incident was brought to a conclusion when Prime Minister Thatcher ordered in a team of SAS soldiers who quickly overcame the hostage takers and released the officer who was still being held hostage.

After a further serious incident a week later in another prison the Scottish Prison Service responded by curtailing all but the most essential activities in every prison and confining all prisoners to their cells. It was well understood that this could be no more than a very temporary arrangement and there were high-level discussions about what should happen in the longer term. In addition to my responsibility for Greenock Prison at the time I was also chairman of the Scottish Prison Governors' Committee, which represented all senior prison personnel, and I had an active role in the national deliberations. Throughout these months there was intense media interest in Scottish prisons and I was frequently called on to provide comment on behalf of other governors. On occasion my views were not to the liking of senior government officials and I had to defend my position robustly. It was decided that all the prisoners who had been directly involved in any of the riots, about 60 in total, would be transferred to Peterhead in order to make it possible for all other prisons to return as quickly as possible to a normal regime.

As part of its plan to restore long-term stability to the Scottish prison system the government decided in May 1988 that there should be a radical restructuring of the top management of several major prisons, and as part of these changes I was asked at very short notice to leave Greenock Prison and to take over as Governor of Peterhead. In fact, the notice could not have been shorter. In normal circumstances a Governor would be given a reasonable period of time to conclude outstanding business in his current prison and to hand over the reins to his successor in a measured fashion. The process would then be repeated in reverse at the new prison. This was especially important if the new charge was a more senior one in a high-profile prison, as was the case on this occasion.

My transfer to Peterhead was confirmed on Wednesday 27 May 1988 and I was instructed to travel to Peterhead the following day to take command on the Friday. One of the reasons for the haste was that the government wanted to be seen to be taking decisive action and the Minister with responsibility for prisons wished to come to Peterhead on the following Monday to unveil me to the media as the new Governor. As far as leaving Greenock was concerned, the haste of my departure could not have been more precipitate. On the Wednesday I had to inform the staff and prisoners that I was leaving that very day and I had to brief my deputy, who was to take over interim charge of Greenock Prison. I had been told in confidence a few days previously about what was to happen and so had been able to have a brief discussion with my family about immediate domestic arrangements.

On Thursday I drove the 200 miles to Peterhead and checked into the local hotel. The following morning I reported to the prison to receive a briefing from the outgoing Governor before he formally handed over to me. I had known him throughout my prison career as a man much senior to me and highly respected in the service. He had been in charge of the prison for over six years, having also worked there twice previously in less senior positions. In addition, he had attended school in Peterhead when his father had also worked in the prison; so he had in effect grown up alongside many of his current staff. In normal circumstances he would have been looking forward to a planned retirement within a few years. Instead he had been given two days' notice that he was to be transferred to an administrative post and was summarily to hand over to me. We had always got on well together professionally and he received me in a generous manner in his office which he was about to vacate in my favour, although it was clear that he was quite distressed by the turn of events. After a brief discussion he proposed that the Chief Officer[2] should escort me on a tour of the prison, which I had visited several times previously during my period working in headquarters, while he cleared his desk and prepared to leave the prison. As I walked round the prison being introduced to staff it became clear to me that not only the Governor but the whole prison was in a state of shock and needed time to come to terms with what was happening.

I decided that the outgoing Governor deserved better treatment and on my return to what was still his office I told him that I was grateful for the briefing he had given me but that I now intended to return to Greenock in order to give him an opportunity to say a proper farewell in Peterhead. After he had departed I would return on the Sunday evening in time to meet the Prisons Minister and the Director of the Prison Service when they arrived in the prison on the Monday morning. I then got into my car and drove the 200 miles back to Greenock. I learned later how grateful both the outgoing Governor and the staff had been for what I had done. He had come back to the prison on the Saturday to say his farewells and to clear his desk. That evening at the end of duty all staff remained in the gate muster room, intending to see him out of the prison for the final time in a respectful manner. He had been so overcome with emotion that he refused to leave his office until all the staff had left the prison.

On Monday I returned to the prison early in the morning to take over as Governor. The weather was unusually bright and sunny for Peterhead and in due course the Minister, Lord James Douglas Hamilton, and the Director arrived. We gathered in the boardroom where the Minister addressed the assembled media and the three of us then took our places outside the main gate of the prison in front of the cameras which recorded my formal appointment.

Since the incident the previous October all the prisoners had been held in solitary confinement in their cells and a number had reacted by covering their cell walls with their excrement. On coming on duty each day staff, with the exception of the governors, donned what was euphemistically described as protective clothing, which consisted of body armour and helmets, elbow and knee pads and Perspex shields. Precisely at this juncture the High Court trial of the prisoners who had been involved in the rooftop hostage incident was set to begin in Peterhead courthouse. This was the world which I entered on 30 May 1988.

More than 30 years after that life-changing experience I can identify a series of events which epitomised the radical change which I was seeking to bring about in that prison. One of my priorities as a prison governor was always the requirement to be as open as possible with both staff and prisoners, to have regular discussions with each of these groups and to encourage them to have discussions with each other. Prisons are not democratic institutions and there have to be clear parameters which define what is and what is not open for debate and from the outset I operated on this principle at Peterhead. My first meetings were with staff, individually, in groups and through their trade union, the Prison Officers' Association (POA). The POA branch committee were supportive of the need for change. They described the stress which their members felt coming to work each day to put on their 'protective clothing', never knowing what might face them each time they opened a cell door. They wanted the regime to be more positive and less oppressive. At the same time, they had a clear message for me: 'Governor, never again must we see one of our colleagues dragged across the roof of the prison with a chain around his neck.' That was a red line which we all acknowledged.

As part of our statutory duties my deputy or I was required to visit on a daily basis each prisoner who was confined to his cell. On occasion our exchanges would be very brief, with the prisoner reluctant to engage in conversation; on other days there would be extensive discussion on any of a number of topics, more often than not about the man's current situation. At times the conversation would be civilised, if not cordial; on other days it might be less so. I remember one day standing directly in front of a prisoner, as was my custom, while he embarked on a tirade about his treatment for which, not unreasonably, he held me entirely responsible. This man had previously been involved in a serious hostage-taking in another prison during which, unknown to him, I had been Incident Commander of the team which brought the incident to a peaceful conclusion. He had been writing a letter as I entered his cell and he walked in an agitated manner from one side of the cell to another, shaking his ballpoint pen about in front of my face. I considered that I had the situation under control but suddenly I felt a firm pair of hands on my shoulders and I was lifted bodily out of the cell by the senior officer who had been standing behind me. "I'm sorry, Governor, that was just getting too tense," he explained. I had to accept the senior officer's judgement – the last thing he wanted was the Governor to be assaulted on his watch.

I also had regular sit-down joint meetings with small groups of prisoners and the staff who were directly responsible for them. In June 1989, after I had a year under my belt and decided that I had built up sufficient credibility with staff and prisoners, I invited a senior reporter from the *Glasgow Herald* newspaper to spend a day in the prison, agreeing that he could speak to any officers or prisoners who were prepared to talk to him. I had dealt with him on previous occasions and trusted him to write an even-handed report of what he observed. He sat in with us in a meeting which I was due to hold that day in one of the halls. As frequently happened, exchanges at one point became quite heated and he duly included this in his subsequent newspaper report:

> The transformation in the fortunes of the country's most notorious institution, the end of the road, the dustbin, is startling; so much so that it seems like tempting fate to describe it. While they may never come to love each other, the majority of Scotland's most difficult, dangerous and subversive prisoners are at least in dialogue with their prison officers, working out a future which will allow both sides to exist decently. Yet to spend a day in the life of Dr Coyle is to experience the emotion and the tension which still attend every hour inside the red granite fortress …
>
> As we reach a point in the open discussion where the governor momentarily appears to become heated, Chris, a young man serving eight years, interjects, 'Come on, Mr Coyle man, you're not on form today. You're losing it.' The tightly packed room

> dissolves in laughter but Dr Coyle has made his point: 'Was all the fault on our side?' David, a lifer with years of time left for a horrifying murder, snaps back, 'There were faults on both sides, but you people screwed down security so much that you suppressed all means of protest and then the lid blew.' (Freeman, 1989)

Around the same time a senior researcher in the Scottish Office[3] came to the prison to discuss with me the possibility of organising a conference in the Prison Service College on the subject of long-term imprisonment. This would be a first attempt at an analysis of the causes behind the recent spate of violence in Scottish prisons holding men serving long sentences. He proposed that those attending should include senior prison personnel and academics who specialised in prison research. I agreed to this proposal but suggested that the best place to organise such a conference would be within the walls of Peterhead Prison so that a number of the prisoners who had been involved in the violence could take part. He required some convincing about the merits of this proposal, but I later took him round the prison and we floated the idea with various prisoners and staff who responded enthusiastically. He agreed to take the proposal back to Prison Service Headquarters. To cut a long story short, the Director of the Service eventually gave approval that the conference could go ahead in the prison.

Throughout early autumn we held a series of meetings with the prisoners and staff who had expressed an interest in taking part about the main issues which should be aired at the conference. Some of the group expressed a fear that it would merely be a talking shop with no subsequent action. The researcher responded blithely, 'Better to light a candle than to curse the darkness.' Back came the quick-witted Glasgow reply, 'Not when the bastards keep blowing out the candle!' One prisoner suggested that the issue of 'conjunctive visits' should be on the agenda. When I realised that he was referring to conjugal visits, I told him that would be a bridge too far at this stage. One of the younger prisoners, who had been involved in a particularly serious hostage incident, was initially enthusiastic about taking part but later said that he wished to withdraw. I sensed that there was a hidden reason for this and I asked one of the senior staff who knew him well to have a word with him. A few days later the officer came back to me with a smile on his face. During the conference all the participants were to have lunch together in the prison sports hall. The prisoner had reluctantly explained that he would be unsure how to hold his (plastic) cutlery properly and did not want to be embarrassed. This from a man in his early 20s who had a fearsome reputation for violence. The officer had promised to give him some confidential lessons in the finer arts of dining and the problem had been resolved.

The conference duly took place over two days in late October. The Director of the Prison Service, his deputy and a number of other senior officials and personnel from other prisons attended, along with some 30 individuals including academics, psychiatrists and psychologists. Crucially, a dozen Peterhead staff and nine prisoners also took an active part. At the most basic level, the fact that the conference took place at all was a significant step forward. It concluded without incident and the prisoners involved, several of them in Category A, the highest security category, and many highly dangerous, presented themselves in a sensible light. It was also a good learning experience for several key officials from headquarters who were accustomed to dealing with the individual prisoners on paper but had never previously come face to face with any of them. A week or so later we held a review with all the Peterhead participants, staff and prisoners. There was general agreement that the experience had been worthwhile and some surprise was expressed that in general staff and prisoners had presented broadly similar opinions.

Discussion at the conference and indeed its dynamics throughout helped me to advance my own thinking about the management of prisons and the relationships between prisoners and staff. I harked back to one of my early exchanges with one of the most influential prisoners when he had remarked privately to me, "One thing we all respect you for, Governor, is that you never give up; you just keep coming back for more." Years later after he was released I kept in touch with him and got to know him quite well, but when I first arrived in Peterhead he was on 'dirty protest' with his cell covered in his excrement. I visited him every day while he was in this condition. With staff in full riot gear outside the open cell door, the two of us stood inside the filthy cell, he covered with his blanket and I in my suit and tie, frequently having a serious conversation. One day he said to me, "You know, Governor, you have taken everything away from me; I have nothing left, yet still you do not have complete power over me." I thought of the implications of what he said many times over succeeding months.

The following January I attended a conference in Glasgow on self-determination and power which was addressed by the distinguished American political philosopher Noam Chomsky. I later published an article with some reflections on the theme, inspired in part by the discussion we had that day in Peterhead. In it I wrote:

> The distinction between power over what a person does, extreme though that may be at times, and power over him or her as a person is not a semantic one. It is a distinction which I and those who live and work in similar environments must never forget in our professional lives. Those of us who exert power in a personal capacity over what other people may do must never be seduced into the illusion that this implies having power over who the other person is, with the unspoken assumption that we can somehow force the other to change as a person. To be seduced in that manner threatens our own self-determination. (Coyle, 1990: 33)

The reservation expressed by a prisoner before the conference that it would merely be 'a talking shop with no subsequent action' was not realised. On the contrary it was an important stimulus for discussions, in which I was heavily involved, which went on in the succeeding months about the future management of long-term imprisonment in Scotland. The eventual outcome was the government's policy paper *Opportunity and Responsibility* published in May 1990, which laid out a template for the future (Scottish Prison Service, 1990). This became a watershed report for the Scottish Prison Service and it provided the foundation for the development of prison management in Scotland for many years.[4] In his introduction to the report Secretary of State for Scotland Malcolm Rifkind wrote:

> The Government's penal policy is that the prison sentence should be imposed upon those, and only those, for whom an alternative disposal is not appropriate. But we are also concerned that, so far as is consistent with the deprivation of liberty and the protection of the public, the disruption to family ties and work prospects consequent on a sentence of imprisonment should be minimised, and the prisoner should be given opportunities to address his offending behaviour and to contribute positively to society on discharge. (Scottish Prison Service, 1990)

In putting that aspiration into practice it was decided that Shotts Prison in Lanarkshire, where I had been deputy governor a decade previously, would become the main high-security prison in the country and that the bulk of the high-risk prisoners in Peterhead would be transferred to Shotts. As part of that process I was to become Governor of Shotts Prison, and my tenure at Peterhead came to an end and. By the time I left Peterhead we could point to several significant improvements.

The number of men being held in solitary confinement had been reduced from 60 to less than ten. Staff no longer had to don 'protective clothing' each day and had reverted to wearing their normal uniforms. The number of assaults by prisoners on staff had fallen dramatically and the level of staff sickness absence had plummeted. Peterhead remained a very problematic prison but its darkest days were behind it. One of my last tasks before leaving was to make arrangements for the Princess Royal to visit the prison in her capacity as Patron of the Butler Trust, a charity which honours the work of prison staff. Her visit, which took place some months after I had handed over the reins to my successor, would have been unthinkable two years previously.

My personal opinion, unsolicited at the time, was that the transfer of the high-security prisoners to Shotts could have provided the opportunity to commence the closure of Peterhead Prison. The history embedded in the walls of Scotland's former convict prison meant that it should have had no place in a modern prison system. However, politically that was clearly unacceptable. Shortly after I arrived in Peterhead I had been visited by the recently elected local Member of Parliament, Alex Salmond, who had a single message for me: 'Governor, I just want you to know that Peterhead will never close.' Some staff, long-standing members of the local community, were under the mistaken impression that I had come with the secret remit of closing the prison and they probably had a word in the ear of their new MP, who stuck to this line thereafter. Over a decade later Alex Salmond, by then First Minister of Scotland, finally accepted that the former 19th-century convict prison was no longer fit for purpose but he maintained his commitment to his constituents and a new prison was built within the boundaries of the original prison, much to the chagrin of senior officials in the Prison Service. Looking out onto the North Sea as its predecessor had done and known as HM Prison Grampian, it was described officially as 'the first community facing prison in Scotland'. Today it holds almost 500 prisoners, relatively few of whom come from the north east of Scotland.

Brixton

In 1991 I transferred to HM Prison Service of England and Wales, where I had been asked to take over as Governor of Brixton Prison, at that time the most problematic prison in the country and described by some commentators as ungovernable (Lewis, 1997: 43–4).

Brixton is the oldest prison in London, having opened in 1819 as the Surrey House of Correction. Throughout most of the 20th century its main function was to hold all prisoners who were awaiting or under trial in all the Crown Courts in the south east of England, of which there were 14 in the early 1990s. They included iconic courts such as the Central Criminal Court (the Old Bailey) as well as the Court of Criminal Appeal in the Royal Courts of Justice. Brixton staff were responsible for conveying prisoners to and from each of these courts every sitting day and also for staffing the court cells and dock areas. The prison had the biggest annual budget and largest number of staff of all the country's prisons, around 200 of whom travelled each day from the prison to work in the various courts. On any one day over 200 prisoners left the prison early each morning and a similar number, but not necessarily the same prisoners, returned into the late evening. All of them had to be processed in and out of the reception area with all their personal possessions. The logistics involved were extremely complex and Brixton prided itself in getting everyone to and from the correct court on the correct day.

However, there was a terrible price to pay inside the prison for that achievement. In 1990 HM Chief Inspector of Prisons had published a coruscating report on the prison, describing it as 'a corrupting and depressing institution' (HM Chief Inspector of Prisons, 1990). Following an inspection that same year the Council of Europe CPT found that the 'pernicious combination of overcrowding, inadequate regime activities, lack of integral sanitation and poor hygiene' amounted to inhuman and degrading treatment (Council of Europe, 1991a).

In 1991 the buildings were little changed from the Victorian era. In comparative terms, Brixton fulfilled the functions of a very large prison inside the envelope of what should have been a much smaller prison. It commonly held well over 1,000 prisoners, despite only having a capacity for around 650. That meant that there were two and often three men in a cell built to hold one person. Prisoners who were not due in court would spend most of each day, perhaps months at a time, locked in small cells with no immediate access to sanitation. There was little organised activity of any kind. On my first day in charge I remember entering one of the largest accommodation blocks and being struck at how quiet it was, with not a prisoner in sight. The principal officer in charge of the wing saluted smartly and announced, "350 prisoners, Governor, all present and correct!" Accustomed as I was to the daily hustle and bustle of a long-term prison, I looked around and said, "But where are they all?" The principal officer, whom I later got to know well and to respect for his capabilities, looked at me quizzically: "They're all in their cells of course, Governor." I asked him to open some cells for me and, sure enough, in each small cell there were three prisoners, one sitting on the single chair and the other two lying on the bunk beds. Plastic chamber pots were under the bed and most of the men were smoking so the air was completely foetid.

There were two groups of prisoners who contributed to Brixton's unique profile and who were to be a particular focus of my attention. Since Brixton held all prisoners who were waiting for trial in the highest criminal courts in the land, it followed that a number of the more notorious of them were considered to be particularly dangerous, with some likely to attempt to escape. When attending court these prisoners would be taken in a special security van with armed police in escorting vehicles, and if they were thought to be very high-risk there would also be a police helicopter hovering overhead. In 1991 there were 60 of these, all in the highest security category. They were held in a small wing with additional security and higher staffing levels. Given its age and condition Brixton did not meet many of the requirements of a high-security prison. This had been recognised for some time and arrangements were in hand to re-organise the distribution of prisoners throughout the main London prisons. Crucially, Belmarsh, a new maximum security prison in south east London, was nearing completion and the 60 high-security prisoners in Brixton were due to be transferred there in early autumn 1991.

There was another disturbing aspect to what Brixton was being asked to do. In addition to holding prisoners awaiting trial it also held all men who had been remanded from any of the 37 magistrates' courts in London for psychiatric assessment. At any one time the prison would hold about 300 of these men and most of them were located in one of the main prison wings. Officially designated F Wing, it was universally known as 'Fraggle Rock' after a popular children's television show of the time. I have previously recorded details of many of my experiences in Brixton and other prisons. This is what I wrote about F Wing:

> I shall never forget the first day I walked into F Wing. Nothing in my twenty years in the prison service, not even the extremes of Peterhead, had prepared me for what I encountered. The walls were painted bottle green. Permanent semi-darkness meant that artificial lighting had to be kept on all day. The all-pervading smell was over-powering: a combination of urine, faeces and stale food. And the noise. An unrelenting cacophony of keening, wailing, shouting and banging, which went on even during the night. Each cell had a large flap in its door. These were usually open. A face, usually a black face, peered out from most of them, hungry for human contact. (Coyle, 1994: 115)

For many years, largely ignored by the rest of the Prison Service, its senior management and government ministers, Brixton had been left to do the impossible. Staff were proud of the way that they consistently achieved what they described as 'the daily miracle', yet for anyone who cared to look it was clear that there would soon have to be a day of reckoning.

The final straw: 7 July 1991

Worse was to come and on Sunday 7 July 1991 the unthinkable happened. The Governor's journal entry for the day tells the story in its barest form:

> At about 10.10am two category A prisoners charged with terrorist offences and awaiting trial at the Central Criminal Court escaped from the prison using a firearm. They were Pearce Gerard McAuley and Nessan Quinlivan. An officer was taken hostage and they gained freedom by entering the builders' yard to the south of the prison and scaling the wall which was compromised by lower structure.

The two escapers had been due to appear at the Old Bailey accused of Irish Republican Army (IRA) terrorist crimes, and along with the other high-security category A prisoners they were to have been transferred to Belmarsh Prison later in August. As they were being escorted from the prison chapel after Sunday service one of them produced a miniature gun which was fired at an officer, injuring him slightly, and escaped over the prison wall onto the main road at Brixton Hill where they were able to flag down a black taxi which took them to central London where they disappeared from sight. They were later traced to the Republic of Ireland.

Alongside the subsequent police investigation into the escape, the Home Secretary instructed the Chief Inspector of Prisons, Judge Stephen Tumim, to carry out an urgent inquiry into how the escape had been possible. I had already accepted an invitation to take over the running of the prison when the current Governor took early retirement, which had been arranged for the autumn. While the Chief Inspector's inquiry progressed I was asked to go immediately to Brixton to work alongside the Governor. It was a delicate situation for both of us and had a number of parallels with the circumstances in which I had taken over at Peterhead. Even before this incident Brixton had been under a massive cloud and the Governor had been told that his tenure was coming to a premature close. There was little doubt that, justifiably or not, he would carry much of the responsibility for this final disaster. There was uproar in Parliament and across the media with strident calls for the resignation of Home Secretary Kenneth Baker. I took up residence in a corner of the Governor's office, leaving him at his desk as he was still legally in charge, although much diminished in authority. We reached a modus vivendi in which he dealt with the aftermath of the escapes and the daily business of the prison while I concentrated on preparing for the future.

The Chief Inspector of Prisons submitted his conclusions to the Home Secretary at the end of July and on Monday 5 August the latter announced the findings of the inquiry in the House of Commons. It contained extensive criticism of security procedures and practices in the prison. As a consequence the Governor was to be relieved of his command with immediate effect and to take early retirement. Earlier that morning I had been summoned to meet the Home Secretary and Prisons Minister Angela Rumbold and had been informed of what was to be announced. The meeting was relatively brief and businesslike. The Home Secretary said, "I have only one thing to say to you, Governor: there must be no more escapes." This resonated with the instruction I had been given by the Scottish Prisons Minister when he appointed me to Peterhead: "You have one main priority, Governor: Get Peterhead Prison off the front pages of the newspapers."

When I returned to Brixton later that morning the former Governor had already departed and I was in the hot seat which I was to occupy for over five years. That afternoon I called a meeting of all staff in the largest building in the prison, the chapel, to introduce myself, to explain the events of the day and to reassure them that by working together we would ensure that the prison would recover from its current trauma. The following morning I chaired a meeting of senior managers and followed that by meeting the branch committee of the POA, who I knew would be important for my future relationships with all staff. The branch chairman was Irish and the secretary was a Scot. They told me that they had checked me out with their colleagues in the Scottish Prison Service who had advised them that I was 'all right' – high praise in trade union terms. I spent the rest of that day and the following one going round every corner of the prison, talking to staff and prisoners and, more importantly, listening to them. In the hospital wing I was approached by an older prisoner who, I later learned, had been a well-known London gangster and carried a great deal of influence with other prisoners. Quietly he informed me that he had been making inquiries among acquaintances 'north of the border' and he mentioned several names which were well known to me. They had told him that I was 'a man of my word' and he promised me he would put that message around in Brixton. To get both the POA and the prisoners on side at the outset was a promising beginning.

The challenge of governing Brixton was different in complexity to what I had experienced in other prisons. In Greenock the challenge had been to create a new environment for men serving long sentences. This had been successful and the 'Greenock way' had provided a working model for wider application. The challenge in Peterhead had been to restore a degree of humanity to the treatment of the most difficult prisoners in the Scottish prison system and in doing that to contribute to a new template for the management of long-term prisons. My task at Shotts Prison had been to demonstrate that this new template could be applied successfully on a wider scale. In each of these prisons, particularly in Peterhead, the different challenges were operationally demanding but in each case the strategy which had to be developed and implemented was relatively straightforward. The situation with Brixton was much more complicated.

On top of the problems at Brixton the Prison Service of England and Wales was still recovering from the trauma of the major riot in April 1990 at Strangeways Prison in Manchester, which had been copied in a number of other prisons, including Brixton although in a less violent fashion. The seminal report into the riots by Lord Justice Woolf had been presented to Parliament in February 1991 (Woolf, 1991),[5] and the Prison Service was in the final stages of preparing its response which was published in September of that year (Home Office, 1991). Among other changes at a senior level it had been announced that the Director General of the Prison Service was to retire. Now the circumstances surrounding the escapes from Brixton had put the Home Secretary under an intense political and media spotlight which, among other things, had led him to take the highly unusual step of seeing me personally on the morning of my appointment to emphasise that I too would be under the spotlight.

At a local level, Brixton Prison, and by extension its staff, had been found badly wanting and morale was at a very low point. In addition to the forced retirement of the Governor, several senior members of staff, including the Deputy Governor, were transferred or retired within a matter of months. This latest unforeseen disaster had happened just as the prison was about to embark on a series of major changes which would involve Brixton losing its unique role for the main courts of south east England. At the same time it would forfeit its place as a maximum security prison once the category A prisoners were transferred to the new prison at Belmarsh. Staff were also aware of the direct consequences for them since Brixton would no longer be able to justify the fact that it had the largest staff and the biggest annual budget of any prison in the country. In sum, the mythology of the unique position of Brixton was shattered and my task would be to set a new direction for the oldest prison in London.

Charting the way forward

My experience in other prisons had given me an appreciation of the key elements of strategic change in an operational setting. They would have to be implemented in concert but a number would require immediate attention. At that point Brixton was the highest-profile prison in the country, regularly on the front pages of the national press, and there was a great deal of interest inside the service as to how it would respond to the diverse challenges which it was facing. For many of my new professional colleagues I was an unknown quantity, having been recruited from Scotland, although what I had been doing there had obviously attracted a degree of professional interest. This worked to my advantage when we advertised across the service to fill senior vacancies and we were able to recruit a number of competent individuals who clearly welcomed the challenge of being part of the process of radical change.

In the medium term there also had to be a significant reduction of staff at all levels; for example, within a few months the excessive number of middle and junior governor grades was reduced by 50 per cent. There was a fine balancing act between treating everyone fairly while at the same time making sure that those who remained were best suited for what was required. This was particularly important in respect of staff who had responsibility for care of the men who had been remanded for psychiatric assessment. In the first month a local psychiatric care task force was set up, chaired by an external medical doctor, and negotiations began with local psychiatric hospitals for the transfer of some of the patient/prisoners. As was the case in most prisons at that time, the majority of staff working in what was known as the 'hospital wing', including the infamous F Wing, were prison discipline officers who had little more than basic training in health care and some of them, particularly at a senior level, were despondent at the criticism they were facing and found the prospect of fundamental change to their working practices too threatening. Some chose to take early retirement immediately while some asked to be transferred to other prisons. I selected a number of junior staff to fill the vacant senior positions and this led some others who had not been selected to offer their resignation.

Once the senior positions were filled I established a small strategic management group consisting of the heads of each department and I set about slimming down the cumbersome daily schedule of meetings, many of which served little purpose. The strategic management group met briefly each Monday morning to review the previous week and to consider what was expected to happen in the coming week. It met again later in the week for a slightly longer period to discuss matters which merited deeper consideration and also once a month to carry out its long-term planning function. The format of these meetings, especially the monthly ones, underlined the collegiate responsibility of the strategic group. In most prisons at that time almost all communications were vertical, very few were horizontal and the vertical ones were from the top down, rarely in the other direction. This meant, for example, that the heads of each department would meet personally with the Governor but would rarely meet formally with each other. The new structure meant that each member of the senior management team had the opportunity to contribute input on issues across the entire prison and to challenge other colleagues about the implications of decisions in one department for other areas of the prison. I retained ultimate authority and responsibility when it came to decisions concerning operational command, but as regards strategic decisions about the future direction of the prison I wished to encourage corporate responsibility. Within a short period of time this senior group understood and warmed to the new structure, and I encouraged each of them to set up parallel communication structures in their own departments.

Within three weeks of my arrival the newly appointed Director General of the Prison Service, Joseph Pilling, visited Brixton and I took the opportunity to explain to him my nascent plans for the prison. He responded positively and thereafter remained supportive. I also obtained his approval to take all the members of the strategic management team to the Prison Service College in Newbold Revel for five working days to hammer out a preliminary strategic plan for the prison with the help of an external facilitator. Understandably the Director General was initially quite hesitant about allowing the entire senior management team to be out of the prison for such a period, particularly in view of the continuing pressures which were on the prison both internally, externally and, crucially, politically. I explained that I had been having regular meetings with staff at all levels and was confident that the prison would continue to run smoothly in our absence. One of the senior deputies was about to retire and he would remain in charge of the prison along with a number of other middle-ranking governors who were about to be transferred elsewhere. The Director General accepted my assurances and the planning week took place at the beginning of December.

Each member of the strategic management group held discussions with staff in their departments to prepare input for the planning group. Before we went to Newbold Revel I had a meeting with all staff to explain what was to happen, and similarly on our return they were informed of the broad tenor of our discussion and conclusions. Over the winter months the strategic plan for the prison was further developed and discussed with staff groups, and by April 1992 the completed document was ready for circulation and consultation both within the prison and with various interested parties in Cleland House, the Prison Service Headquarters. The plan was entitled *Brixton 2000* to emphasise its strategic nature and the fact that it might well take that length of time to implement it fully. As the final part of this planning I was able to secure funding for the heads of each department to go away for several days with their senior staff to discuss how they would implement their section of the strategic plan.

Brixton 2000 stood the test of time. Progress was discussed at the monthly meetings of the strategic management group; as a means of articulating this new style of management the head of each department was given the title Director and they were collectively known as the Brixton Board. After some time I was fortunate to secure the services of a highly experienced pro bono non-executive Director from the private sector who attended the monthly meetings and also made himself available for one-to-one discussions with each Director. The plan was updated annually and every quarter I held a meeting with all staff to discuss progress and identify areas of concern. I had less success in having the plan acknowledged in the various prison headquarters departments. The only one which showed any interest was the one responsible for building and maintenance, where the architects and engineers were familiar with the need for long-term plans and welcomed the opportunity to have a strategy to implement.

Encouraging public scrutiny

In the early 1990s prisons were much more private places than they are now, sometimes described as the last great secretive institutions of the age. This was particularly true of Brixton, and for more than ten years virtually no press or media had been allowed into the prison. There were relatively few visitors from outside the prison service or even from inside the service; it was as though people feared contamination by association. There were two consequences of this isolation. The public, through the media, were led to believe that something terrible was going on in Brixton, and the staff, who in reality were doing their best in impossible circumstances, had the feeling that they must have something to be ashamed of. During problematic times in Scotland I had learned the value of being proactive with the media, answering questions directly with up-to-date information whenever possible, and developing positive relationships with key commentators. At an early point I invited the editor of the local weekly newspaper, the *South London Press*, to see the prison for himself and to have a discussion with me, but I knew that could only be a first step.

The next initiative was to offer a facility visit to major national daily and weekend newspapers. It required considerable effort to convince colleagues in the Home Office press department that there was more to be gained than lost by this initiative, although given the barrage of negative publicity up to this juncture their caution was understandable. I also briefed staff and prisoners in advance of the visit, telling them that the intention was to give the public an idea of what life inside the prison was actually like for both prisoners and staff. Staff were to feel free to speak to the journalists about how they went about their daily work and the challenges they faced. Prisoners were also told that they could speak to the press visitors if they wished. This was clearly a high-risk exercise. There was a danger that staff would be dismissive of all that was being done or that they would be seen to be uncaring in their attitude to the prisoners. Similarly, there was a possibility that prisoners would be highly critical about the way they were treated by staff. In the event the visit achieved all that was intended. The journalists and cameramen spent a half-day in the prison and were able to see the reality of life in an old, overcrowded, under-resourced local prison. Staff explained the manner in which they tried to carry out their duties in a humane way. Prisoners said what a terrible place Brixton was but distinguished that from the way they were treated by staff. The copy in the newspapers the following day reflected this reality. The articles documented the problems of overcrowding, of the mentally ill and of the lack of facilities. But they also demonstrated that staff were making the best of a bad job and that they showed concern in the way they dealt with prisoners.[6] A start had been made in the rehabilitation of Brixton.

In early January 1992 we turned our attention to television and I invited a *Channel 4 News* team to spend two days in the prison to prepare a ten-minute piece for their evening news programme on the changes which were taking place in the prison. Following these experiences we were approached by the editors of *Public Eye*, at that time BBC Television's prime weekly investigative programme, and agreement was reached that the presenter Peter Taylor and his team would spend two weeks in the prison recording material for two hour-long documentary programmes. These were transmitted in February with one programme focussing on the plight of the mentally disordered men in F Wing. It showed the shocking conditions in which they were being held but also demonstrated that staff were as caring as they could be in impossible circumstances. The root of the problem lay not solely in Brixton but also in a system which sent men such as these to prison.

The reaction to the programmes was as we had hoped. Shortly after transmission I received a call from one of the most senior officials in the Department of Health. "Governor," he said, "I think perhaps I should pay a visit to Brixton." "Doctor," I replied, "you should have done that a long time ago." Following his visit there was a marked improvement in contacts between the prison and local psychiatric hospitals and other community health providers and, importantly, there was enhanced provision for diverting appropriate individuals from the criminal justice system before they reached prisons such as Brixton. Another significant outcome from these media initiatives was that staff now felt that their work was much better understood and they had an added confidence as they went about their daily duties. One young officer who worked in F Wing and who had spoken impressively on camera about the difficulties of his work told me about what had happened after the programme. He explained that he had never told friends in his social circle anything about where he worked or what he did because, he admitted, he was slightly embarrassed and did not know how they would react. After the programme several people in his local pub were keen to tell him how impressed they were with what he did and the manner in which he had spoken on camera. The most satisfying outcome came later that year when the last of the remaining mentally ill prisoners were transferred into a new health care ward and F Wing, 'Fraggle Rock', finally was no more.

Over the succeeding five years Brixton was gradually rehabilitated. By 1993 the Chief Inspector of Prisons, who had previously described the prison as 'a corrupting and depressing institution' reported on its 'remarkable transformation' (HM Chief Inspector of Prisons, 1993). He attributed much of the change to 'a very positive optimistic and professional attitude amongst staff which translated into a very good rapport with inmates'. The change was summed up in a comment made to the Chief Inspector by one prisoner: 'The difference in this nick from two years ago is that staff now show us some respect' (Mills, 1993).

Comment

I had governed three prisons in Scotland, staying in each for an average of two years, which was a typical length of tenure for a governor. In each I had successfully completed the task which I had been set which was to drive through a process of radical change and I had then handed over to someone else. At Brixton an opportunity for me to move on presented itself following the positive inspection report in 1993, by which time the prison had emerged from its darkest days. Having at that point completed five years in the top rank of Governor it might have been expected that I would then take on a senior headquarters post and it was made clear that was what was expected of me. However, having for a fourth time steered through an initial change process and set a future course for a prison, I decided that I wished to remain in Brixton to oversee the subsequent stage, which was to attempt to embed the change process in the bones of the prison and in each of its departments; to demonstrate that change in a prison was not a once and for all event but rather an ongoing process which had to be regularly reviewed, adjusted and developed. There have been many past (and current) examples of prisons which appeared on the surface to have changed for the better, only to sink back at a later stage. Indeed, the Prison Service itself seemed to encourage such a vicious circle and so many times after a serious failure or a critical inspection report there would be an announcement that 'a new Governor has been appointed and change is already underway'. There was ample evidence that such a response might well lead to an immediate improvement in performance but that this would be temporary with a likelihood that any positive change which had been achieved would soon ossify and the previous failings would recur in a vicious circle. At Brixton I hoped to demonstrate that it was possible to ingrain cultural change in an institution in a lasting manner which would outlast any individual Governor or group of senior staff.

By March 1997 I concluded that I had done all that was possible to establish the principle of long-term and constantly renewing change in Brixton and I decided that I should put my hard-won experience and knowledge to use in another environment. However, within a few short years there was evidence that my optimism had been misplaced. By autumn 1999, according to media reports, it was as though the prison had reverted to the situation in which it had been in 1991.

On 4 November 1999 Paul Boateng, Home Office Minister of State with responsibility for prisons, gave a press conference inside Brixton Prison, subsequently reported the following day in the local newspaper, the *South London Press*, at which he announced: 'Brixton must in its current state be regarded as a failing institution. The level of resources it currently absorbs, while at the same time failing to deliver to acceptable standards of performance overall, can no longer be tolerated.'

Later that month Boateng invited me to a breakfast meeting to share with him my opinion about the current situation in the prison. In preparation for that meeting I wrote a paper for the Minister and the Director General of the Prison Service with my reflections on the issues at stake. In a conclusion to the paper I offered an assessment of what had happened at Brixton in the two and a half years since my departure. I wrote this not to highlight the achievements during my tenure but to draw attention to what I thought were systemic failures in the way that prison systems are managed. I might have added a further one, which is the lack of any strategic thinking on the part of government about prisons and their function. Paul Boateng lasted for less than three years as Prisons Minister, which now seems an eternity compared to the ministerial merry-go-round in recent years. This is an extract of what I wrote:

> In the light of what was recognised by many both inside and outside the Service as a significant success, one inevitably asks what has happened over the last two years to bring Brixton to a situation where the Minister can describe it as being once again 'a failing institution'. The answer to this question is of particular interest to me. I chose to remain as Governor of Brixton for almost six years with the express intention of ensuring that the changes incorporated in *Brixton 2000* became part of the fabric of the prison. It would now appear that I have not been successful in that aim. Why should this be so? There are a number of contributory factors.
>
> *The nature of the strategic changes which were happening at Brixton were not recognised by the rest of the Service*
> In the early years of the change there was a searing memory in the organisation of recent history and an enthusiasm for the changes being implemented at Brixton which were likely to make it a less problematic institution in future. As Brixton began to settle, other national priorities emerged and the willingness to provide the capital resources needed to complete the process of strategic

change at Brixton evaporated. The opportunity to use Brixton as a model for change in other similar prisons was lost.

Line management above the prison did not share ownership of Brixton 2000

The Area Manager at the time was entirely supportive of what we were doing at Brixton, but subsequent events indicate that neither he nor the Operational Director above him saw this as other than the method in which I personally chose to manage the prison. It was not regarded as a model which was important for the continuing good health of the prison nor as one to which they were committed. This meant that when a new Governor came to the prison he was not put under any pressure to continue this model of strategic management. There were no questions asked when the new Governor chose to revert to a more traditional form of management. This was noted by junior staff at the prison who saw the planning to which they had committed themselves for six years being replaced by a completely different way of working.

The lack of institutional memory

Towards the end of my time at Brixton I became increasingly aware that there was little institutional memory of things which had happened even a few years before. Instead people concentrated on the problems of the day, even if that meant continually reinventing the wheel. Within a few years, for example, many people in Brixton had forgotten that F Wing had ever existed and the tremendous progress that had been made in dealing with mentally disordered offenders. This fact is significant when one remembers that the spark for the present difficulty at Brixton was precisely this issue and it emphasises the need for the Governor and senior management team in a prison to have an understanding of the organisational memory of the prison. A change in the individual composition of the team should not be an occasion for a complete change of direction.

I include these comments here because they are relevant to any attempt at prison reform, whether in the United Kingdom or elsewhere in the world. I have discovered in many countries that positive change in prisons tends to come about in the wake of some disaster which attracts the attention of the public momentarily, or because of the presence of one charismatic individual, as we shall see in some of the following chapters. But too often that change is like a comet, shining brightly for a short period before burning itself out. That recognition has led me to conclude that, while attempts at prison reform and improvement are always to be encouraged, ultimately they can only have limited success until such time as there is a root and branch re-examination of the principles on which imprisonment is based and the manner in which it is currently (over)used in many countries at great social and fiscal expense. I shall write more about these matters in the final chapter of this book.

A short time after our meeting Minister Boateng announced his intention to market test Brixton Prison; that is, to invite tenders from commercial companies willing to take over the management of the prison. In the event no company was willing to submit such a tender; one can only assume that their cost-benefit analysis concluded that the risks were too high and the expected profit margin too narrow. The prison remained in the public sector and yet another new Governor, the third in as many years, was appointed. Over the past 20 years Brixton has had a chequered history of ups and downs under a succession of Governors. Some have been credited with 'turning the prison around' during their tenure; others have been severely criticised for failing to do so.

3

Prisons of the world

From the outset of my career in the Prison Service, in my search to understand the principles which underpinned the concept of imprisonment, I had developed an interest in prison matters beyond the United Kingdom and read all that I could find about the history of prisons and about the philosophical, social and judicial traditions on which it was based. My first direct experience of prisons outside the United Kingdom came in 1984 when I was awarded a Winston Churchill Memorial Trust Travelling Fellowship which enabled me to spend several months in North America studying the management of long-term prisoners in Canada and the United States. That circle was rounded some 30 years and over 70 countries later when I was asked to provide support to a number of legal initiatives to reduce the current excessive use of solitary confinement in prisons in those two countries. The experience of preparing expert evidence for court cases in California, British Columbia and Ontario over the last decade brought home to me forcefully that, while there had been many developments and some improvements in the treatment of prisoners since my first encounters with prisons in the region, some fundamental issues had not been resolved and may even have regressed, notwithstanding the fact that these two countries were among the most advanced in the world, prided themselves on being at the forefront of what was now described as 'corrections' management and were home to some of the world's leading academic writers and teachers on criminal justice. These two sets of different experiences decades apart could be considered as a paradigm for the circuitous and often repetitive nature of all discussions about prisons and imprisonment and form a useful introduction to the description which follows in succeeding chapters about the prisons of the world.

Canada and the United States: 35 years of progress?

In 1984 the Federal Bureau of Prisons (BOP) held around 45,000 prisoners, significantly less than the 170,500 it held in 2020.[1] Over a period of a number of years there had been a dramatic increase in levels of violence within federal prisons, with serious assaults on both staff and prisoners and in an attempt to manage this the BOP had established what it described as a control unit within its most secure penitentiary in Marion, Illinois. Given that the whole of Marion was already a maximum security institution the Bureau had to invent a new description for the even higher level of supervision in the new unit and so was born the concept of 'super maximum', usually referred to as 'supermax'. When a prisoner in the control unit was to be taken out of his cell for any reason he first had to put his hands through the grilled front of his cell to be handcuffed and he was then escorted along the unit corridor by several staff. On two separate occasions on one unforgettable day in October 1983 two prisoners who were being escorted in this way managed to collect weapons from other prisoners and attacked two escorting officers with fatal results. Following these incidents the BOP created a new ten-cell segregation unit *within* the control unit which was *within* the maximum security penitentiary.

During my visit in 1984 BOP Director Norman Carlson discussed these developments with me and he shared with me his real concern that this immediate and short-term response to the incidents in Marion might lead the Bureau down a blind alley from which there would be no return; that this might lead to the creation of similar isolation units within other prisons and that the concept of 'supermax' would be self-perpetuating. Developments over the last 40 years have proved that Carlson's fears were justified. Most US State Departments of Corrections now have at least one 'supermax' facility, and the concept has been exported to many other countries.

In 1984 the Correctional Service of Canada (CSC) was also facing serious questions about the manner in which it was holding some of its most difficult prisoners. In 1977 it had set up a Special Handling Unit in Millhaven Correctional Center in Ontario. Despite the close staff supervision, just as in Marion, violence had continued in the unit; over a short period two prisoners had been murdered and there had been several serious assaults on staff and prisoners. A report into the unit had characterised the atmosphere in the Unit as one of 'idleness, tension and fear' with a 'high degree of paranoia', and prisoners were labelled as 'particularly dangerous' (Vantour, 1984). The report noted that staff responded to these labels when dealing with the prisoners and in turn the prisoners expected violence in the unit. During my visit to Canada I had discussions with the lead author of the report, James Vantour, and he shared with me his concerns for the future management of these violent prisoners, concerns which resonated with those I had heard earlier from Norman Carlson.

Pelican Bay, California

Over the last decade I have been involved in a number of court cases challenging extreme prison conditions which have their roots in regimes which were introduced in prisons such as Marion and Millhaven many years ago. In the United States I was asked to provide an expert witness report in a class action filed in 2012 on behalf of ten men who had been held for between 11 and 22 years in the Special Housing Unit (SHU) in the 'super maximum security' Pelican Bay prison in California. The applicants were among over 1,000 men held in the SHU in small concrete cells with no windows. They were taken out of their cells to 'exercise' on their own in a small enclosed concrete yard for less than one hour a day. Meals were served through a small hatch in the cell door. There were no face-to-face visits with families and no organised activities or education. I submitted my report to the court in March 2015, and in September of that year the plaintiffs and the government of the State of California agreed a settlement which was expected to point the way to an end to indeterminate solitary confinement, the end of gang affiliation as grounds for allocation to solitary confinement and a programme designed to return those currently in solitary confinement to the general population.[2] In April 2016 Jules Lobel, one of the lead advocates in the case, organised a conference in the University of Pittsburgh attended by many of those who had contributed to the action, including academics, lawyers, psychologists and doctors as well as the then current and a former United Nations Special Rapporteur on Torture. There were moving presentations by a number of people who had spent many years in solitary confinement, including Albert Woodfox, one of the 'Angola Three', who had spent 40 years in solitary confinement in the infamous Louisiana State Penitentiary.[3] The issue remains far from resolved as the State of California has yet to deliver on the terms of the agreement. Many prisoners in California remain in solitary confinement, and in 2021 there were still ongoing appeals in this case.

Ashley Smith, Canada

The most troubling legal case in which I was involved was that of Ashley Smith. In October 2007 Ashley, aged just 19 years, died by her own hand in a federal prison in Canada. She had first been arrested at the age of 15 near her home in New Brunswick for throwing crab apples at a mail man. She was sent to an institution for children where she was very disruptive towards staff and regularly injured herself. Staff found her impossible to handle. She was taken to court on several occasions because of her behaviour and received additional custodial sentences totalling six years. As soon as she turned 18 she was transferred to the custody of the CSC, the federal prison system which holds adults serving over two years in prison. In the final year of her life Ashley was transferred 17 times between various prisons across Canada. She was held in continuous segregation, which meant that she was in an isolation cell and had no contact with anyone other than the staff who supervised her and that was usually through the hatch in her cell door. While in these conditions she continued to abuse herself and to be difficult towards staff. Several times she tried unsuccessfully to kill herself. Prison psychologists advised that her suicide attempts were 'attention seeking behaviour' and that she should not be 'rewarded' for this. On that basis senior prison management ordered staff that if they observed Ashley apparently trying to kill herself they were not to intervene. On 19 October 2007 19-year-old Ashley Smith strangled herself to death with a strip of cloth while staff watched on closed-circuit television from outside her cell. An hour elapsed before they realised that she was dead. The tragic death of this young woman and its consequences became a major political and media issue in Canada. In October 2013 I spent two days in a coroner's court in Toronto, giving evidence at the coroner's inquest into the death of Ashley Smith. The inquest was held over an extended period between September 2012 and December 2013. On 19 December 2013 the jury delivered its damning verdict; it was a hammer blow for the CSC: 'Cause of Death: Ligature strangulation and positional asphyxia. By what means: Homicide.'

The jury made 104 recommendations. The first of these was:

> That Ashley Smith's experience within the correctional system is taught as a case study to all Correctional Service of Canada management and staff at the institutional, regional and national levels. This case study can demonstrate how the correctional system and federal/provincial health care can collectively fail to provide an identified mentally ill, high risk, high needs inmate with the appropriate care, treatment and support. This case study can also demonstrate the lack of communication, cohesiveness, and accountability of a large organization such as Correctional Service of Canada.[4]

The jury also recommended that its verdict and recommendations should be made publicly available on the CSC website.

The case of Ashley Smith was not an isolated one in Canada. In 2016, 2017 and again in 2018 I submitted expert evidence in solitary confinement court actions in Ontario and British Columbia. In all of them the courts found against the prison authorities. These are salutary tales of what happens when a prison service loses its moral compass. For a number of years previously the CSC had been held up as a model of what a prison service should be, which was one of the reasons that I had gone there in 1984. It aspired, as do a number of other prison services, to be 'a world leader in corrections'. Yet young Ashley Smith killed herself in the full gaze of staff of the CSC. What seemed to me even more shocking, if that were possible, was that the week before I gave evidence the Commissioner of the Correctional Service also gave evidence in the case and claimed that the segregation cell in which this young woman died 'can be the only safe place for the mentally ill'. Astonishingly he went on to caution jurors against making any 'costly recommendations', saying that 'there is no free pocket money that we can go to to implement these things'. This implied that any identified failures in the Correctional Service could only be resolved by an increase in resources. The Commissioner appeared to be unwilling to accept that any failures might be caused by a lack of moral focus within the organisation.

Comment

These two sets of experiences, a career lifetime apart, tell a story about the changing and also the unchanging features of imprisonment. They also open up many issues for further discussion. The United States, with over two million men, women and children in prison, detained in a spectrum of federal, state and county prisons and jails, has an imprisonment rate of 639 per 100,000 of its national population; an overall rate which hides gross disparities, particularly of race.[5] Canada on the other hand has less than 40,000 prisoners and an imprisonment rate of 107 per 100,000. How is one to explain the fact that one of these countries has proportionately over six times as many people in prison as the other? In 1984 the Director of the US Federal BOP had told me of his concern that his short-term response to specific violent incidents by creating isolation units within 'supermax' facilities might lead down a self-perpetuating blind alley. His fear has been realised beyond his wildest nightmares. And in Canada, could James Vantour have ever conceived that solitary confinement imposed on a vulnerable young woman who had originally been taken into custody as a child for throwing crab apples at a mail man would lead to her death and a finding of homicide against the correctional authorities?

These were two examples of the unanswered conundrums which led me inexorably to a detailed academic study of the nature of imprisonment and from there to an intimate knowledge of the use of imprisonment around the world.

4

International Centre for Prison Studies

What is this thing we call the prison?

When I began to work in prisons in 1973 I had little appreciation of the world I was entering. Yet, even allowing for this ignorance, I remember that one my first sensations was of a lack of clear direction. There was no obvious point of reference for this new environment in which I found myself. In common with many reasonably well-informed members of the public I had been aware of the existence of the prison system. From time to time I read about it in the press in a detached manner, but more than that I did not know. I re-read recently what I wrote over 25 years ago about my early reactions:

> From the outset I felt a personal need to place the prison system and the whole notion of imprisonment within a context. I soon found that there were so many obvious inconsistencies in how prisons operated and uncertainties about their purpose. It was necessary to go back to the beginning, to learn something about the development of punishment in our society and how imprisonment came to have such a central role in the expression of that punishment. I set myself the task of learning about the history of imprisonment in the hope of gaining some idea about how imprisonment, if it was thought to be necessary in the future, might be better organised. (Coyle, 1994: 4)

As I read myself deeper into the subject I became ever more intrigued when I attempted to relate what I was learning in the course of my studies to my daily experiences in the actual world of prisons. In 1981, having worked in Edinburgh Prison, Polmont Borstal and Shotts Prison, I transferred to work in Scottish Prison Service Headquarters in Edinburgh as one of the small number of people there who had operational experience in prisons. This environment gave me an added insight into the opinions which members of the administrative civil service had of the Prison Service and of those who worked in it, an opinion which was often less than flattering.

Over the years I had become involved in a variety of criminal justice-related organisations, including the Centre for Criminology in Edinburgh University, which at that time was somewhat unusual for a prison governor. My appointment to headquarters meant that I had a much more predictable timetable, generally working office hours with weekends off. This provided me with the opportunity to take my external involvement a step further and in 1981 I was accepted to study part-time for a PhD in Edinburgh University School of Law. Academically this was an exciting time to be studying at Edinburgh. Derick McClintock, who was then Dean of the School of Law, was one of the leading criminologists of the time. There was the opportunity for regular exchanges with other academics in the school, including Neil MacCormick and David Garland, as well as regular seminars given by European scholars such as Nigel Walker from Cambridge, Tony Bottoms from Sheffield, and the *enfants terribles* from Oslo, Nils Christie and Thomas Mathiesen. Derick McClintock agreed to supervise my PhD and the subject of my thesis was 'The organisational development of the Scottish Prison Service with particular reference to the role and influence of the prison officer'. I successfully defended my thesis and was awarded a PhD in 1986.

International Centre for Prison Studies

I maintained my links with the academic community both in Scotland and also later when I moved to London, contributing to academic journals and speaking at conferences. In 1993 I accepted an invitation to become chair of the Institute for the Study and Treatment of Delinquency (ISTD) which was based in King's College London, having been a long-standing member and latterly chair of ISTD's sister organisation the Scottish Association for the Study of Delinquency. Once I had decided to leave the Prison Service in 1997 to pursue my interest in developing new thinking about the purpose of imprisonment and its use I had to find an academic home and, given my existing contacts, the obvious place to look was King's College, one of the two founding colleges of the University of London. I discussed my plans with the Head of the School of Law, Ian Kennedy, and Andrew Ashworth whom I knew well. They both responded positively and together we took our proposal to the College Principal who agreed that an International Centre for Prison Studies (ICPS) should be established in the School of Law and that I should be appointed its first Director. Such matters were much simpler to arrange in the late 1990s than they are today.

During my time at Brixton Prison I had been invited to assist in the work of Penal Reform International (PRI), a non-governmental organisation which had been established in 1989 to work at an international level to improve access to justice and to reduce excessive use of imprisonment. Within a very short period of time PRI found itself being increasingly called on to help develop penal reform strategies in a range of countries around the world and when my duties at Brixton allowed I advised in several countries as well as being asked to assist intergovernmental organisations such as the United Nations and the Council of Europe. In particular at that point in time requests for assistance came from a number of countries which had until a few years previously been members of the Soviet bloc. Most of these, notably Russia, had very high levels of imprisonment, a legacy of the Gulag system of labour camps. I also became involved in several countries in the Caribbean and sub-Saharan Africa where many prisons were crumbling institutions dating from the colonial period. Several of my activities in these countries are described in the following chapters.

In the course of this work it had become clear that in many countries there was little or no understanding of what were the parameters that should inform the manner in which prisons were managed and how prisoners should be treated. Alongside these failures, and partly an explanation for them, was the fact that often there was no separate national prison service. Instead, prisons and other places of detention were the responsibility of the police or the military and personnel were often allocated to this work because of failure in other mainstream roles. Put another way, work in prisons was not regarded as a good career move for an individual. It was these findings that prompted the establishment of ICPS with two main objectives:

- to develop a body of knowledge, based on international covenants and instruments, about the principles on which the use of imprisonment should be based, which could be used as a sound basis for policies on prison issues;
- to build up a resource network for the spread of best practice in prison management worldwide to which prison administrators would be able to come for practical advice on how to manage prison systems which were just, decent, humane and cost effective.

In the spirit of the time, these objectives were expanded into a Statement of Purpose which made clear that ICPS aimed to assist governments and other relevant agencies to develop appropriate policies on prisons and the use of imprisonment. As a centre within one of the leading university law schools in the UK it also undertook to make the results of academic research and projects widely available to policy makers, practitioners and administrators, the media and the general public in order to increase an understanding of the purpose of prison and what could rightly be expected of it.

ICPS moved into the School of Law at the end of March 1997. Six weeks later there was a General Election in the UK which returned a new Labour government and in October Home Secretary Jack Straw formally opened the centre by delivering a lecture on the new government's intended approach to crime and punishment to a packed audience in the Great Hall of King's College (Straw, 1997).

Shortly after ICPS was established the United Nations Commission for Human Rights based in Geneva approached PRI and ICPS with a request to draft a manual on human rights training for prison staff. This project fitted exactly with the objectives and statement of purpose of ICPS and it became the first substantive piece of work carried out by the new centre. The finished document was published by the United Nations in 2005 (Office of the High Commissioner for Human Rights, 2005). It also provided the stimulus for ICPS to write what became its flagship publication *A Human Rights Approach to Prison Management: Handbook for Prison Staff* (Coyle, 2002). It was clear from the outset that this handbook met an international need. Requests were soon made for it to be translated into several languages; for example, the Ministry of Justice in Brazil was given permission to translate it into Portuguese and to print 40,000 copies for distribution to prison staff. It has since been translated into 18 languages, with a second updated edition published in 2009 and a third edition (co-authored with Helen Fair) in collaboration with the International Committee of the Red Cross in 2018.

Within a very short time ICPS, with the support of a distinguished international advisory board, was more than fulfilling the objectives which had been set and was justifying its founding premise that there was a demand for its work, particularly in countries which had a very poor record on human rights in general and prison treatment in particular. In Latin America it was working with governments, non-governmental organisations and universities in Argentina, Brazil and Chile as well as with the UN Latin American Institute for the Prevention of Crime (ILANUD) in Costa Rica. It was involved in a number of countries of the former Soviet Union in Eastern Europe and Central Asia. It was also engaged in research cooperation with academic institutions in several European countries and had developed links with various departments in the United Nations, the Council of Europe and the Organisation for Security and Co-operation in Europe as well as working on the reduction of tuberculosis infection in prisons with the World Health Organisation and the International Committee of the Red Cross.

This work continued in succeeding years as ICPS extended its reach to sub-Saharan Africa, Australasia and the Far East, developing its applied research into the use of imprisonment; organising international conferences and seminars; responding to requests from governments, non-governmental organisations and prison services for practical assistance; publishing a series of reports based on the work which it carried out in collaboration with other academic and intergovernmental institutions and bodies; and developing online resources, notably its World Prison Brief with data on the use of imprisonment in almost every country in the world. In 2014 ICPS merged with the Institute for Crime & Justice Policy Research in Birkbeck College, University of London.[1]

Comment

Over the course of 30 years, alongside many admirable colleagues, I have worked on prison-related issues in countries in every continent, from the frozen expanses of Siberia to the searing heat of sub-Saharan Africa, from the steppes of Asia to the pampas of South America, throughout North and Central America, the Caribbean and Australasia as well as in most countries across Europe. These experiences have not given me answers to all of the questions and queries about imprisonment, its use and abuse, which have pursued me for almost 50 years. They have, however, given me an insight into my question: 'What is this thing we call the prison?' The following chapters in this book will describe a number of my experiences in a manner which I hope will open a window onto the prisons of the world.

5

Women: the forgotten minority

Some 93 per cent of prisoners in the world are male, so it is not surprising that much of the narrative about prisons is male oriented. That is also the case with this book since the bulk of my experience has been in the male prison setting. However, we should not lose sight of the fact that there are over 700,000 women in prisons around the world. The journey which has taken them to prison will often be quite distinct from that of their male counterparts, and their experience of imprisonment will also be different, especially if they are the primary carers of small children or are pregnant when they are sent to prison. In a word, they are the forgotten minority who should be given a voice.[1]

'Ill-adapted correctional policies borrowed from models designed for men'

> *Ministers have rejected hospital proposals which would have ended the controversial practice of shackling pregnant women prisoners to prevent escapes*
>
> Secretly filmed footage, broadcast on Channel 4 last week, showed a Holloway prisoner, named only as Annette, shackled to warders only an hour after giving birth. Witnesses said she had been restrained when she was having contractions.
>
> Anne Widdecombe, prisons minister, said it was not policy to restrain women during labour and claimed that in Annette's case, once full labour had been established, she had not been shackled.
>
> 'The Prison Service has a duty of care to the mother, but this must be balanced against the needs of the service to keep all prisoners, including pregnant women prisoners, in secure custody,' she said. (Mills, 1996)

In September 1994 and January 1995 two groups of high-security male prisoners escaped from two maximum security prisons in England. Following an inquiry into the operational lapses which had led to these escapes, new security procedures were introduced in all prisons in England and Wales. One of these was that all prisoners who were being escorted to a public hospital for any reason were to be handcuffed and chained at all times. This regulation was interpreted literally and it later transpired that pregnant women prisoners who were taken to hospital to give birth were being restrained in this way. There was a media outcry when this was discovered and the (female) Prisons Minister responded as in the aforementioned extract.

I recalled this sequence of events a number of years later when visiting the main prison for women in Costa Rica. There had recently been an escape from a men's prison and the Minister for Justice had issued an instruction that the perimeter security in all prisons had to be reinforced with an additional external high-security fence. A significant amount of money was made available immediately for this work to be done. The prison for women was well managed and there was a good relationship between prison staff and the women in their care, including some who had small children. The director of the prison told me that there was always a shortage of funds to support all the positive activities which she wanted to introduce to prepare the women for life after release. With some frustration she pointed to the shining new five-metre-high fence topped with steel razor wire which had been installed outside the existing security fence surrounding the prison. "We have never had an escape from this prison," she said. "The original fence gave us all the security we needed. We could have spent the funds used for this so much more usefully on other things."

One of my most heart-rending experiences was in a women's prison in Romania in 1993. The cowed prisoners were dressed in shifts made of a serge material with vertical stripes, a replica of the uniforms worn by prisoners in Nazi concentration camps during the Second World War. The similarities did not end there. The single shower room in the prison was a large barn-like building, completely bare apart from 40 shower heads which protruded from the ceiling. The place reeked of the shame and the humiliation which must have been felt by these women each week as they went to the large ante-room, took off all their clothes and then were herded into this shower room. It was possible that the guards did not set out to be cruel or to degrade; they simply no longer saw the humanity and the individuality of the women for whom they had responsibility. In becoming prisoners the women had been stripped not only of their own clothes but also of their dignity as human beings.

Correctional Service of Canada

Inhuman incidents such as this have occurred in other countries which consider themselves to be models of decency and humanity. In

April 1994 a series of shocking events took place in the segregation unit of the Kingston Prison for Women in Canada. Stated briefly, following several days of unrest and violent confrontations between women prisoners and a number of correctional staff in the segregation unit of the prison, on the evening of 26 April the Warden called in an Institutional Emergency Response Team (IERT) from the neighbouring male Kingston Penitentiary to conduct 'cell extractions' (that is, to forcibly remove each woman from her cell) and to strip-search the eight women in the segregation unit. The IERT was an entirely male group and they had never before been called into a women's prison. As was customary when the IERT was deployed, the cell extractions and strip-searches were videotaped. In February 1995 a copy of this videotape was broadcast on Canadian television. It showed the eight women having their clothing cut off and being stripped naked by members of the IERT, assisted by some female staff, and then being handcuffed and chained while partially covered only by skimpy paper gowns. The programme caused a public uproar and led to the appointment of a distinguished judge, the Honourable Justice Louise Arbour, to chair a commission of inquiry into the events and their aftermath. The commission's report was published in April 1996 and was scathing in its conclusions, both in respect of the events at the prison and also of the subsequent inaction of the senior management of the CSC once it had become clear what had happened (Arbour, 1996).

> [W]hat is particularly disturbing in watching the video is not only the men 'witnessing' the naked inmates, it is the combination of the inevitable brutality of this type of intervention, combined with the necessary physical handling of individual women by several male IERT members, while each woman is completely naked for a period of time, and then very improperly covered by a paper gown or bib. When properly understood in its full context, these events raise a legal and moral question much more basic than merely whether it technically constituted a 'strip search'. It raises the question of whether the treatment of the inmates was cruel, inhumane, and degrading. I think that it was.
>
> The process was intended to terrorize, and therefore subdue. There is no doubt that it had this intended effect in this case. It also, unfortunately, had the effect of re-victimizing women who had had traumatic experiences in their past at the hands of men. Although this consequence was not intended, it should have been foreseen.

> I find that the conditions in which the inmates were left in their cell at the completion of the IERT intervention were, frankly, appalling and I see nothing in the evidence to indicate that these conditions were genuinely dictated by a serious security concern. These women were left barely covered by a paper gown, on a cement floor in an empty, small cell, with absolutely nothing to sit or sleep on, not a mattress, not a blanket or a towel, while the windows were left open for a considerable period of time. They were left in body belts, shackles and leg irons, and they were kept in that condition until mid-afternoon on the 27th when they were each given a security blanket.

In the preface to her report Justice Arbour made a more general comment on women and the criminal justice system: 'The history of women and crime is spotted with opportunities most of which have been missed. We hope that history will not dictate our future.' She went on to observe that 'decades of neglect and ill-adapted correctional policies borrowed from models designed for men, have failed to produce the substantive equality to which women offenders are entitled'.

Following publication of the Arbour Report the Canadian government decided that plans should be put in place for the closure of the Kingston Prison for Women and that five dedicated facilities for women prisoners should be built across the country. As this gradually happened the number of women held in Kingston slowly reduced and the prison was finally closed in 2013. But, as we shall see in later chapters, building new prisons and units does not necessarily lead to improved treatment of those held within them as was demonstrated by the tragic case of Ashley Smith, who died inside her segregation cell at the Grand Valley Institution for Women in Kitchener, Ontario as described in Chapter 3. And it would appear that the treatment of women in Canadian prisons continues to fail. In his annual report for 2018–2019 the Correctional Investigator strongly criticised the treatment of women held in maximum security units, describing it as 'an arbitrary system that results in discriminatory outcomes, exists outside the law and that disproportionately limits federally sentenced Indigenous women classified as maximum security from accessing services, supports and programs required to facilitate their safe and timely reintegration'. Alongside his report the Investigator also published the Correctional Service's response to his findings: 'In keeping with law and policy, Correctional Service of Canada (CSC) makes every effort to ensure women in the secure unit have access to the programs, services, and interventions required to address their individual risk and needs.' There appeared to be no official response to the Investigator's conclusion that the practice was 'outside the law' (Office of the Correctional Investigator, 2019).

The numbers

The proportion of women in prison systems throughout the world varies in individual countries between two and nine per cent, with only 19 jurisdictions having a higher proportion than that (Walmsley, 2017). These figures do not mean that the number of women in prison is small since the world total is estimated at around 714,000, with one third of these in the United States.

The number of women and girls in prison worldwide has increased by some 53 per cent since the year 2000. This rise cannot be explained in terms of global population growth (United Nations figures indicate that the global population rose by 21 per cent between mid-2000 and mid-2016) or by growth in the total number of prisoners. The worldwide male prison population has increased by around 20 per cent since 2000. The female prison population has risen in all continents over the last decade. In Africa the rise has been somewhat less than the increase in the general population of the continent, and in Europe the increase in prisoner numbers has been similar to the general population increase. By contrast, rises in the female prison population in the Americas, in Asia and in Oceania have been respectively about three, four and five times the increases in the general population of those continents.

Prisons are primarily male institutions

One consequence of the proportional imbalance of the sexes is that prisons and prison systems are designed, built and organised primarily to meet the needs and requirements of male prisoners and this applies to architecture, to security provision and to all other facilities. There is a recurring tendency that any special provision for women prisoners will be something which is added on to the standard provision for men. This is despite the fact that the profile of women prisoners is very different from that of male prisoners and particular attention needs to be given to their special needs.

In most countries the majority of women will have been imprisoned for non-violent property or drug-related offences. If their crime has been a violent one, the victim may well have been someone close to them. Many women prisoners are likely to have suffered frequent physical or sexual abuse throughout their lives. They will often have a variety of untreated health problems. In addition, the consequences of imprisonment and its effect on their lives may be very different for women. A large number will be single parents, often with dependent children. When a man is sent to prison, his partner may well do all in her power to keep the family together. When a woman goes to prison, there is less likelihood that her partner will be able or willing to do the same (Scharff Smith, 2014).

In a number of countries tough anti-drugs legislation has had a significant effect on the numbers of women in prison. Another feature of this and similar changes has been an increase in the proportion of foreign national prisoners who now form a large percentage of women prisoners in some countries; many of them having been convicted of transporting drugs from one country to another at the instigation of male drug traffickers. All of these additional factors mean that prison authorities need to pay special attention to the way women prisoners are treated and the facilities which are provided for them.

The health profile of prisoners in general is poor, which is hardly surprising, given the fact that in most jurisdictions prisoners in general are drawn largely from marginalised groups and many will have untreated health conditions. A high proportion of them may well be addicted to one or other form of drug abuse, with the added possibility that they may suffer from infectious hepatitis, tuberculosis or from HIV. The incidence of mental health problems among all prisoners is also very high. If that is their condition when they enter prison, the environment in which they will then live is likely to exacerbate their problems. In many instances living conditions may be badly overcrowded, sanitary arrangements may be poor, diet will be inadequate, there will be limited access to fresh air and exercise and health provision will be unsatisfactory. For women in prison, many of these problems are writ even larger (Hatton and Fisher, 2009; Drucker, 2011).

What this can mean in practice

Gatesville, Texas

A number of towns in the United States, usually with small populations in rural areas, are known as 'prison towns' because they have a high concentration of state correctional institutions. There are a variety of reasons why this has come about. It might be that there is an absence of employment opportunities in the area and a prison will provide a substantial number of secure, relatively well-paid jobs. In some cases the town originally had poor infrastructure and stood to benefit from the utilities and other services including highways which the state has to provide to support the prisons. There is a third anomalous reason which is that some financial support from federal and state sources is calculated according to the number of residents in a town – and for these purposes prisoners count as residents, although they are not on the electoral roll.

The small conurbation of Gatesville in Coryell County, Texas is one such prison town, with five of the eight correctional institutions for women in the State of Texas located within its boundaries. In 2006 when I visited Gatesville the town's population was just under 16,000, of whom 2,600 were employed by the Texas Department of Criminal Justice and another 8,500 (that is, more than half of the total) were prisoners; of the latter 5,500 were women.

In April of that year I was invited to speak at a conference with the title 'Opening up a closed world: what constitutes effective prison oversight', organised by the University of Texas at Austin. At the end of the conference some of the international contributors were invited to visit the Mountain View Unit, one of the women's prisons in Gatesville, which includes a section which holds women who have been sentenced to death. Our party included the President of the European CPT, the Swedish Prisons Ombudsman and the Chief Inspector of Prisons for England and Wales, all of them women.

We were taken first to the 'death row' section where we were able to talk to the five women who were waiting for news of their pending execution; a number of them had been there for several years. We spoke to them in a group and the women, all dressed in the prison uniform of white tops and baggy trousers, were keen to talk as we stood in the small open area outside their cells. They did not want to discuss their personal situations; instead they were keen to question us about prison conditions and the treatment of prisoners in our relative countries.

A couple of us took the opportunity to talk to the senior officer who was in charge of the unit. Like the five prisoners in the unit and most of the staff she was African American, a friendly, almost gentle woman, who clearly had a good relationship with her charges. She was happy to talk to us about her work and answered our rather intrusive questions with good grace.

"What about executions?" we asked. "How do they affect you?" "Well," she replied, "it's not easy. Recently I had to go with a woman to the execution chamber at Huntsville. She had been in here a long time and she had no family, so she asked me to go with her to her execution, to be with her at the end. So I went with her to Huntsville and was there in the death chamber when she was killed. It wasn't easy. Since then I have been thinking about it a lot." She then turned the question on its head. "Tell me, how do you manage executions in your country?" She had no idea that in the majority of countries in the world capital punishment has long since been abolished; that for all of us the notion of judicial execution, particularly of women, was unthinkable. For her, God-fearing woman that she was, looking after women in white uniforms on death row who were waiting to be killed was normal, all in a day's work. We left the death row unit in a subdued manner, unusually silent.

We were then taken to the administrative segregation unit which, as in all United States prisons, held prisoners who were not allowed to be in 'general circulation'. This could be for a variety of reasons; perhaps because of mental instability, or because of past behaviour, or because of problems with some other prisoners. Once admitted to 'ad seg' it would often be difficult to return to general population, and a person might be held there for years on end. That afternoon in Mountain View there were 78 women in the unit, each held in a cell closed by a reinforced steel door with a small inbuilt vision panel covered with netting; none of them had a 'mountain view'.

Before we were allowed into the unit we were told we had to put on stab vests, heavy padded jackets, this despite the fact that all the women were inside their secure cells. All of us in the party had extensive experience of high-security prisons, many of us in infamous locations all over the world. Not one of us had ever before been asked to put on a stab vest. There was discussion among the staff as to whether we should be asked to wear helmets and gas masks but it was decided that it was not necessary.

The unit was dark and the atmosphere forbidding. Architecturally it resembled a huge, wired cage with little light and no colour and rolls of razor wire between each of the three floors. In the semi-darkness we could see faces behind the narrow slits in the doors and we attempted as best we could to have conversations with some of the women. One woman named Joanna told me that she had been in the segregation unit for three years. She explained that the decision to release a person from segregation was made by a committee that met in the department headquarters in Huntsville. She wasn't sure how they made the decisions but she was, she said, hopeful that she might soon be moved.

Staff then showed us the exercise cage which was in effect simply a cell with wire walls, about six feet by ten feet. They recounted how sometimes a woman would climb the wire in the cage and refuse to go back to her cell. In a very flat manner staff explained that they then donned gas masks before spraying the woman with tear gas. When she fell from the wire of the exercise cage they would strip her and take her back to her cell. We asked how often this would happen and back came the reply, "Nearly every day." On the day of our visit all the staff on duty were male. Clearly neither the guards themselves nor those in charge of the prison thought that this was in any way untoward.

It was obvious that the staff in the administrative segregation unit thought that what they did on a daily basis, if they thought about it all, was just a job; like the woman in charge of death row, for them it was 'normal'.

El Salvador

In a later chapter I describe the reality of imprisonment for men in Mariona prison in El Salvador which I visited in October 2016. On that same occasion I inspected the new high-security prison for men which was being built in Izalco with spaces for 5,000 prisoners. One kilometre away was a new prison for women, Granja de Izalco, which would eventually have capacity to hold 1,000 women. In 2016 it already had accommodation in three large dormitories, a series of vocational workshops, a small farm where some women grew vegetables and similar produce and a family visits area as well as a unit for conjugal visits. It was clean, bright and spacious throughout; the women were dressed in light-coloured uniforms, and clearly there was a good relationship between them and the staff. It was the complete opposite of the male prison at Mariona.

The most striking aspect of the prison was that it had a separate unit where up to 160 women lived with their small children. Some were recently born and all were able to stay alongside their mothers until they reached the age of five years. Infants were kept in a nursery during the day while their mothers worked, looked after by other prisoners who had been given some basic training in childcare. Those who were older attended the school which was just inside the entrance to the prison. In some ways it was a model of its kind. And yet it raised as many questions as answers about the principle of the imprisonment of women and particularly those with small children.

After we passed through the entry to the prison I paused and said to another member of our party, "Listen. That is the saddest sound you will hear in a prison." She was not attuned to the nuances of the prison world and after listening for a moment asked me what I was talking about. I explained that I was referring to the excited chatter of the small boys and girls who were sitting in orderly rows in the open area which served as their school. All were dressed neatly, the girls in white blouses and black skirts, the boys in white shirts and black trousers. We were introduced to them and they peppered us with questions about who we were, where we were from and what it was like in our countries.

The director of the prison explained that the mother and children facilities allowed the women to foster a good relationship with their children and also ensured that the children did not lose out on their schooling. Construction of the facilities had been sponsored by the government of Taiwan to the tune of over $700,000. Those children who were approaching five years were given specific support about how to cope with life when they had to leave their mothers behind. Some would go to be cared for by other family members and those who had no families would be taken into official care. We had one more chastening experience when we went on to the education unit for the women. In one room was a class which was preparing mothers of the four-year-old children for the emotional trauma which they might well experience when their daughter or son was taken away. As a mere male I wondered what on earth might be on the curriculum of a course on how a mother should prepare to give up a child.

All of this brought into sharp focus in a very real manner the dilemma about mothers who are imprisoned and their subsequent relationship with their children: what are the issues affecting the mothers and what is to be done for the good of the children? This vexed issue of children living with their imprisoned parents and arrangements in a number of countries is discussed in Scharff Smith (2014: Chapter 15).

Australia

In March 2000 I visited Bandyup, a women's prison in a suburb outside Perth in Western Australia. In my notes at the time I wrote: 'A large number of women were crammed into a small site.' It was the only prison for women in the Perth metropolitan area and held all who were awaiting trial or who were sentenced. Originally opened in 1971 it had accommodation for 68 women but as time went on it had to find space for many more. After a public outcry about the fact that some women were obliged to sleep on mattresses on floors, new units had been built increasing its capacity to 180 but since then overcrowding had returned. As it was the only facility available for women in the area it was classified as a maximum security prison although only a small minority of women fell into that category. At the time I visited different levels of security were applied to the women. Some who had been classified as a low security risk were living in small houses inside the perimeter where they cooked and cared for themselves. The relationships between staff and prisoners appeared to be good but there was little employment, education or other activity for the women.

There was a unit where mothers could live with their newly born infants. It was spacious with a shared kitchen and rooms for various activities. The mothers had large single rooms with space for a cot or crib and were able to care for their babies on a continuous basis until they reached their first birthday. At that point the infants were taken away from their mothers and either given over to the care of other family members or put into care. This arrangement is common in many countries with a variety of cut-off points for the small child to be taken from the mother.

Equal outcomes require different approaches

Over a 13-month period between 2002 and 2003 six women killed themselves in Styal Prison in England. These shocking fatalities prompted the UK government to commission Baroness Jean Corston to undertake a review into the treatment of women in the criminal justice system, and her seminal report was published in 2007 (Corston, 2007). Her principal conclusion was that there are fundamental differences between male and female offenders and as a consequence there has to be a different and distinct approach to the manner in which women are treated within the criminal justice system. She summarised some of these differences as follows:

- Women with personal experiences of violence and abuse are over represented in the criminal justice system and can be described as victims as well as offenders.
- The biological difference between men and women has different social and personal consequences.
- Women commit a different range of offences from men. They commit more acquisitive crime and have a lower involvement in serious violence, criminal damage and professional crime.
- Relationship problems feature strongly in women's pathways into crime.

- Coercion by men can form a route into criminal activity for some women.
- Drug addiction plays a huge part in all offending and is disproportionately the case with women.
- Mental health problems are far more prevalent among women in prison than in the male prison population or in the general population.
- Outside prison men are more likely to commit suicide than women but the position is reversed inside prison.
- Self-harm in prison is a huge problem and more prevalent in the women's estate.
- Proportionately more women than men are remanded in custody before trial.
- Prison is disproportionably harsher for women because prisons and the practices within them have for the most part been designed for men.
- Levels of security in prisons in general were put in place to stop men escaping.
- Because of the small number of women's prisons and their geographical location, women tend to be located further from their homes than male prisoners to the detriment of maintaining family ties, receiving visits and resettlement back into the community.
- Women prisoners are far more likely than men to be primary carers of young children and this factor makes the prison experience significantly different for women than men.
- Thirty per cent of women in prison lose their accommodation while in prison.

Her concluding recommendations on how to achieve equality for women inside prison can be paraphrased succinctly:

- A narrow focus on equal treatment of men and women will not of itself result in equality.
- Genuine equality will only be achieved once there is a distinct woman-centred approach.

Baroness Corston's report deals with the situation of women in prison in England and Wales but its assessment and recommendations have equal application in all countries.

In Scotland the Commission on Women Offenders (Angiolini, 2012) reached broadly similar conclusions to Corston about the need for a new and targeted approach to dealing with women who are involved in offending. To date progress on the Angiolini Commission's recommendations has been disappointingly slow, as is also the case in respect of the Corston Report.

Comment

The cameos in this chapter describe some of the worst and a few of the better examples of the treatment of women prisoners held in systems which have been designed and are managed primarily by and for men. How is this imbalance to be addressed? In the first place, its existence has to be acknowledged. Only then can steps be taken to deal with it.[2] The opening paragraph of the Report of the Scottish Commission on Women Offenders in 2012 (Angiolini, 2012) stated: 'Many women in the criminal justice system are frequent re-offenders with complex needs that relate to their social circumstances, previous histories of abuse and mental health and addiction problems.' If we stand this sentence on its head we might begin to see the possibility of an alternative approach. The sentence would then read: 'Many women with complex needs that relate to their social circumstances, previous histories of abuse and mental health and addiction problems end up in the criminal justice system and are frequent re-offenders.' Expressed in this way we will then be driven to ask an obvious question: why should we expect the criminal justice system to provide the answers to all these complex needs relating to the 'social circumstances, previous histories of abuse and mental health and addiction problems'? The conclusion of the Commission on Women Offenders was quite clear. The solution to these problems lies beyond criminal justice systems in general and beyond prison systems in particular. The Report of the Scottish Commission underlined the need first to look for alternatives to prosecution (which are likely to be found outside the criminal justice system); then if there has to be a criminal justice process to look for alternatives to remand in custody before trial; then if there is a court case and a finding of guilt to look at appropriate disposals short of custody. Only when all of these factors had been exhausted should imprisonment be considered. The exponential increase in the rate of women's imprisonment, demonstrated in the figures quoted earlier, is a startling consequence of the failure to apply the approach recommended by Angiolini.

A radical structural review of this nature will be likely to result in a significant reduction in the number of women who are held in prison in most countries. This will in turn provide opportunities for the development of conditions of detention and treatment which are not 'add-ons' to a male oriented system but which will guarantee what Corston has called 'a distinct woman-centred approach'. Then, and only then, will we have responded to Justice Louise Arbour's finding that 'decades of neglect and ill-adapted correctional policies borrowed from models designed for men, have failed to produce the substantive equality to which women offenders are entitled'.

6

The legacy of the Gulag

I first became involved in work in the prisons of the former Soviet Union within a year of its break-up in 1991, beginning with Russia in 1992, Kazakhstan and Kyrgyzstan in 1993 and Belarus in 1994. For more than a decade thereafter I was a regular visitor to the region in various contexts: as a member of the Russia/Council of Europe programme on the Reform of the Prison System in the Russian Federation; as an expert member of the first two visits of the CPT to Russia and its first visit to Armenia; with the Council of Baltic Sea States, the World Health Organization and other bodies for work in tackling the problem of tuberculosis in places of detention; to several countries for work on the abolition of the death penalty; as well as on a number of ICPS long-term projects on improving human rights in places of detention.

In later sections I describe the terrible conditions in the post-Soviet pre-trial detention centres (SIZOs) which I witnessed in the early 1990s. Once a prisoner was convicted and sentenced he or she would be transferred to a labour colony. Colonies were classified according to the severity of their regime and in passing sentence the judge would specify the severity of the regime to which the convicted person was to be allocated according to the nature of the offence, the length of sentence and the number of previous convictions.

Prisoners in Soviet times were regarded as enemies of the State – outlaws, literally placed outside the law. One thing which the State could demand from them in return was labour. This principle was added to the earlier Tsarist system of exile to far-flung parts of the Empire (Rybakov, 1988). At one level the Gulag[1] described by Solzhenitsyn (1973) was an unstructured archipelago of camps and colonies which happened to exist wherever they were placed. At another level it was a sophisticated organisation which was a key contributor to the economy of the country, and the Soviet labour camps were units of production (Dallin and Nicolaevsky, 1947; Shifrin, 1982). Until the early 1990s the forest camps in Siberia were administered as a separate prison administration. Other camps were clustered geographically. For example, the city of Pawlodar which I visited over a period of years is located in the part of Siberia which is now in Kazakhstan and it grew up around the conglomeration of penal colonies which turned it into an industrial town with a population of over 300,000. The city's population of Kazakhs and ethnic Russians with significant minorities of Germans as well as Ukrainians and Tatars was testimony to the numbers who had been forcibly transported there in Soviet times as well as families of former prisoners who had settled there after release and had no means of travel back to their former homes in Moscow and other western cities.

The individual colonies in Pawlodar and elsewhere were part of a vast industrial network. Wheels for heavy goods vehicles might be made in a colony in Siberia; their chassis would be made in Ukraine; their cabins in Georgia; and the various elements would all be brought together, say, in Moscow to be put together. I witnessed the result of this arrangement when visiting a large industrial warehouse complex attached to the institute for training prison staff in Domodedovo outside Moscow in the early 1990s. It was a testament to the industrial enterprise which existed in the Gulag. Ploughshares and tractors were on display alongside astronauts' suits and internal aircraft fittings made for Aeroflot. In another section there was a whole range of domestic furniture, clothing and kitchen equipment; all made in the camps and available for purchase.

The main obligation on prisoners was that they should work. The Soviet administrators may have had a vague expectation that through this work prisoners might change their attitude to society but that was a far second to the requirement for economic production. This priority was apparent in the way camps from Riga to Vladivostok were physically organised. One section or zone consisted of a great series of industrial factories. A separate zone included all the living accommodation, in some ways similar to a group of impoverished working men's hostels. The whole area would be surrounded by a security fence with a small administrative block near the entrance and the level of security would be greater or less depending on the location of the colony. If it was close to an urban area this might include watchtowers with armed guards and fierce dogs roaming in the area between the two fences. In more remote areas, the location itself would be the security: there was nowhere to escape to.

Many of the industrial complexes in these colonies operated for 24 hours each day, seven days a week, 52 weeks a year. In some instances prisoners worked in three shifts of eight hours each; in others they worked two twelve-hour shifts. They were expected to work without stinting. When the work quota was completed they returned to their living accommodation and were left largely to their own devices.

The fact that these colonies, far from being a drain on the economy, were an important contributor to it had implications in the way the camps were financed. The central authorities in Moscow paid the salaries of the staff who guarded the prisoners. In every other respect the colonies were self-sufficient. Income from the goods which were produced was used to maintain the living areas, to buy food, to pay for new equipment and the salaries of industrial staff. In addition, contributions paid by the colonies for services such as electricity, water and sewerage subsidised these facilities for the local population. A proportion of the income from industrial production, usually about 50 per cent, was paid as tax to the authorities in Moscow.[2]

With the collapse of the Soviet Union this whole structure disintegrated. The penal complex in the 15 states of the Soviet Union had previously been controlled from Moscow. From then on the independent countries such as Estonia, Moldova and Kyrgyzstan had to develop their own central prison administrations. Suddenly the lorry chassis which was built in Ukraine could not be linked up with the cabin which was built in Georgia or with the wheels made in Siberia. Industrial production in the Gulag, which had been an important element in the economy of the Soviet Union, was no longer relevant to emerging independent States.

Throughout the 1990s the colonies remained in existence but instead of contributing to the common wealth they became a drag on the public purse. The consequences of this cataclysmic shift were felt at a number of levels. On one hand, the underlying justification for the penal system in the countries of the former Soviet Union had been called into question. The industrial work sheds which had previously operated round the clock now stood empty. I found a typical example in a colony which I visited in the mid-1990s in the north east of Kazakhstan. The rows of work sheds were like great cathedrals, echoes of another era. They stood eerily silent with mountains of rusting machinery. In the distance shadowy figures floated in and out. In one corner a small number of prisoners were engaged in some minor repairs. The works manager who showed us round was still resplendent in full major's uniform, including highly polished knee-length boots. He proudly told us how the machines had worked unceasingly in the past and how he always exceeded his production quota. He spoke with certainty, as if to convince himself that these days would return if only the proper products could be identified.

Life also changed dramatically for the prisoners. The demanding hours of heavy industrial labour had all but disappeared but nothing had replaced them. In some instances the authorities maintained the pretence, and each morning prisoners marched to the industrial sheds as they had done for generations and were left there throughout the day to work around the machinery in a desultory fashion. In others, prisoners simply remained in their living quarters all day with virtually nothing to do and in this meaningless environment monotony could lead to violence. There was another important consequence. The previous disciplined routine at least meant that prisoners were in the fresh air each day, if only as they marched to and from their work places. They had a full day of vigorous activity and they came back to their barracks only to rest and to sleep. Now, many of them spent all day in their living barracks, many of which were of a poor physical standard, badly ventilated and with little natural light. With large numbers of prisoners in them throughout the day they had become breeding grounds for infection and disease.

Belarus: an unreconstructed outlier

Belarus is a country of over 9.4 million people, bordering Lithuania and Latvia to the north, Russia to the east, Ukraine to the south and Poland to the west. It is frequently described as the last dictatorship in Europe, ruled since it became independent in 1991 by Alexander Lukashenko. I first visited the country and its prisons in late 1994. This was a period of great social optimism and considerable political uncertainty in the newly independent countries of Eastern Europe, with enthusiasm in some about the exciting possibilities which were opening up in their new democracies, while in others there was a nostalgia, at least on the part of those in power, for the certainties of the old days of the Soviet Union. In several of them, especially those in the latter group, it was not at all clear what the future might hold. Even in those early post-Soviet days it was obvious that the forces of democracy would face a daunting challenge in what was then known as Byelorus (White Russia), and that was to become even clearer in the course of my first visit there in October 1994.

I went to Belarus on behalf of PRI at the invitation of the Belarus League for Human Rights, a small non-governmental organisation which had been established to enhance human rights across a wide spectrum of the nascent civil society, including the justice system. The League was organised by Evgeny Novikov, an impressive medical doctor who was also a deputy in what was still called the Belarus Supreme Soviet. Along with two colleagues I arrived in Minsk one late evening at the end of October. Evgeny took us immediately to the League's offices where we met a group of former prisoners and families of serving prisoners who made emotional statements about prison conditions and the brutal treatment of prisoners. It was a chastening introduction to what lay ahead. Afterwards we checked into our hotel and Novikov escorted the three of us to dinner in a local restaurant.

After our meal we took the ten-minute walk back along a broad avenue and onto a short cul-de-sac to the hotel. It was 10 o'clock at night and there was no sign of any traffic. Suddenly we were aware of a very noisy car coming up behind us at speed. I instinctively looked back and realised that the car was very hard into the kerb. I pushed the person who was walking beside me onto the grassy verge and as I stepped back the car passed within inches. I realised immediately that Evgeny Novikov, who had been walking in front of us, had been knocked down. The car had hit the briefcase he was carrying and the force of the blow had knocked him down. By this time the car had driven to the end of the cul-de-sac, turned round and drove past us at speed. When it reached the main road it again turned and drove back towards us. It stopped when it reached us and the driver got out. He appeared to be quite drunk.

Until this point there had been no one else in the vicinity but suddenly a man appeared, walking a dog. He went up to the car driver and, according to Evgeny, said, "You drunken killer. We'll get the militia." Evgeny stepped in and said that no harm had been done and that there was no need to take any action. He encouraged the three of us to walk away towards the hotel. We left the driver and the pedestrian arguing and eventually saw the car drive off. Evgeny had a bad cut to his eyebrow which would clearly need to be stitched. (The next day he admitted that his body was quite badly bruised.) He insisted that he was fine and that nothing needed to be done. He impressed on us that we should not say anything about what had happened. The car had passed us within inches of the kerb and had maintained that position until it hit Evgeny, and it was hard to imagine that a drunken driver could have been able to drive with such precision. We were left wondering why he had returned and got out of the car to find out what had happened.

Novikov pointed out that militiamen would normally be stationed at all the main road intersections. He found it difficult to believe that a drunken driver would have come so far without detection and would have been able to drive along a cul-de-sac leading to one of the city's main hotels where foreigners often stayed. He also suggested that it was extremely rare in Minsk for a passing stranger, the man walking the dog, to involve himself in any way in such an incident, particularly since there were four of us and it was late in the evening.

It was possible that this was no more than an incident with a drunken driver. On the other hand, it was equally likely that this was not an accident. In most of the government departments which we were to visit there was a reforming faction and also a conservative one. Evgeny told us that he personally had been threatened several times because of his work with the League for Human Rights, and his strong opinion was that this incident might well have been organised by one of the reactionary factions, for example, in the Belarus KGB. A possible theory was that the driver had intended to knock over one or other of us. Having failed to do so, he returned hoping that we would call the police. They would then discover that we had been drinking at dinner, with the supposition that we had been walking in the middle of the road. That would have been a grave embarrassment to us as foreigner visitors and also to Novikov as a Supreme Soviet Deputy. It would doubtless have led to the cancellation of our visit. An interesting first evening in Minsk.

The following morning we met with Valentin Sukalo, Minister of Justice. He told us that prior to the break-up of the Soviet Union he had been First Deputy Chairman of the Supreme Court of the USSR and that now his Ministry had three priorities for the criminal justice system in Belarus: to draft a new constitution; to introduce a democratic electoral system; and to observe human rights.[3] Our next meeting was with Colonel Leonid Tsurko, Head of the Penitentiary Department, and his deputy whom I had met the previous month at a Council of Europe seminar in Poland. Before our arrival Novikov had been told directly by the Minister of the Interior that it would not be possible for us to visit any prisons. In the course of our meeting with Tsurko we repeated the request and, after some hesitation, he said that he would recommend to the Minister that we should be allowed to visit the pre-trial prison in Zhodino, a town some 60 kilometres from Minsk. He joked with us that we would only be shown the front part of the prison. I responded that I knew enough about prisons to be able to smell the back part as well. Later that day we received word that the Minister had agreed that we could visit Zhodino pre-trial prison the next day.

The town of Zhodino at that time had a population of around 70,000, having been expanded during the 1960s as an industrial centre for truck making. Until two years previously the prison had been a detoxification centre for alcoholics and this was reflected in the relatively light perimeter security, unusual for a SIZO. It was clear from the reaction of the director and his senior staff that they were unused to foreign visitors. We gathered that a decision had been made a few days previously that we would be allowed to visit, and as we went round we were frequently warned to beware of the freshly painted walls and doors. The prison was holding 1,000 prisoners, the majority of whom were held in the standard layout of large rooms with an unscreened toilet in the corner; all were dark, unpleasant and heavy with warm stale air. Most of the cells held at least ten prisoners although there were only eight beds in each. The exercise yards were the standard arrangement to be found in prisons in former Soviet Union countries: a double row of high walled pens covered by steel grilles at high level with staff patrolling on a catwalk above. In discussion the Director told us that his main problems were shortage of finance, recruiting staff of a high quality and low public opinion about prisons.

The following day was taken up with a visit to the KGB headquarters and prison in Minsk. Evgeny Novikov told us that the KGB had been very reluctant to meet us and that he had had several lengthy telephone conversations with its Director and had submitted our full CVs before the Director had agreed to the visit. The KGB building was an imposing complex in the centre of the capital which had been built in 1952 by German prisoners of war. From the outset it was apparent that the authorities had decided, having agreed that the visit should take place, to be as positive as possible. We met with the head of the KGB and four other senior members of his department, accompanied by the head of their press office and a journalist from the government-sponsored newspaper. We were told that until this point it had been unthinkable for the KGB to receive any foreign visitors and we were undoubtedly the first foreign delegation to any of its prisons. The prison itself, the only KGB prison in Belarus, was a rotunda building on two floors. It had accommodation for 100 prisoners and we were told that it normally held about 30, mostly militia who were serving sentences. The facilities were well above the usual prison standard and had the atmosphere of an army detention centre.

We continued our high-level meetings by going to see the Procurator General for Belarus, who was accompanied by his deputy, the procurator for the Minsk region and the procurator responsible for the Minsk pre-trial isolator. At one point in our discussion I asked the Procurator General how many criminal trials resulted in a not guilty verdict. At first he did not quite understand the question but then asked one of his staff to find the exact figures. Five minutes later the answer came back that during the period since January 1994 there had been 98 not guilty findings out of 50,000 cases; that is 0.2 per cent. I expressed surprise that the figure was so low, explaining that around 26 per cent of remand prisoners in Brixton would ultimately be found not guilty.

The Procurator threw up his hands and exclaimed, "But that means that your police must be arresting innocent people!"

One of the intended benefits of our visit was that it had provided Evgeny Novikov with the opportunity to have direct access to very senior officials who would not otherwise have seen him. He had clearly done his lobbying well as we met all the most senior people who were available, and Evgeny used the discussions to raise practical issues of concern at each meeting. At that juncture, as in several countries in the region, the future direction of political travel was not at all clear. In so far as there was an ideological struggle going on within each government department, our presence added strength to the reforming elements. This debate was seen, in some instances literally, as a matter of political life and death. In that context it seemed perfectly probable that the incident with the car on the first evening of our visit was not an accident as there were undoubtedly people who did not welcome our visit and the official recognition being given to Novikov.

When I next visited Minsk in January 1997 our first meeting was with Vladimir Khomlyuk, Director of the Prison Service, now retitled Chairman of the Committee for the Execution of Punishment, which Novikov suggested was an indication of a wish on the part of some to return to the Soviet days of committees and chairmen. Khomlyuk had been in post for six months. In 1994 he had been head of the staff training centre and had subsequently exchanged places with Colonel Tsurko whom we had met on our previous visit. We were informed that his wife was a sister of the Minister of the Interior, and Evgeny suggested that they were among a group of younger people who reckoned that the future of the country lay in looking towards the West rather than East to Russia.

That afternoon we visited Pre-trial Isolator (SIZO) No 1, to which we had been refused access on our first visit. Located in the centre of Minsk it had at its core a medieval castle. In every major city in the Soviet Union the pre-trial isolator was a place of great symbolism, usually an impressive construction, in many cases dating from Tsarist times. It was where accused persons would be held after an initial period in police custody until their trial and any appeal process had been completed and before they were transferred to a labour colony. We were told that SIZO 1 had places for 2,000 prisoners but actually held 2,700, including 250 women and 160 juveniles. In one corridor there were 15 rooms holding a total of 200 men overseen by one guard. We were shown into one large cell which was dark, with an overpowering unhealthy smell. As in other pre-trial places we had visited there were many more men than beds. The air was foetid and most of the prisoners were stripped to the waist or wearing dirty vests. We were then shown a cell holding nine women prisoners, the youngest of whom said she was 19 years old. One woman did all the talking. She told us that she would not like to be in prison in England since she had heard that prisoners there were 'too well looked after'. She was unusually familiar towards the head of the prison who was with us. We then went to a cell holding nine male juveniles, the youngest of whom was 15 years old. Two adults were in their own clothes; one of them was slightly older than the other prisoners and the second was much older. We were told that he was 'the father figure'; his responsibility was to keep order in the cell and he was clearly a dangerous presence for the younger men.

Director Khomlyuk told us that the prison held 41 prisoners who had been sentenced to death, and out of the blue he asked if we would like to visit the 'death row'. Until this point I had never been allowed to see this section of any prison which I had visited in a former Soviet Union country. We were taken to the basement section of one of the prison blocks and into a long corridor which was dim, musty and eerily quiet with no natural light. The director told the officer accompanying us to open one of the cell doors. It was completely black inside until the guard switched on a dim electric light. The three men in the cell jumped up as the door opened and immediately faced the back wall with their hands clasped behind their heads. The director told them to turn round and then to place their arms by their sides. They were then ordered to lift their heads and finally to open their eyes. They wore dirty uniforms with horizontal stripes and their pallor was grey. The director questioned one of them who said that he was 23 years old. He had been in that cell for ten months and was awaiting execution. He explained that one evening he had been in a long drinking session in his flat with a couple who were neighbours. He said that he woke up the following morning to find them dead by his side. He had no other memory of what had happened but accepted that he must have killed them. In a subdued voice he told us he was married with a three-year-old daughter but he was not allowed any visitors and did not expect to see his family again. We asked the director if the men had access to fresh air. He replied that they did and pointed to the small window high up in the wall which was slightly ajar. There was no sign of beds, bedding, table or chairs.

As in most countries in the region at that time prisoners on death row were never told when their execution was to take place. Each time the cell door opened, as it had for our visit, the prisoners did not know whether their last moment had come. If it had, they would be ordered out of the cell to walk along to the end of the corridor to a spot where they would be summarily shot in the back of the head. The first their family would know of this would be when their few personal belongings were handed over to them. In the course of the next few years all other countries in the region either abolished the death penalty or implemented a moratorium as this was a condition of entry to the Council of Europe. Belarus has never done so and retains the death penalty to this day.

We then visited a labour colony close to the centre of the city. We were told that it had places for 1,500 but on that day it was holding 3,000 prisoners. The main industry was a wood factory and some prisoners were just finishing their shift as we arrived. It was like something from darkest Solzhenitsyn. Hundreds of men in dirty ill-fitting uniforms walked past, most of them wearing caps, shaven heads visible on those who did not. Each clutched a lump of black bread as they went into their living zone where they milled around with very little noise. Our small group of visitors walked through them without comment and no sense of fear. At the time I contrasted this with an experience I had of visiting the Modelo Prison in Bogotá some time previously where we had been surrounded at all times on our tour of the prison by a posse of armed guards to protect us from prisoners. How was one to contrast the humanity, or rather its absence, in the two prisons? In Bogotá the prisoners had enough life in them to pose a physical threat. In Minsk life had seeped out of the prisoners so that they did not present a threat. Where was the greater inhumanity?

In the middle of the colony was the Central Medical Hospital, holding 300 prisoners in large dormitories with bunks in triple tiers. The doors to the dormitories were open and the men were free to walk between them. The medical director's office was on the dormitory floor and he would walk out into a milling group of prisoners. Many of the prisoners looked quite ill yet there was no evidence of any segregation on health grounds. We were told that there was no medication in the hospital other than a few aspirins. Many of the men had been brought there from provincial colonies after swallowing razor blades or other sharp items known generically as 'foreign bodies'. One could only surmise what conditions must have been like elsewhere if prisoners were to take such extreme steps to get to this so-called medical centre.

It was clear to us that the political situation in Belarus was unstable, and this was reflected in the relationships between government officials and the League for Human Rights. In November 1994 we had a distinct sense of physical danger. Evgeny Novikov himself was clearly *persona non grata*, and the prison administrators were very unsure about what they should show us. On the other hand, we had met the entire senior management of the KGB and had been shown the KGB prison. Three years later there was little indication of any change on the part of the Procuracy but the prison administration was keen to show us everything. Novikov indicated that he was being courted because of his Western connections and it appeared that the younger administrators were preparing for stronger ties with Europe whenever the time became ripe.

The sad reality is that the time has never become ripe and indications over the last 25 or so years are that Belarus more than any other country in the region has retained many of the worst features of the Soviet justice system. This was confirmed by the reaction to the so-called democratic elections of August 2020. The fact that for many years Belarus has been the only country in Europe to retain and to use the death penalty is a clear marker of this and of itself has justified the country's continued exclusion from the Council of Europe.

Going into any prison is an unsettling experience. There is always a degree of prurience in entering a cell or room where men or women are held against their will and cannot escape the sensation that they are being observed rather like animals in a zoo. The only justification for doing so is that one is there with a purpose, whatever that may be. In terms of my work the justification has usually been that one is attempting somehow to ameliorate the situation, either for individuals or within the system as a whole. That is always predicated on the belief, however tenuous, that those in a position of power are interested in change and want improvement. One of the first questions one asks when visiting a country is whether there is a political will to change. If that is present, then one can always search for the means to begin the process of change. Only once have I come in contact with a prison system where I reluctantly had to conclude that there was neither the political nor the practical will to change and that by continuing to be involved with that system one would merely be providing a veneer of respectability to an immovable structure. That one time was in Belarus in 1997.

More than two decades later nothing has changed.[4]

Moscow SIZO No. 2 (Butyrka) 1992

The first international seminar on 'Penal Reform in Former Totalitarian Countries' was held in Petrovo Dalnaye near Moscow in November 1992 and was attended by over 200 people from most countries in the former Soviet Union and several from Central, Eastern and Western

Europe, as well as a few members of PRI from other regions of the world. Until the final moment it was not at all certain that the seminar would be allowed to take place. The two Russian organising bodies Prison and Liberty, led by its charismatic founder Valery Abramkin,[5] and the Moscow Helsinki Group had informed governmental authorities that the conference had been arranged and had invited them to send representatives but the response had been, to say the least, ambivalent. The organisers had also indicated that the international participants would welcome the opportunity to visit a Moscow prison but the reply had been that this would be most unlikely to be approved. Despite official ambivalence about the conference the Deputy Chairman of the Legislative Committee of the Russian Federation Supreme Soviet accepted an invitation to chair it. It was also to be addressed by the Chairman of the Supreme Soviet Committee on Human Rights, and issues discussed included the use of the death penalty, the criminal justice system for juveniles, monitoring of human rights violations and alternatives to prison.[6]

As the conference drew to a close we received word that permission had been given for the international participants to visit SIZO No. 2, more commonly known as Butyrka. Insofar as we were aware we would be the first foreign group to make such a visit. Even as we were driven from the conference hall into central Moscow we did not know how we would be received or what we would be allowed to see.

Novoslobodskaya Street is a wide boulevard in central Moscow. In the new environment of the city in the early 1990s the shop fronts were brightly lit. The buildings which lined the street were mostly solid early 20th-century Soviet style, with a sprinkling of newer office and accommodation blocks. One particular 1970s apartment block was very much like all its neighbours, and one could pass by an anonymous steel-covered vehicle entrance without a second thought, certainly without an inkling of what lay behind. But to go through this door was to enter another world, one which came from a different age but which was still very much with us at the end of the 20th century. For behind the modern apartment block, which was built during the Khrushchev era, stood SIZO No. 2, Butyrka investigative isolation centre. The massive fortress style construction had changed little since it was built in 1771. It has an infamous place in Russian history, mentioned by writers from Tolstoy and Dostoyevsky to Anatoly Rybakov as one of the main city prisons for those awaiting trial and the point at which those who had been sentenced to exile or the Gulag were gathered to begin their long walk to Siberia. In Tsarist times these journeys could take up to a year and those who set out from Butyrka faced the possibility of dying en route. The period of sentence for these prisoners began only when they had arrived at their destination.

Once our group had passed through the entrance security we were taken to the office of the prison director. A dozen or more of us crowded round the small meeting table as the director, Colonel Oreshkin, stood in front of us. On the wall behind him was a Russian flag and beside it a large, framed photograph of Felix Dzerzhinsky, himself a prisoner in Butyrka during Tsarist times and later first director of the Cheka, the feared and brutal Soviet secret police. There could be little doubt where the director's political sympathies lay. He was clearly nonplussed at our presence and far outside his comfort zone. It was obvious that he had been instructed to facilitate our visit but he had no idea what that implied or what restrictions he should impose on us.

In response to our questioning he explained that Butyrka was designed to hold 3,500 detainees but on the day of our visit it held 5,200. Of these, 4,500 were pre-trial including 452 women. He said that the average time awaiting trial was six to eight months but that some of the accused waited as long as three or four years. Director Oreshkin was at pains to point out that all decisions regarding a prisoner's treatment and what he or she was allowed lay in the hands of the prosecutor. Rooms or cells had beds for 40 prisoners but he acknowledged that as a matter of course each would hold between 70 and 100 persons. The prisoners spent all day in these rooms, taking it in turns to sleep on the available beds. On occasion prisoners would be taken in a group from their room to penned yards on top of the accommodation blocks for fresh air. The director said that many of the prisoners had mental health problems and that there was a continuing and increasing problem with the incidence of tuberculosis.

We then asked if we could be shown round the prison. The director hesitated and asked which parts we would like to see. The rest of our party looked to me as the most experienced prison person present and I replied, "Everything." Sounding less than enthusiastic, the director instructed some of his senior staff to take us wherever we wished to go and off we went for what might be described as a journey into hell.

Butyrka at that time was the second largest prison in the Russian Federation. The largest was SIZO No. 1 in St Petersburg, Kresty Prison, which I describe in the next chapter. With a capacity for 3,000 prisoners Kresty regularly held up to 10,000. Speaking in May 1998 the Director of Kresty described the reality of holding 12 or 14 prisoners in a cell of eight square metres which was originally intended to hold two men. He said that it was quite common for prisoners to say to him, "Citizen Director, I am ready to plead guilty just to get out of this place and be sent to a camp." These were also the conditions which we observed in Butyrka.

Descriptions such as these do not convey the daily horror of what overcrowding meant in these massive SIZOs. The main effect, as we found out in Butyrka, was experienced in the living accommodation. The majority of prisoners were held in rooms with an average size of 80 square metres. In a typical cell of these dimensions there were about 30 to 40 double bunks squeezed close together against the two side walls. This left a space in the middle of the room for a long wooden table and two benches. In most of these rooms there were fairly large windows along the outside wall but the windows had shuttering on the outside and security grilles on the inside. As a result the rooms were in constant semi-darkness and there was little circulation of air. We were there in winter when the cold could be so extreme that prisoners had to huddle together for some warmth. We were told that conditions in the height of summer were even more unbearable and that even when stripped to their underwear prisoners would still drip with sweat. During our visit when the room doors were opened for us we were met with a solid wall of foetid air, rank with disease and infection.

The rooms had originally been painted green or brown, although it was often hard to be certain about this since generations of smoking, coughing and other activities had turned them into an indefinable smudge. In one corner of each room there was an open toilet, stinking and filthy, around which the prisoners had placed some rudimentary screening. Close by there was a dripping tap and small sink and in many cases a sign above the tap warned that the water was not suitable for drinking. Prisoners solved this problem with ingenious electrical arrangements which boiled small amounts of water. Lines of personal clothing festooned the room as they dried in the damp atmosphere.

A typical room held more than 80 prisoners. Even before subtracting the space taken up by the bunks and the long table that meant less than one square metre per person. Because the bunks were crammed so close together the ones in the middle of the row at the lower level had no light or air. The prisoners had a strict hierarchy which decided who was allowed to have what. We learned that the majority of prisoners slept in shifts of three per bed. The youngest or weakest was allocated the day shift for sleeping, which meant that they had to choose between sleep and the daily hour in the fresh air. It also meant that they had to spend all night awake, sitting or standing as best they could.

In 1994 the UN Special Rapporteur on Torture visited a number of SIZOs in Moscow. Sir Nigel Rodley's subsequent report captures the full horror of what he encountered: 'The Special Rapporteur would need the poetic skills of a Dante or the artistic skills of a Bosch adequately to describe the infernal conditions he found in these cells' (UN Economic and Social Council, 1994).

This level of overcrowding also put great pressure on all the services of the prison. The sewage system, which in many instances had hardly been upgraded for 100 years, could not cope with the pressure placed on it. The electricity was undependable and in any event was liable to be cut off because bills had not been paid. The cooking facilities were often quite primitive, even when the cook had sufficient rations to feed the prisoners. If the prisoners were lucky they would be given a bowl of weak porridge in the morning and in the evening and a bowl of watery soup at lunchtime. Two or three times a week there would be bread and often no liquid was provided. This meant that the home-made facilities for boiling water were a matter of survival. In many instances prisoners only survived because their families brought them food and drink.

During the pre-trial investigation the prosecutor could place restrictions on the detained person's access to family, either by visit or by correspondence, as well as access to parcels of food and other items. The period awaiting trial regularly stretched over many months, sometimes years, and it was hardly surprising that disease and illness were rife, with men and women who came into prison in a healthy condition subsequently contracting serious illnesses. There was little effort on the part of the authorities to hide the terrible situation in the pre-trial prisons. Speaking before a special session of the Duma in 1994, the then Head of the General Penitentiary Department (GUIN) Yuri Kalinin said:

> I have to confess that sometimes official reports on prisoners' deaths do not convey the real facts. In reality, prisoners die from overcrowding, lack of oxygen and poor prison conditions … cases of death from lack of oxygen took place in almost all large pre-trial detention centres in Russia. The critical situation in SIZOs is deteriorating day by day. (Quoted in Moscow Centre for Prison Reform, 1996)

This was the reality of what we observed in Butyrka in the course of our visit in 1992. It was reinforced in several further visits over the succeeding decade. In December 2018 the Russian prison service announced its intention to close Butyrka and to replace it with a new prison to be built on the outskirts of the city. At the time of writing it remains in use.

Moscow and Ryazan, 1993

In the first week of October 1993 the Department of the Execution of Punishment in the Ministry of the Interior of the Russian Federation arranged a conference on *Punishment: Legality, Justice, Humanism* in the Department's Higher Training School in Ryazan, a city some 120 miles south east of Moscow. The majority of those attending were academics and senior prison personnel from across Russia as well as from several states of the former Soviet Union. The foreign guests were Nils Christie from the University of Oslo, Martin Fincke from the University of Passau, Roy King from the University of Wales and me.

During the week prior to the conference there was a great deal of uncertainty about the political and security situation in the country. The constitutional battle between President Boris Yeltsin and the Congress of People's Deputies had reached crisis level and came to a head on 21 September when Yeltsin announced his intention to dissolve Congress and its Supreme Soviet despite the fact that the constitution gave him no authority to do so. Congress responded by impeaching Yeltsin and proclaimed Vice President Aleksander Rutsky as acting President.

Throughout the final week of September I was involved in a series of frantic telephone and fax exchanges with the Russian authorities; these were the days before the existence of email and other internet communications. It was clear that despite the political upheaval and the fragile security atmosphere the Russians were determined that the conference should go ahead and that they wanted us to attend. On Saturday 2 October Roy King and I along with our interpreter Kathy Judelson flew to Moscow and made our way to the apartment home of friends of Kathy, where we were to stay until our planned departure for Ryazan on the Monday. We spent Sunday on a tour of the Vladimir region with our Russian hosts and when we returned to Moscow that evening we learned that violence had erupted around the parliament buildings. Armed protestors opposed to Yeltsin had overturned barriers around the Congress of People's Deputies (the 'White House') and entered the parliament in support of opposition politicians. They had also taken over the nearby high-rise building which housed the office of the city mayor and had attempted to invade the Ostankino television centre.

We made contact with the Ministry of the Interior and were told that, while we were unlikely to be in personal danger, we should remain inside the apartment where we were staying and must on no account go near the centre of the city. In common with most Muscovites we spent the greater part of Monday in front of a television set watching the violence unfold in the city centre and listening to news bulletins on the radio. The assault on the television centre had been repulsed but the situation around the 'White House' was far less clear. The army had initially indicated that it would remain neutral in what it saw as a political struggle, but early in the morning of 4 October it responded to an order from President Yeltsin and stormed the parliament building, arresting the leaders of what had now become an attempted coup. By midday it appeared that the immediate violence was coming to an end. In the suburb where we were staying there was no sign of any unrest and in the afternoon we felt confident enough to take a short walk in the neighbourhood.

The Ministry of the Interior remained insistent that the conference should go ahead and advised us to be ready to depart on Tuesday morning for the journey to Ryazan. We were joined by Nils Christie and Martin Fincke, who had spent the previous day in a Ministry hotel within the sound of gunfire around the 'White House'. Despite the relative calm we were accompanied on our journey and throughout the conference by a senior armed officer. The journey was covered at speed; our minibus had a flashing blue light, as did the military cars which went before and behind us. In Ryazan we paid an initial courtesy visit to the Higher School where the conference was to be held before travelling on to the sanatorium on the outskirts of the town where we were to stay. That evening over dinner Nils Christie, in his usual frank manner, gently chided our hosts: "I have no objection to travelling by air; I have no objection to travelling by road; but I do object to travelling halfway in between them!"

The next morning we were driven back to the city centre, passing through the main square where the previous evening we had spotted a large statue of Lenin with his arm outstretched in the style which was to be seen in every town and city in the former Soviet Union. I nudged Nils who was sitting beside me. "Look," I whispered, "Lenin has disappeared." Indeed the statue had been carted off in the dark of the night, just as was happening at the same moment in many public squares across the country.

In the course of the conference we discovered more about the tenacity within the Ministry of the Interior that the conference should take place. The Head of the Prison Service, Major General Yuri Kalinin, found time to play a major part in the conference as well as meeting us on our arrival in Moscow and also immediately prior to departure. We learned that in the previous days the Head of the Ryazan Higher School, Sergei Ponomaryov, had despatched several lorries with uniformed staff and students to Moscow to support President Yeltsin in his hour of need. Shortly after this action he was promoted to the rank of Major General.

Debate at the conference itself reflected the momentous changes which were taking place in the Russian Federation at that juncture. One of the early speakers was Alexander Zubkhov, Deputy Chief of the Scientific Research Institute of the Ministry. An impressive looking grey-haired general, in some respects he personified the history of the GUIN and clearly questioned the basis of the new dispensation within the organisation. He was not at ease with the presence of foreign 'experts' and in many meetings over the coming years I was to have challenging discussions with him. A typical comment was, "What do you so-called 'experts' from the West have to tell us about prisons? You only have toy jails; we have real prisons." At the same time he had a rigorous intellectual capacity and was not afraid to criticise previous structures and practices during Soviet times. He talked about the present 'dynamic period' in Russian history and the degree of uncertainty about the future, commenting that the prison service could not be divorced from the current period of momentous change. He acknowledged the importance of not repeating past mistakes and the welcome possibility of discussing the process of change in a manner that would not have been allowed previously.

In succeeding years Zubkhov continued to discuss 'the process of change' in a variety of fora and began to alter his own views. At a conference in Moscow in 2000 which I attended as a Council of Europe expert he expressed his concern that Russia still had a penal policy based on punitiveness, even though it was now acknowledged how destructive this had been. He said that every third adult male in the country had either been marked by a criminal record or had a close relative who had; this despite the fact that many local leaders had themselves suffered under the criminal justice system in the past. He went on to assert that in the long term there would have to be legislative changes to prevent the imprisonment of petty offenders, quoting as an example that 350,000 of those in prison had been sentenced for minor offences such as stealing a sack of potatoes. These people, he said, were not socially dangerous. He claimed that only three or four per cent of prisoners could be described as dangerous and violent. This was a marked change in tone from what he had been saying in 1993.

Early in the conference held in the great auditorium of the Higher School, General Kalinin presented an informative paper which for the first time provided detailed factual information on the situation in penal establishments and the immediate challenges which they were facing. He left the massed ranks of brown uniforms in front of him in no doubt about his vision for the future of the prison system, a future in which international norms and standards would be acknowledged and implemented. A succession of grey-haired be-medalled officers followed him to the microphone to explain why such change would not be possible, certainly not at the rate he indicated. Eventually this prompted Kalinin to return to the rostrum. He apologised for doing so, acknowledging that this was against normal protocol, but went on to speak authoritatively as the Head of the Service: "I think that perhaps you did not entirely understand me. I want you to be in no doubt that these changes will happen and they will begin to happen now. I want you all to work with me on this, but if any of you cannot do this then you will have to go to retirement." This performance helped us to understand why Kalinin had been plucked from relative obscurity as a middle-ranking officer in the Ministry of the Interior based in Saratov Oblast to head the national prison service. I had originally met him in October 1992 in Poland where the Council of Europe had organised the first meeting of Directors of Prison Services in Central and Eastern Europe and had immediately marked him out as someone who might be a force for change.

The closing presentation of the conference was delivered by the Presidential representative for the Ryazan district who brought us back to the reality of the present day. He said that for 70 years the Soviet Union had had an idol, yet the previous night the statue of Lenin had been removed from the main square and it would now be placed in a museum. He ended by suggesting that, based on what he had heard at the conference, the strength of the prison service lay in the fact that it was no longer constrained by an idol. The conference had demonstrated that ideas could be shared and that opinions could be challenged.

After the conference I had a further day in Moscow before returning to London. Natalya Khutorskaya, a senior researcher in the Ministry who had spent several months during the previous year in London familiarising herself with criminal justice institutions in England and Wales, kindly took me under her wing and showed me all the key areas which had come under attack earlier in the week. Her husband Boris worked in the office of Yuri Luzhkov, who had become mayor of Moscow the previous year, and was able to provide access to the mayoral high-rise building, which had been badly damaged on 3 October. He also took me inside the security cordon to point out the damage which had been done to the parliament building, with the top floors of the 'White House' blackened by fire and still encircled by tanks. We also watched the surreal scene of a wedding party who had come to have their photographs taken in the shadow of all the rubble.

Towards the end of the day Natalya and Boris took me to the famous Novodevichy Cemetery which holds the graves of many important Russians, including Anton Chekhov. In the Soviet era many of the regime's leaders had been buried there, as well as leading authors, playwrights, musicians and scientists, and in 2007 the remains of Boris Yeltsin were interred there. As we walked around the cemetery Natalya pointed out many famous headstones. Conscious that at that particular moment the future direction of her country was far from clear, as was how history would eventually record the past, she murmured, "Of course, you should understand that in Russia we have a very unpredictable past."

The stance which Yuri Kalinin took at the conference in Ryazan in October 1993 was a courageous one. Given the dramatic events of the previous few days, there remained great national political uncertainty. The indications were that the old guard of Soviets had been repulsed on this occasion but the long-term future direction of the country was by no means clear at that time. Kalinin would have been instrumental in encouraging Ponomaryev to send his staff and students in uniform to Moscow to support Yeltsin. At the seminar in Ryazan it was obvious that there was a sizeable group of 'old hands' who were not in favour of change but Kalinin decided to challenge them head on and to demand their loyalty. His performance at the conference left me with a clear appreciation of his determination to drive through a process of change and of his confidence that he had sufficient support within the Ministry of the Interior to succeed in this, and I concluded that we should do everything we could to support him.

We had many dealings with Kalinin over the next ten or 12 years and arranged for him to come to conferences in London on two occasions. In November 2002, by which time he was Russian Deputy Minister of Justice, I invited him to King's College London where he delivered a seminal lecture in which he provided a comprehensive overview of changes in the Russian penal system during the previous decade and went on to give an indication of future ambitions to reduce the prison population and provide strong alternatives to prison. The ICPS subsequently published the lecture in English and Russian and it became an important text, much in demand from senior prison officials in other countries in the region (Kalinin, 2002).

Comment

From time to time, whether by accident or design, I have found myself involved in countries which have been in the midst of cathartic political and social change. I think of Cambodia in the immediate aftermath of the Khmer Rouge atrocities, in South Africa as it emerged from apartheid, in Chile in the period after two decades of brutal dictatorship and in the Middle East in the midst of the second intifada. The experience which was the most intense and lasted the longest was in countries of the former Soviet bloc following the collapse of Communism. In a number of newly independent states in Central Asia, such as Kyrgyzstan and Kazakhstan, in the early 1990s reform of the former Gulag system was seen as an important indicator of positive change. In Poland the impetus for change within its prisons was driven internally by a group of charismatic academics and others, while the Council of Europe became an important early influence in the Baltic states. Without doubt the greatest challenge lay in the country which had been at the core of the Soviet Union: the Russian Federation.

At a distance of some 30 years there is a temptation to overlook the uncertainty and even danger of those early years. In political terms it was not at all clear what even the immediate future would hold or which of the competing political factions would win out; in Natalya Khutorskaya's phrase, the country had 'a very unpredictable past'. The extent of that uncertainty was epitomised during the groundbreaking conference organised in Petrovo Dalnaye in November 1992 and the confused response from the government which ended with the authorities opening the door to the closed world of the infamous Butyrka prison to its first small group of international visitors. At that point the winds of reform were blowing strongly in at least some of the upper levels of what was then called the Main Administration for the Execution of Punishment (GUIN), part of the Ministry of the Interior. One year later the political uncertainty had become even more pronounced when GUIN itself hosted the first conference at its Higher Staff Training School to which it invited foreign experts notwithstanding the attempted coup which was taking place in Moscow at that time. In the course of that gathering the foreign guests witnessed at first hand the playing out of the struggle which was underway for the future direction of the Russian penal system.

For the next decade and a half the drive for reform waxed and waned. In 1996 Russia was admitted to the Council of Europe and two years later it took the significant step of ratifying the European Convention for the Prevention of Torture which opened its places of detention to independent inspection by the CPT as detailed in the following chapter. In the same year responsibility for the prison administration was transferred from the Ministry of the Interior to the Ministry of Justice, and the balance of administrative power fluctuated, affected in part by changes at Ministerial level.[7] For a short period Yuri Kalinin was transferred to another post in the Ministry but in 2004 he was reappointed as head of what was then entitled the Federal Penitentiary System, where he remained until 2009, when he was again appointed a Deputy Minister of Justice. Over the years the number of people in prison in Russia has fallen dramatically from a high of over one million in the year 2000 to its current level of 400,000, although this is still very high in comparative terms. Prison conditions, particularly in pre-trial detention facilities, remain a matter of grave concern as reported in the latest published report of the CPT (Council of Europe, 2013), with levels of overcrowding in some cases of up to 40 per cent. The report also noted that the European Court of Human Rights had found that some conditions amounted to inhuman and degrading treatment.

While it is probably no longer true to say that Russia has a very unpredictable past, its prison system still does have an unpredictable future.

7

European Committee for the Prevention of Torture

The United Kingdom

The Council of Europe's Committee for the Prevention of Torture and Inhuman or Degrading Treatment or Punishment (CPT) was established in 1989 under the European Convention of the same name. It is a mechanism designed to prevent ill-treatment from occurring and it implements its remit by carrying out regular inspections of all places where people are detained in countries which have ratified the European Convention. The background to the enactment of the European Convention for the Prevention of Torture and Inhuman or Degrading Treatment or Punishment is analysed in detail in Evans and Morgan (1998).

The CPT carried out its first round of inspections in 1990, visiting Austria, Malta, the United Kingdom, Turkey and Denmark. Its visit to the United Kingdom took place in the summer of that year and it had a heavyweight membership. Led by the President of the CPT, a distinguished Italian jurist, it included the two vice presidents, a Danish medical doctor and a Swiss psychiatrist, as well as a Norwegian doctor and an Austrian lawyer. Its visit came in the aftermath of the April riot at Strangeways Prison while Lord Justice Woolf was carrying out his subsequent inquiry and the team had a meeting with Woolf. The Committee submitted its report to the UK government in March 1991, one month after the Woolf Report had been submitted to the UK Parliament:

> *Report on the visit of the CPT to the United Kingdom in 1990*:
> The CPT's delegation found that the conditions of detention in the three male local prisons visited [Wandsworth, Brixton and Leeds] were very poor. In each of the three prisons there was a pernicious combination of overcrowding, inadequate regime activities, lack of integral sanitation and poor hygiene. In short, the overall environment in which the prisoners had to lead their

> lives amounted, in the CPT's opinion, to inhuman and degrading treatment. (Council of Europe, 1991a)
>
> *Response of the UK Government to the CPT Report*:
> It is difficult to judge when inadequate facilities and an unpleasant environment can be said to constitute 'inhuman and degrading treatment'. The Government's view is that the conditions at Wandsworth, Brixton and Leeds prisons at the time of the delegation's visit needed considerable improvement but were not so poor that the prison authorities could be said to be treating prisoners in an 'inhuman and degrading manner', and it therefore disagrees with the delegation's assessment. (Council of Europe, 1991b)

As described in Chapter 2, I had taken over as Governor of Brixton at the beginning of August 1991 and immediately became involved in commenting on the final draft of the UK government's response to the Committee's report. Immersed as I was in the pressing challenge of restoring a degree of normality and sanity to the battered and demoralised prison, I found myself dancing on the head of a pin as the Home Office drafters sought a form of words to refute the CPT's finding that prisoners in the UK were being subjected to 'inhuman and degrading treatment'. UK Ministers were prepared to concede that there was overcrowding, that there were inadequate regime activities and that there was a lack of integral sanitation and poor hygiene but could not stomach the reasonable conclusion that this amounted to 'inhuman and degrading treatment'. The concession in the final response was merely an admission that the conditions in which prisoners were being held 'needed considerable improvement'.

This response by the UK government was symptomatic of a wider expectation on the part of many countries in Western Europe that the CPT would become a mechanism for drawing attention to failings in the Council of Europe's new accession states in Central and Eastern Europe and would act as a spur to improve their detention arrangements. The original member states of the Council did not expect that their own arrangements would come under criticism. Some Scandinavian countries, for example, took offence when their practice of holding individuals who were awaiting trial in conditions which amounted to virtual solitary confinement were the subject of negative comment. In subsequent reports the CPT has repeated its criticism of prison conditions in the United Kingdom and its most recent report, published in April 2020, concluded that 'the ineluctable fact remains that the prison system [in England and Wales] is in deep crisis'. During the 2019 visit, the CPT's delegation found that the local male prisons visited remained 'violent, unsafe and overcrowded, with many inmates enduring restricted and isolating regimes and/or long periods of segregation. A similar state of affairs was also found in the two young offender institutions visited' (Council of Europe, 2020).

Committee for the Prevention of Torture

The primary objective of the CPT is to protect individuals deprived of their liberty rather than to condemn States for abuses, and on that basis after each visit to a State it submits a confidential report to the government concerned and requests a confidential reply to the issues raised in the report. States are invited to request publication of the CPT's report together with the government's response and, with some notable exceptions, this generally happens.

The membership of the CPT is made up of one person appointed from each member state which has ratified the European Convention for the Prevention of Torture and Inhuman or Degrading Treatment or Punishment, currently 47 countries. The members serve in an individual capacity (that is, they are not representatives of their own country) and do not take part in visits to their own country. Members are independent and impartial experts drawn from a variety of backgrounds, including lawyers, medical doctors and specialists in prison or police matters. Each delegation consists of anything between three and five members. Depending on the issues at stake and the complexity of the situation in a particular country the CPT has developed the practice of also inviting ad hoc experts to be part of some delegations. The development of the working arrangements of the CPT in its early years has been described by its first President, Antonio Cassese (1996).

After I moved to King's College London the Committee invited me to become one of its experts and I carried out this function for a number of years. During inspections to different countries I witnessed some terrible examples of the ill-treatment of human beings and on occasion examples of how the individual human spirit can shine through in the most challenging circumstances. I inspected an old inner-city prison in Reykjavik which had places for 16 prisoners and was making the best possible use of inadequate facilities. In order to avoid overcrowding, all but the most serious offenders waited at home after sentence until advised by the prison authorities that a place was available. The person then had 14 days to put their affairs in order before reporting to the prison. Since prisoners were required to report on a specific day but not at a set time, most would report at the prison between 10 pm and midnight on the given day. That same year I was part of the inspection team in Butyrka pre-trial prison in Moscow where arrangements were completely different. I also inspected prisons in Armenia where there was rampant tuberculosis with hundreds of new cases being reported each year. The situation had become so dire that the International Committee of the Red Cross, after much soul-searching about a possible breach of its mandate, had provided funding for a 200-bed prison hospital to care for the most extreme cases.

In a visit to Turkey our inspection focussed on the treatment of high-security prisoners and in one prison I entered a cell to speak to the prisoner inside and found myself facing Mehmet Ali Aja who had attempted to assassinate Pope John Paul II in St Peter's Square in Rome in 1981. He had served 19 years in prison in Italy before being deported to Turkey where he had been returned to prison to serve a previous outstanding sentence. The two of us had a lengthy conversation about religion and matters theological. He explained to me that he had no particular hostility towards Catholicism or Christianity; his animus, he claimed, extended to all religions and especially religious leaders. That discussion did not find a place in my final report.

The two CPT inspections which made the strongest impression on me were those which I made to the Russian Federation in 1998 and 1999.

Russia

Throughout the early 1990s an increasing number of countries in Central and Eastern Europe gained entry to the Council of Europe and went on to ratify the Convention for the Prevention of Torture and Inhuman or Degrading Treatment or Punishment which brought them within the scope of the CPT. In 1994 the Committee inspected places of detention in Hungary; in 1995 it went to Romania, Slovakia, Bulgaria and Slovenia, and in 1997 to Albania, Estonia and the Czech Republic. Russia ratified the Convention in May 1998 and it came into force there on 1 September of that year. A mere two months later the CPT made its first inspection visit to Russia and I was invited to be a member of the delegation. I received a similar invitation for the CPT's second visit just ten months after the first.

As described in the previous chapter, I had visited Russia in connection with a variety of prison reform initiatives virtually every year since 1992. The Russian Federation became a member of the Council of Europe in February 1996 and shortly thereafter I was invited by the Council's Director of Legal Affairs to join a steering group which was being set up in partnership with the Russian government to develop initiatives to reduce the prison population in the Russian Federation. This steering group met alternately in Strasbourg and in different locations in Russia, and earlier in 1998 I had attended two of its meetings in Moscow. All of this activity meant that among the members of the CPT's first two delegations to Russia I had the greatest first-hand knowledge of what we were likely to find in the course of our inspections.

The first visit took place over two weeks in November 1998 and focussed on conditions for persons in pre-trial detention. For the first week we were based in Moscow, concentrating on Butyrka pre-trial detention centre (SIZO), which I had visited in 1992, and police facilities in the city. During the second week half of the delegation went to Nizhny Novgorod (known as Gorky in Soviet times) on the Volga River and the other half to Saratov further downstream on the Volga and 860 kilometres south east of Moscow. I was a member of the latter group, and the domestic flight gave me another opportunity to experience travel by Aeroflot. We carried our own luggage across the tarmac in Moscow's Domodedovo airport in sub-zero temperatures directly onto the plane, entering through its belly and depositing our cases in the hold wherever we could find a space before ascending to the cabin. Fellow passengers wandered along the aisle as we took off. Cabin crew cooked our meal (chicken, as I remember) on open gas burners and wheeled samovars of tea, which were also standing on gas burners, to our seats. As we landed in Saratov our fellow passengers burst into a round of applause, presumably grateful that we had completed the flight without mishap.

I have already described the terrible conditions which we had found in Butyrka in 1992, and the 1998 CPT inspection discovered that little had changed over the period of six years. We discovered similarly shocking conditions in the main detention centre in Saratov.

The CPT's second inspection visit to Russia took place in August and September 1999. It was very unusual for the CPT to make two visits to a member state in such quick succession but then the situation in the Russian Federation was indeed most unusual. According to the available data, at the time there were more than 700,000 convicted prisoners in penal colonies and another 270,000 men and women in pre-trial detention centres under the supervision of the prison administration. The SIZOs had a throughput of about 500,000 detainees a year. In addition an unspecified number of suspects were held, sometimes for lengthy periods, in police detention cells. In comparative terms there were more prisoners in Russia than in the rest of the member states of the Council of Europe combined, and the rate of imprisonment was second only to the United States in world terms.

The delegation began its second visit in St Petersburg City and Leningrad Region. I had paid a short visit to St Petersburg in April 1992, taking advantage of attendance at a conference in Helsinki to travel by overnight ferry to Russia's second largest city for two days to marvel at the magnificence of the former Tsarist capital which only the previous year had reverted to its historic name, having been known as Leningrad throughout the Soviet era. At that point there were very few tourists or foreign visitors and we were able to walk easily along the Nevsky Prospect, sail on the canals, cross to the Peter and Paul Fortress and climb to the top of St Isaac's Cathedral; even the Hermitage Museum was largely uncrowded. With the CPT in 1999 my focus was on another less salubrious ancient monument, Kresty SIZO, Investigative Isolator No. 1.

Kresty

Located on a prominent city centre site on the banks of the Neva River the prison was built largely by prisoner labour and was completed in 1890. The main accommodation was in two large buildings, each five storeys high in the shape of a cross, hence its name, with four radial spokes meeting in a central tower. In other words it was built on the panopticon style favoured by 19th-century prison architects in the United States and similar to Pentonville Prison in London. Between the two main blocks was a large church dedicated to St Alexander Nevsky. The prison had 960 cells and was originally designed for 1,150 detainees. At the time of our visit it was holding 10,000 men, 90 per cent of whom were pre-trial. The basement level of some blocks had been converted into living accommodation. The punishment unit was in one spur and others held men who were mentally disturbed.

We were told initially that one block held the 354 men in the prison who had tuberculosis. However, the two medical doctors in our team had private discussions with the prison doctors and examined the medical files. They found evidence that a total of 1,200 prisoners either had registered TB or were under investigation for the illness and that in the first eight months of 1999 there had been 13 deaths from TB. These frightening figures confirmed data which we already had of the incidence throughout prisons not only in Russia but in all the countries of the former Soviet Union (Stern, 1999).

Our team divided into pairs, each with an interpreter, to spend two days inspecting the prison and interviewing prisoners, at first in groups within their cells and then singly with those who asked to be interviewed in private. A colleague and I spent a day in a section which held 350 prisoners who were being detained either in strict or special regime conditions as well as others whose death sentences had been commuted to 25 years' imprisonment. In practical terms the only difference between special and strict regime in SIZOs was that those in the former category were held in cells with two locks on the door. In the centre of the block there were a number of guards with Alsatian dogs which barked in a threatening manner whenever a prisoner was taken past.

As was normal practice with the CPT, we asked the guard to unlock cell doors for us and we along with our interpreter went into the cell, pulling the door behind us so that the prisoners could feel they were able to talk to us without intimidation by staff. Shortly after we entered the first cell the door was thrown open and a major entered. He informed us that he had been told 'from the top' that he had to stay with us in the cell 'as the prisoners were so dangerous'. We said that this was not acceptable and asked to be taken to see the director of the prison. We found him in his office along with the regional director who had come to greet us. They informed us that prison rules were quite clear and the director could not agree to us interviewing these particularly dangerous prisoners with the door closed. We had a stand-off for 20 minutes while we argued that this was normal practice for the CPT and that we had operated these arrangements during our first visit in November 1998. The regional director eventually agreed but said that additional staff would be detailed to stand immediately outside the door. In the event the additional staff turned out to be one slightly built young lieutenant.

One of the consequences of overcrowding was that, as we had seen elsewhere, prisoners did not have their own bed; for example, in one cell which contained 84 prisoners there were 34 beds. In the largest rooms this meant that up to three prisoners shared one bed, sleeping on a rota basis, with the strongest men using the bed at night, while weaker ones slept during the day. In large rooms bunk beds were packed together so as to leave some communal living space. This meant that men who had lower bunks in the middle of a row were in a particularly dark, airless environment. In smaller cells holding up to eight men, the typical arrangement was to have two sets of double bunks. The remaining prisoners laid out thin mattresses on the stone floor as best they could. On one occasion as I sat on the edge of a bunk bed talking to prisoners who were crowded round, my interpreter cautioned me to be careful where I placed my feet as they were right beside the head of a man who was asleep on the floor under me. When we asked an 18-year-old man if he took fresh air, he said that he did not because his allotted time to sleep was during the day. That meant that he spent every night standing or crouching as best he could. As one prisoner graphically expressed it, "People sitting on each other's head is a torture." If anything, the pressures of overcrowding in smaller cells could be worse than in the large ones. In Saratov, for example, we had visited a cell of less than eight square metres which was holding eight men. Prisoners lived in this situation for virtually 24 hours each day. As in Butyrka, in many of the rooms there was virtually no natural light as the windows were covered by shutters and grilles, sometimes on the inside of the room as well as on the outside.

In June 1999 I had attended a conference in Moscow jointly organised by the Council of Europe and the Russian government concerning the issue of the abolition of the death penalty. In the course of the conference a message of support from President Yeltsin was read out in which he confirmed that he had just signed a moratorium on the death penalty and the commutation of the death penalty sentence to life imprisonment for all prisoners currently under sentence of death in Russia. He expressed his hope that the conference would lead to the abolition of the death penalty in the Russian Federation.

In Kresty the prisoners whose death sentences had been commuted were held in a basement unit which had little natural light. Each cell had between four and six prisoners. It had two concrete, raised bed blocks and there was space for two additional mattresses on the floor. This meant that in cells with more than four prisoners, they could not all sleep at once. The cells were black with dirt, with very little natural light. The whole unit was dark and cramped, with a smell of death. The prisoners wore black uniforms with white horizontal stripes painted on them. They had been in these cells for between two and six years. There was no electricity point in the cells which meant that these prisoners could not boil water, as other prisoners did, but had to take drinking water straight from the tap, despite signs in all other rooms that the water should not be drunk.

One prisoner for some reason was still under sentence of death and was in a cell on his own. Initially we spoke to him through the hatch in his cell door and indicated that we would like to come into his cell to talk with him privately. He agreed and we asked the guard to unlock the cell door. Before we realised what was happening, the guard told him to put his hands through the hatch and he was handcuffed for our visit. The guard then unlocked the door for us. The CPT has a provision that prisoners should not be handcuffed while being interviewed. When the cell door was opened it was quite obvious that the man was very agitated and so we decided to go ahead with the interview despite the handcuffs since we concluded that his agitation would have become even worse if we had taken a stand. Staff stood outside the door. The man, clad in a white pyjama-style uniform, slippers and no socks, was very nervous and pale but talkative. He told us that he had been sentenced to death four years earlier but expected that his sentence would soon be commuted to 25 years' imprisonment, at which point he would be sent to a colony. In his cell he had a Bible, paper and a pencil. He was taken to the exercise pen for one hour each day and was allowed a ten-minute shower once a week. He was handcuffed whenever he came out of the cell.

All rooms used for permanent accommodation in the SIZOs, whether large or small, had one Asian-style toilet and one washbasin with a cold water tap, both of which were invariably in a filthy condition. Some prisoners told us that their main daily activity involved joining one of three queues: for the toilet, for the water tap and for fresh air at the window. In the smaller cells there was often a wall one metre or so high around the toilet which offered a degree of privacy. In larger rooms prisoners had usually constructed some sort of screening.

On the roofs of the accommodation blocks there were pens where prisoners would be taken for a short period each day for 'exercise'. These pens were best described as walled rooms with the ceilings replaced by metal grilles. All the prisoners from one room had to take exercise at the same time which meant that the degree of overcrowding in the exercise pen was the same as in the accommodation room.

There could be little argument that some of the conditions in Kresty, as in the other SIZOs we inspected, amounted to extremely serious examples of inhuman and degrading treatment of those who were detained there and that some of what we had observed amounted to torture.

In the administration block in the central rotunda there was a well-appointed museum which documented the history of Kresty with full records, artefacts and photographs. We learned to our amazement that the administration had embarked on a private enterprise to provide additional income. Each weekend the public could join a tour of the prison at a charge of 50 roubles for Russians and $10 for foreigners. Four groups of 15 people were accommodated each day. The tour walked through the centre of one of the main blocks, up to the fourth floor of one section, into the former chapel and through the small unit which had been converted into the museum. Each tour lasted one hour, during which the rest of the prison was closed up. Apparently it was not uncommon for former prisoners to bring wives and girlfriends to show them where they had been held.

Kresty SIZO was closed in 2018 and its prisoners transferred to a new prison with 4,000 places in Kolpino on the outskirts of St Petersburg. It is informally known as Kresty 2.

After St Petersburg the CPT delegation divided into two groups. One went to Ognenny Ostrov in Vologda Region some 450 kilometres north of Moscow to inspect a high-security colony which held prisoners serving life sentences and others who had previously been sentenced to death. The colony was in a former medieval monastery on a small island in a remote location. They later reported that they were welcomed by the director who had on his desk a copy of a handbook on human rights training for prison staff which ICPS had published earlier that year. He informed the delegation that the manner in which the colony was managed had 'Andrew Coyle's seal of approval'! Their subsequent findings did not bear out this assertion.

Chelyabinsk

I was part of the other group which travelled across the Ural Mountains to Chelyabinsk on the east side of the border between Europe and Asia. Our first visit was to a strict regime colony where we were met by the regional prison director who informed us that we were the first delegation to visit the region from Europe. He explained that there were 22 penal institutions in the region holding a total of 34,000 prisoners. With the population of the region being 3.5 million, this implied a rate of imprisonment of almost 1,000 prisoners per 100,000 of the population, a disturbingly high rate, even higher than that of Texas in the United States. The director talked about the recent movement of the prison service from the Ministry of the Interior to the Ministry of Justice which had led to a much simpler line of management as he now reported directly to the national headquarters in Moscow. He told us that the main problem was lack of funding, pointing to the fact that in the previous year only 56 per cent of the agreed budget had actually been received.

The colony had a standard layout. The external perimeter was surrounded by a wooden fence with an inner wire fence and coils of barbed wire laid on the ground between the two fences. Guards with dogs patrolled the inner perimeter, and the external perimeter was guarded by 13 watchtowers. As in all colonies there were two main areas, the industrial zone and the main zone which included 13 living units, a kitchen, dining hall, shower area, infirmary, security services and a concert hall. The official capacity of the colony was 1,520, and on the day of our visit it held 1,750 men. They had all been sentenced to strict regime, which implied that they were recidivists or first offenders who had been convicted of a serious crime. The average length of sentence was five to eight years, the longest being 20 years.

The living units each held an average of 150 prisoners. In the Soviet era the men would have spent eight to 12 hours a day in the industrial zone, many of them involved in heavy engineering work. This activity had all but dried up and most prisoners now spent all day in the living units with little to keep them occupied. Each unit had an external compound surrounded by a wire fence and the prisoners were able to come and go within this as they wished. This ameliorated the gross overcrowding within the units. In one of them we found 172 prisoners sleeping in a dormitory with triple bunk beds squeezed together two deep against both walls. We calculated that the average space per person was between 1.0 and 1.4 metres. The toilet and washing facilities in the units were appalling. We inspected one toilet block serving up to 300 prisoners which was a filthy, stinking building with six holes in the ground. There was no flushing arrangement, simply small piles of lime, and no toilet paper. One of the prisoners expressed the novel opinion that "the degree of civilisation in a country could be judged by the state of its toilets".[1] Given these conditions it was no surprise that our medical colleagues discovered a high level of infection among the prisoners and this was confirmed by the presence of a separate isolation unit for 80 prisoners who had active tuberculosis.

Beyond the living zone was the industrial zone where the landscape repeated what I had seen in so many colonies throughout the 1990s, with great echoing factories empty save for ghostly glimpses of a small number of staff and prisoners. Heavy machinery was rusting all around as it lay unused. Many of the lights were off 'to save electricity'. There was a significant shortage of both orders and of raw materials. The head of industry said that the units were working at 30 per cent capacity but that looked to be a significant overestimate. He told us the story which one heard everywhere about how they used to work 24 hours a day to meet production requirements and now they worked from Monday to Friday, 8–11 am and 12–3 pm. About 450 prisoners were employed in this way. The only area which seemed to be working was where old car and lorry tyres were being recycled to produce asphalt.

On a more positive note there was a technical school which had been built in 1961 and trained around 180 men each year on a nine-month course in crane operating, electrics and welding. The course was a mix of academic and practical work with a nationally recognised certificate at its conclusion.

Each year prisoners were entitled to have three 'short' visits lasting four hours and three 'long' visits lasting 72 hours. The former took place in a room with cubicles behind glass and using telephones. As in other colonies, the unit for the 72-hour visits was relatively well appointed with accommodation for 14 visits at a time. There was a common room for all the visitors furnished with easy chairs, a television and children's toys and also a fully equipped kitchen. The visitors, who brought their own food for the three days including that for the prisoner, could be parents, grandparents, children, grandchildren, spouses or foster relations. The private rooms were furnished with either a double or two single beds and folding beds which were provided if there were children, as well as two chairs, a mirror, clothes hooks, a shelf, crockery, an electric kettle and a radio. Roll call was taken each evening and the unit was then locked from the outside. Eleven of the units were in use on the day of our visit. A small child was running about and a young woman stood peeling potatoes in the kitchen. Not surprisingly, we were told that many families could not afford the time or the costs of travelling extensive distances to visit three times a year but clearly a number did somehow manage to do so. In the midst of all the terrible conditions which we were uncovering we had at last found one practice where the Russian authorities were more humane to families, as well as to prisoners, than their counterparts in the United Kingdom and many other countries.

Zlatoust

The town of Zlatoust, with a population of around 22,000, lies some 150 kilometres east of Chelyabinsk. The prison close to the city centre was one of only 13 of its type in the Russian Federation in 1999, used to hold convicted prisoners before they went on to a labour colony and also to hold prisoners who required a closer level of supervision than was provided in the colonies. The early records of Zlatoust prison had been lost but it had certainly been in use since 1914, originally as a transit prison for those on their way to the labour colonies in Siberia. At the time of our visit it functioned both as a local SIZO and as a prison, with a capacity for 600 in the SIZO and 1,200 in the prison. In September 1999 it was holding almost 3,000 in the SIZO and 873 in the prison. Our main investigation centred on the prison but we discovered that the conditions in the SIZO mirrored the worst that we had found in Kresty and elsewhere.

In the prison 268 prisoners were in general regime and 605 in strict regime, the main difference in their treatment being that those on strict regime were not eligible for long visits. Three hundred and five had been sentenced to prison regime directly by a court while the remainder had been transferred from colonies because of some disciplinary infraction. Those sent directly from court would spend three to five years in the prison before going to a colony while those transferred from the colonies would spend up to three years in prison before being sent back to a colony. On admission, all prisoners served the first 12 months on strict regime. The vast majority spent all the time in their cells with the exception of a short exercise period each day.

A maze of stone faced corridors ran under each area of the prison, creating a dark, overpowering atmosphere. One sensed that the history of the years when the prison held political prisoners seeped out of the walls. The admission unit where prisoners were brought on arrival was completely underground with no natural light. The whole area was clad in grey stone, unchanged since it was built in 1938 for political prisoners. Prisoners were initially held in a series of rooms with stone benches round the walls, no natural light and minimal electric light and an open toilet in the corner. We were advised that prisoners were kept there for a very short period but there were indications that they could be there for longer periods.

They were then taken to an admission unit, known as 'quarantine', until a decision was made about their long-term allocation which would usually be made in two weeks. This unit, which in addition held prisoners who had been in trouble in other units, was also in the basement and had no natural light in the corridors or common areas. The dark grey stone of the walls gave it the real feeling of a dungeon. I interviewed one prisoner there who told me that he had been transferred there two weeks before from a colony in Siberia where he had been for five years. He said that he had 'asked for his rights' and as a consequence had been classified as incorrigible. He was then taken before an internal court and accused of using drugs although he said that no evidence of this was presented. He was told that he would be sent to a closed prison, and it was only after he reached Zlatoust that he was handed written confirmation that this would be for a period of two years.

In the main accommodation units in the prison men were held seven or eight to a small cell where they spent 23 hours each day. Once again the windows were covered with external shutters which excluded all natural light. The main block, which held over 500 prisoners, had one small washing unit with four showers. A number of prisoners told us that they had not been provided with soap for two years. In the course of an interview one man told me, "The main difference between the colony and the prison is the absence of any freedom of movement here. One gets used to being here, learns to suppress all responses and all emotions." Without question, the level of overcrowding, lack of natural light, of proper ventilation and of sanitation in the blocks amounted to inhuman and degrading treatment.

Prisoners were taken out of their cells once a day for 'exercise' in yards on the roof of the block. As in Kresty, these consisted of 18 high walled pens with a grille and wire across the top. Given the high number of prisoners in each pen there was little room for proper exercise; instead people shuffled about or stood against the wall. Staff patrolled along a gallery above the pens. A corrugated iron cover had been installed on top of the whole structure so that the yards could be used when it was raining or snowing. As a consequence, the whole area was dark and the prisoners could see not see the sky. One disturbing feature was that loud music, which could be heard all over the prison, was played whenever prisoners were in the yards. We were told that this was to prevent prisoners talking to those in other pens. This form of daily exercise was obligatory and the whole scenario conjured up much of what was worst about the Gulag.

While other colleagues inspected the kitchen and the sparse medical facilities I went to the laundry which was under the control of a woman who told me she had been a guard until her retirement the previous year. A large solidly built 'babushka', she looked at me intently for a moment as I came in before asking, "Are you from Europe?" I confirmed that I was and she said, "I have never met anyone from Europe; I am going to hug you." She then clutched me to her ample bosom in a tight embrace to the great amusement of the guards and prisoners who were around.

Convicted prisoners subject to general regime in the prison were entitled to three 'long' visits each year, similar to those which we had observed in Chelyabinsk. The prisoners on strict regime were limited to two short visits each year. These were held in a room with individual booths, prisoners and their visitors sitting on either side of a glass screen. We were told that the visits operated every weekday from 8 am to 5 pm and that a visit could last for up to four hours. There were only six booths for the whole prison and none were in use during our visit. Given the travelling distances and the expense involved it was clear that very few prisoners received visits.

Comment

The first two visits of the CPT to Russia in 1998 and 1999 were of great symbolic significance for the Council of Europe and for the Russian Federation. At that time there were 41 member States in the Council and a total of approximately 1.8 million prisoners in all countries. One million of them were held in places of detention in Russia. Among the countries of the former Soviet Union which had joined the Council, the Russian Federation above all still existed within the shadow of the Gulag. Many of its places of detention had a history of grotesque abuse of human beings throughout the 70 or so years of Communism and some even stretching beyond that back to Tsarist times. During these two inspection visits we had been in Butyrka, which had been the gathering point for millions of men and women who were about to embark on the long and arduous journey east to the deadly mines and forest camps 11 time zones away in Siberia. We had also been to the grim prison in Zlatoust which had been a transit site for prisoners from Moscow and elsewhere in the Soviet Union on the final stages of their journey to work in the mines of Kolyma and the far east.[2] Moving forward to modern times, some of us had been to the former monastery on Fire Island in Vologda which had been a much feared prison colony in Soviet times and was now being used to hold men who until recently would have suffered the death penalty in conditions which would crush all but the strongest character.

Some months before the first visit to Russia I had reported for the CPT on prison conditions in Iceland, another member State of the Council of Europe, with a total of 100 or so prisoners. How could I possibly compare the two inspections? What, if any, could be the read across between the two countries?

There was no question that many aspects of conditions of detention in the Russian Federation remained completely unacceptable in a democratic society. To mention but three examples:

- The levels of overcrowding which we witnessed were appalling. Taken in conjunction with extremely low levels of hygiene and sanitation and the almost total lack of any meaningful activity, such conditions amounted to inhuman and degrading treatment.
- Conditions for those held for long periods in prisons, particularly for those held under strict regime, were excessively harsh. This applied particularly to those prisoners serving life sentences or whose death sentences had been commuted where some of the conditions of detention could be described as torture.

- Throughout the 1990s there had been a growing understanding of the dangers posed by the epidemic of tuberculosis in many Russian prisons, and the reality of what this meant in practical terms was demonstrated with terrible clarity in a number of the prisons which we visited. The medical members of our delegations emphasised that the conditions of detention contributed significantly to the spread of this epidemic, which presented a real threat to the public health of the whole country.

At the same time we needed to acknowledge that this was a period of great change within Russia and also in the General Penitentiary Department in terms of its administrative structure and the management of prisoners after its transfer from the Ministry of the Interior to the Ministry of Justice. In the late 1990s there was what appeared at the time to be a justifiable degree of optimism about the direction in which the country was moving and there was a wish on the part of the Russian government to play an active role in bodies such as the Council of Europe and to cooperate with intergovernmental agencies and human rights bodies. Within a decade or so, sadly, this optimism was called into question.

After each visit, the CPT sends a detailed report to the State concerned. This report includes the CPT's findings and its recommendations, comments and requests for information. When sending the report, the CPT requests the State to provide a detailed response to the issues raised in its report. Since the inception of the CPT it has been the custom that the State concerned invites the Committee to publish its report along with the State's response, and this happens with all but a few countries. In the years between 1998 and 2020 the CPT visited Russia on 29 occasions, a number of which have been specifically to the Chechen Republic. Only four of the 29 reports have been published. They do not include those on either the first or the second visit.

8

Regional contrasts: Cambodia and Japan

Cambodia: coming out of Year Zero

In 1975 the Khmer Rouge (Communist Party of Kampuchea) took control of Cambodia, renaming it Kampuchea, and governed through a reign of terror and mass murder until 1979 when neighbouring Vietnam invaded, overrunning most of the country. Following the example of the French Revolution in 1789, the Khmer Rouge designated 1975 as Year Zero. Cambodia was re-unified by the Paris Peace Accords of 1991 and was then governed by a United Nations Transitional Authority (UNTAC) until democratic elections in 1993.

In 1994 as Cambodia began to take its first tentative steps towards establishing a new democracy in the wake of the nightmare of the years of Khmer Rouge terrorism the Royal Cambodian Government requested the United Nations Centre for Human Rights to conduct a review of the situation in the country's prisons. The ensuing report (UNCHR, 1994) painted a grim picture, beginning with its stark opening paragraph: 'Cambodia's prisons are in a state of crisis. Penal administration is in disarray. Prison buildings are in many cases literally falling down. Medical care is often non-existent and disease and malnutrition are rampant.' Also in 1994 a medical team led by Physicians for Human Rights undertook an assessment of health conditions in the country's prisons. Their subsequent report (1995) documented 'a pattern of mistreatment including beatings of detainees during interrogation, extreme overcrowding, shackling and other illegal means of physical restraint, decaying buildings, and overflowing septic systems and open sewers'.

Following these investigations I was asked by the United Nations to visit Cambodia to provide expert advice on prison reform. In the course of January 1995 I visited prisons across the country and also had a series of meetings with senior government officials and diplomatic representatives.

The director of prisons

There are few prison systems in the world that are administered by men or women who have themselves been prisoners. One such was in Cambodia in 1995. The story of Na Saing Hieng would be unbelievable if it were not true. He had trained as a lawyer in his native country and was appointed a local magistrate at a relatively young age. He subsequently became a soldier and in the early 1970s rose to be head of the military police in Cambodia under the Lon Nol government. After the Khmer Rouge came to power he escaped to Vietnam. The Vietnamese authorities immediately arrested him and he spent two years in solitary confinement, shackled hand and foot. For a further two years he was held in a concentration camp. After the Vietnamese invaded Cambodia in 1979 he was taken back to Phnom Penh, where he expected to be released. Instead he was confined in Prison T3, the most notorious in the capital. Nine months later he was released and sometime after that he was able to join the smugglers' route to Thailand where he spent a period as a refugee in the border camps. He eventually made his way to the United States and for ten years worked as an engineer with the McDonnell Douglas Company in California. In 1994 he had returned to his native land to help rebuild its democratic institutions and to his surprise he was asked to become Director of Prisons. He was the man who met me on my arrival in Phnom Penh on 14 January 1995 and who was prepared to listen to what I had to say about the management of humane and decent prisons. If ever there was a time for me to be humble, that was the moment.[1]

Prison T3, Phnom Penh

In worldwide prison mythology a small number of prisons have iconic status, invariably for negative reasons. In the late 20th century one of these was Prison T3 on Street 154 in Phnom Penh. The original prison was constructed in 1877 and at the beginning of the 20th century a second prison was built alongside to hold non-natives who had contravened the laws of the French Protectorate. The two prisons were later combined into the Central Prison. The routine in the prison during the period of French rule was harsh and many of the prisoners were taken outside on a daily basis to undertake forced labour on government infrastructure projects. Infectious disease was common and in 1918 the head of the prison asked that an isolation ward and a septic system be provided to reduce the spread of cholera. In 1927 his successor asked to be allowed to separate minors from the general population because of 'malicious promiscuity' among the prisoners, and a few years later the Governor General of Indo-China spoke of the need to extend France's *mission civilatrice* to the prison, which by then held around a thousand prisoners. During the brutal regime of the Khmer Rouge no prisoners were held in T3 but it was re-opened by the Vietnamese who took over the city in 1979, when one of the first prisoners it held was Na Saing Hieng.

In the late 19th century it was customary in many countries to build major prisons in town and city centres and they were often grandiose, impressive, forbidding fortresses; think of Pentonville in London, Joliet in Illinois and La Santé in Paris. One of the main reasons for this imposing architecture was to impress on the local population what was likely to happen to anyone who committed crimes or misdemeanours. This principle was especially important in countries which had been colonised, where there was a need to subjugate the local population. Prison T3 was an obvious example of this type of prison. It stood in the centre of the capital in a bustling inner-city neighbourhood, close by Wat Ounalam, the most important Buddhist temple in Phnom Penh, and it dominated its neighbourhood.

T3 was the first prison I visited in Cambodia and it was obvious even from the outside that the buildings were in serious disrepair. The solid boundary wall was around four metres high but the wall and its massive corner turrets were damp and covered in mould, with vegetation sprouting from the cracked concrete. The wall was separated from the busy main street by a single wire fence approximately two metres high, and the ground between the wall and the external fence was cultivated as a vegetable patch where a few prisoners worked under the supervision of a guard. As we arrived senior staff lined the route between the inner and the outer gates and we were greeted by General Na Saing Hieng and Colonel Burnsorn, the director of the prison.

The prison itself was a rambling group of buildings in a very poor state of repair and extensive parts were not used because of their precarious condition. The prisoners were accommodated in large, high-ceilinged rooms, the majority holding 20 to 30 prisoners and during our visit they were crouched around the walls of each room, all of which included an open latrine and a water trough. The non-governmental organisation Médecins du Monde had just completed the construction of a small hospital block which was not yet in use.

On the day we visited there were 290 detainees awaiting trial and 56 convicted men as well as 26 women prisoners. The director told us that prisoners were allowed out of their rooms in rotation between 7.30 am and 11 am and between 2.30 pm and 5 pm for exercise, to collect food and to wash their clothes. While we were there we observed large groups of prisoners doing physical exercises in the yards. However, it seemed highly likely that this performance had been staged for our benefit and we subsequently learned that the vast majority of prisoners were allowed out of their cells for a maximum of 20 minutes each day. Meals were served twice daily, at 11.30 am and 5 pm, and the director acknowledged that the diet was insufficient but expressed the opinion that for many it was better than they would have outside prison.

The high-security prisoners, those serving sentences between ten and 15 years, were in a block with cells which held three or four prisoners. The youngest of these was 15 years old. One political prisoner, a former general who had been involved in a coup attempt, had a small suite of rooms at the end of a corridor where he lived with his family. Women prisoners were housed in a large room in the same corridor as male prisoners. They were serving sentences between one and 20 years and, like the men, they sat and slept on mattresses laid out on a raised cement block. One woman had her two-year-old son with her. There was one female officer on duty.

There were 116 staff in total, seven of whom were women. Some 60 per cent of staff lived in police accommodation around the perimeter of the prison. In the middle of our visit the director stopped to clean the nose of one of his two small children who were playing inside the prison yard.

There was a generally relaxed atmosphere around the prison with little obvious security at either the inner or the outer gate, both of which lay open. Staff appeared easy-going; they carried no batons or other arms. The reason for all this was simply that the prisoners were locked up for most if not all of each day. When they came out they did so only in small numbers, despite the fact that the staffing ratio was relatively generous.

In April 1994 the government had announced its intention to close Prison T3 and to transfer its inmates to a new prison which was to be built in Prey Sar, 20 kilometres from Phnom Penh. This eventually happened in 2000.

P.J. Prison, Phnom Penh

Close by T3 on Street 51 was the P.J. (Police Judiciare) Prison, which in many other countries would have been classed as a police lock-up, attached as it was to the main police station in the centre of the city. In the early days of the Khmer Rouge regime it had been the notorious interrogation centre S21 until this moved in 1976 to Tuol Sleng. It consisted of one main cell block for male prisoners and a ramshackle wooden building for women prisoners. At the time of the UN Centre's first visit in April 1994 the prison held 216 prisoners and overcrowding was so severe that sewage overflowed into cells with some inmates even having to sleep in the latrine. At that time Physicians for Human Rights had described the facility as 'a public health disaster waiting to happen' (1995: 16). By the time of my visit the number of prisoners had been reduced to 14, including five women, in response to an instruction from King Norodom Sihanouk. The prisoners were held in a large dilapidated wooden barn with little privacy or protection from the weather. The corrugated iron roof had recently been replaced with funding from the Australian Embassy. The women told us that they were allowed out twice a day into a small yard, although it seemed unlikely that this was the case. The door to the women's hut was left open and they were supervised by the male staff.

Takmao Prison, Kandal Province

Takmao lies about 20 kilometres to the south of Phnom Penh. King Sihanouk was opening a new psychiatric wing in the local hospital on the day of our visit so the road to the town was well-decorated with flags and guarded by police. The prison was in a rural setting on the edge of the town and the front gate of the prison, which in any event looked quite insecure, lay open. The buildings had originally been a cotton wool factory and were converted to a prison in 1980. The prisoners were housed in cell blocks built within the former cotton barns. The large prison compound was surrounded by a reasonably secure wall which had been built in 1986. As in most prisons in the country, the visiting area was immediately outside the main entrance.

The prison held 141 prisoners, including five women. The men were housed three or four to a cell. In most of them the grilled front was covered by a wooden or steel door. A long bar ran the length of the range, giving added security to the doors. The women were held in one room at the end of one range. One detainee, who had been there for one month had a four-month-old baby. Another woman, aged 20, had a three-year-old child. Immediately next to the women's cell was a triple cell holding 12 men.

There was considerable potential to develop the regime in this prison. The perimeter wall was in reasonable condition. All that was required was that the gate should be secured and that proper staff surveillance of the perimeter be introduced. The grounds were generous and there was no reason why prisoners should not have spent the majority of their days working these to produce vegetables which could be used to supplement their diet.

Kompong Cham Prison

The provincial capital of Kompong Cham lies about 120 kilometres north east of Phnom Penh on the bank of the Mekong River. The prison was built in 1951 as an agricultural college and converted for use as a prison in 1979. It stood on grounds adjacent to the police headquarters and was approached through the main gate of the police compound. As in other prisons, the gate of the prison lay open. As we left, we photographed the gate officer asleep in a hammock. This prison was also in very poor physical condition and was surrounded by a wall about seven feet high topped by barbed wire to another three feet. The administration building was a ramshackle wooden construction with gaping holes in the wall. The director told us that there had been five escapes since October 1994 caused by prisoners breaking through the walls or roofs of buildings. In one case, he said, a family had brought a saw for a prisoner which they had hidden in food.

There were 114 prisoners of whom 13 were female. The director explained that he kept minor offenders in one cell block and allowed them into the open air each day. This block had two large rooms with 35 to 40 prisoners in each. There was a large water trough in the middle of the room and an unprotected latrine in one corner. Prisoners were crouched along the walls. One room held three boys who told us that they were 12 years of age and had been in the prison for 21 days. The director said that adults had brought them up from Phnom Penh to steal in the neighbourhood and they would probably be released in due course. When asked who had been there longest, one man said 13 months. Next door one man was in a cell with his wife; they were allegedly co-accused. The 13 women prisoners were held in one room which had a toilet/washhouse/storage area screened off. One woman said that she had been there for 11 years.

The more serious offenders were in another block, held in four dark, smelly cells with eight or nine prisoners in each and they told us that they might get out of their cell for about ten minutes each day to wash and exercise. The director was at pains to show where attempts had been made to saw through the window bars and told us that he was leaving the cells in their damaged condition "to show the NGOs" (non-governmental organisations).

We interviewed a number of prisoners in an open-sided covered area beside the cooking pots. This was also where staff took their food and rested on one of two beds while on duty. The director and senior staff crouched a few yards away while we spoke to the prisoners. A 59-year-old woman told us that she was serving an 18-year sentence after "a quarrel with her sister" and had been held in the same room for 11 years. She told us she worked in the garden area from 7 am to 10 am each day and that conditions had improved in recent years, principally in relation to food. She had always been guarded by males but said there had never been any interference, although we had no way of testing the truth of that statement. A middle-aged man told us that he had been detained for 60 days accused of murder. He was the chief of his village commune and insisted that there was no evidence against him. He did not know when he might go to trial. He was the cook and was out of his cell all day. When asked why he was wearing his own clothes he replied that it was because he was the prison cook. It struck us as rather odd that a person with such a serious charge should be given such privileges. We then spoke to a 42-year-old man who had been detained for two months on a murder charge. He shared a cell with 30 others; they were allowed out for half an hour each day to bathe. His family came to see him twice a month and if he could change one thing it would be that prisoners should each have their own eating utensils.

There were 43 staff members, including three women. Many of them had accommodation on site and were on call round the clock. A surprising number of them seemed to be continuously driving in and out of the prison on motorcycles and bicycles.

The director told us that he had joined the police in 1973 and had previously been director of the prison between 1979 and 1981. After a series of escapes in 1994 the former director had been transferred to other duties and demoted and this man had been reappointed as director. He told us that the Ministry of the Interior provided 1,000 riels per day per prisoner (at the time US$1 converted to 2,600 riels) which was intended primarily for food and fuel. There had been problems in the past about the transfer of this money and a new arrangement had recently been introduced which involved the director of each prison going to the Ministry in Phnom Penh each month to collect the cash by hand. This presumably was one way of ensuring that the full amount was received at the prison.

The director insisted that shackles had not been used since his appointment and he had heard that the UN people who had taken the shackles away had sold them and used the money to buy playing cards for the prisoners. In fact I had seen a number of these shackles stored in a room in the UN offices. He did not think that had been a progressive move as the prisoners had then got into fights over the card games. However, he acknowledged that the Red Cross had helped to improve toilets, showers and cooking facilities.

There was a general atmosphere of listlessness and lack of interest among both staff and prisoners. One member of staff, dressed unusually in a black uniform, carried keys and seemed in effect to be the jailer. The other staff were very relaxed as they went about whatever little business they had. The director had made no preparations for our visit. He was superficially polite but various comments indicated that he did not welcome outside interference. The situation was summed up by the guard who was sound asleep at the gate when we left and the best that could be said was that there was no attempt to impress us.

Prey Sar Prison

Prey Sar is a rural area 15 kilometres outside Phnom Penh. The main prison gate from the inner to the outer compound was too rusty to open and pedestrian entry was through a hole in the wall to one side of it. The inner compound of the prison was surrounded by a wall about three metres high topped by a further metre of barbed wire and there was also an inner fence with guard towers at the four corners.

The accommodation blocks were on three sides of the yard and prisoners were held in cells with between 12 and 20 in each one. A concrete platform ran down each of the two main walls of each cell with toilets in a separate area off the main room. The prisoners, who were eating a meal of rice and pork when we were there, were divided into two groups: those who had committed crimes and those who had committed misdemeanours. Those approaching release were held in the latter group and were allowed to work in the yard all day. Prisoners in the other sub-division were allowed out for five hours each day. Visits were allowed at any time because of the distances visitors had to travel. The director estimated that perhaps about ten prisoners received visits.

Sixteen of the 170 convicted prisoners were Vietnamese. We interviewed a number of them, one of whom was a 64-year-old man who had served eight years of a 12-year sentence for murder. He had been held for one year in T3 and six in Kompong Chnang, which he described as being much better, cleaner and not so crowded as the others he had been in. He spent most of the day outside his cell making bamboo baskets for use in the prison. He said that serious criminals were allowed out for one hour in the morning and another in the afternoon. According to him there was little prisoner-on-prisoner violence and no abuse by staff. Each room had a 'boss' prisoner and this man was one of those. In a concluding discussion the director confirmed that each group had a boss prisoner who was chosen by him on the recommendation of the staff on the basis of his crime, his honesty and his behaviour. This prisoner was responsible for cleaning and good order in his room but, it was claimed, he had no disciplinary function.

It was refreshing to visit Prey Sar after the experience of the previous day in Kompong Cham. The director had a clear management style and was making efficient use of existing resources. He had introduced a simple categorisation system which allowed greater freedom of movement to those prisoners who were not thought to present a major threat to security. Staff appeared to be much more alert in this prison, particularly in respect of basic security procedures.

The main issue for discussion in Prey Sar in 1995 was the proposal to build a new prison with 1,000 places at Prey Sar to replace Prison T3 in central Phnom Penh. This plan came to fruition in 2000 with the closure of T3 and the transfer of prisoners to the new prison with 3,000 places in Prey Sar. In January 2020 the General Department of Prisons announced that the prison could not accept any more prisoners as it was already holding 9,000, three times its capacity (Narim, 2020).

Siem Reap Prison

Siem Reap is the provincial capital of the province of the same name in the north east of the country. My visit there coincided with one by Justice Michael Kirby from Australia, the UN Secretary General's Special Representative for Human Rights in Cambodia. As well as going to the prison, Justice Kirby was in Siem Reap to view the work being done by Japanese and other scientists at Angkor Wat and other temple sites in the neighbourhood and I accepted his invitation to join him as he did so. Being part of an official delegation we were given an extraordinary insight into the temple complexes and the work which was ongoing to preserve them by the group of Japanese experts. In January 1995 there was still a strong Khmer Rouge presence in the surrounding countryside and we were accompanied by armed guards throughout. We were virtually the only non-locals, and the people we met in the complex were all local residents. It was quite clear that once the Khmer Rouge threat receded the area would become a massive tourist attraction. This was confirmed when I returned on a personal visit in March 2000 and was able to find accommodation in the restored grandeur of the Raffles Grand Hotel d'Angkor which had been a deserted shell in 1995.

The prison had been constructed by the French in 1944 and was located near the centre of the town. The external prison grounds were surrounded by a wire fence about eight feet high and the exterior gate was locked and had a guard, unlike some of the prisons we had seen previously. Most of the ground was cultivated by prisoners. During the time of the Khmer Rouge the prison held 2,500 prisoners. One assumed that most of them must have been in this external area. The prison proper was surrounded by a secure wall. The buildings of the prison were free-standing and the two-metre distance between them and the wall provided additional security. The gate to the inner courtyard was locked and the prison buildings faced inwards onto a central courtyard; there was a watchtower in the middle of the yard. The accommodation for prisoners consisted of six large cells and eight small ones. A new toilet area had been built in one corner. A small raised covered area at one end of the yard was used as a primitive joinery shed. The other half of the yard was taken up by a large, covered area. The exterior of all the buildings was smart, painted white with blue facings.

At the time of my visit there were 137 prisoners, including two women and five juveniles, 16 and 17 years old. We were told that 15 prisoners were detained accused of being members of the Khmer Rouge and we were shown their detention warrants. They had been signed by a court but we noted that the provisions on their warrant had not been on the statute at the time of their arrest in April 1994.

When we visited all cell doors were open and prisoners were free to come and go within the yard, which was apparently normal practice. One prisoner was doing some woodwork and a number were involved in preparing food. The majority were in the large, covered area watching a video. The deputy director said that the colour television and the video were his personal property. A few prisoners were sitting in the cells. In two of the larger rooms there were blackboards with English lessons written on them. There were six staff on duty in the yard, where the population was increased by two pigs, a dog and puppy and a number of hens.

We were told that one of the women prisoners worked in the house of the head of administration and she also stayed there overnight. The other woman had a single cell in the main yard but had to use the same toilets as the men and to bathe Khmer-style in full view. She was walking about preparing her meal while we were there. Her presence did not appear to excite any curiosity. She had a personal lock and key to her cell. She showed us her cell and we spoke to her privately. She told us that she was 30 years old and was in the eighth year of a 16-year sentence.

The director gave us an overview of the prison routine. He said that 'training sessions' were held each week to encourage the prisoners not to return to crime on release. Better-educated prisoners were used to teach basic literacy and there was also some language teaching in Thai and English. Prisoners were encouraged to become involved in craft and hobby work and also in physical exercise and sport within the small yard. He told us that a special feature was that prisoners were encouraged to prepare and eat their meals in small groups of four or five. Visits took place in the external compound three times each month. The director expressed concern about the health of the prisoners, particularly in respect of malaria and tuberculosis. One female member of staff carried out nursing duties although she had no training. The main medical cover, as in other prisons, was provided by an NGO. When asked about positive and negative features, the director mentioned the absence of escapes and the fact that there were now sufficient rations among the former and the old buildings and poor health of the prisoners among the latter.

The Deputy Commissioner of Police explained the new chain of command which had recently been introduced: he was responsible for the judicial police in the province and as such was operationally responsible for the prison which he visited once a week. The Second Deputy Governor of the province, who had responsibility for judicial matters, approved new buildings. In other respects his remit did not mean much and he had never visited the prison. When asked about the Director of Prisons and the Ministry of the Interior, the reply was that the recent invitation to our forthcoming seminar on prisons was the first contact he had had from General Na.

This was by far the best organised prison which I visited and it demonstrated what could be done with limited resources. My conclusion confirmed that of the UN Centre for Human Rights Report (1994: 49) which favourably contrasted the positive attitude of staff to what they had found in other prisons. However, the numbers in the prison were rising steadily and it was clear that if this continued it would become difficult to maintain the level of freedom of movement and constructive activity for prisoners.

The situation in 2021

At the beginning of 1995 the number of prisoners in the country was around two thousand, and at the conclusion of my visit I submitted a raft of recommendations as to how what I had described as the shocking conditions in the prisons might be improved. However,

I ended my report with a warning that prison reform should only take place as one element of reform of the criminal justice system as a whole and I cautioned that the result of improving prison conditions in isolation might simply be that courts would send more and more people into prison. Unfortunately this was exactly what happened. According to government figures, by 2010 the prison population had increased to 14,000. By 2016 it stood at 22,000 and the latest available figure as at November 2019 was 36,000, 72 per cent of whom were awaiting trial. The total population of the country in 1995 was about 11 million and by 2019 it stood at almost 16.6 million, a much lower rate of increase that that of prison numbers. Today the government is frequently criticised, both nationally and internationally, for the poor state of the prisons and levels of overcrowding. In response it regularly publicises its determination to improve the situation but to little effect.[2]

Postscript: Tuol Sleng

During my time in Cambodia in January 1995 I was very conscious that everyone was living with the ineradicable memory of the trauma of Year Zero and the ensuing horrors of the Khmer Rouge atrocities. Remnants of the Khmer Rouge were still active in the north east of the country, as I saw when I was in Angkor Wat, and I realised that in every town and village I visited not one family had been untouched by the tragedy. Two particular locations stood as living memorials of that time. One was in the Killing Fields of Choeung Ek and the other was Tuol Sleng. In May 1976 the Khmer Rouge converted a former school in the area of Phnom Penh known as Tuol Sleng into Security Office 21 (S-21), the regime's main interrogation and extermination centre. Between 1976 and 1979, S-21 was a place of the most vile torture, murder and inhumanity. In 1980, following the expulsion of the Khmer Rouge from the city it was converted into a historical 'genocide museum'.[3]

During my visit in 1995 I had one free afternoon and I decided to pay my respects at Tuol Sleng. Coming out of the air-conditioned Royal Phnom Penh Hotel I hailed one of the ubiquitous pedal cyclos. When given directions the cyclist displayed no emotion as he cycled down Monivong Boulevard. He dropped me at the end of Street 113 and directed me to a nondescript building which looked exactly like what it had formerly been, Tuol Svay Prey High School. Opened in the 1960s, three-storied concrete buildings with open verandas were constructed around a square, where pupils would have gathered prior to going to the classrooms in the main blocks. To one side were smaller wooden buildings with thatched roofs which had previously been a primary school. The Khmer Rouge made few physical alterations to the buildings when they took them over, merely enclosing the compound with two folds of corrugated iron sheets, covered with electrified barbed wire to prevent any of the prisoners held there from escaping. All the classrooms were converted into prison cells, the windows enclosed by iron bars covered with barbed wire. The classrooms on the ground floor were divided into small cells for individual prisoners; those on the first floor held women, while the rooms on the top each held large numbers of prisoners. The information leaflet produced by the Documentation Center notes that:

> Within each unit there were several sub-units composed of male and female children ranging from 10 to 15 years of age. These young children were trained and selected by the KR regime to work as guards at S-21. Most of them started out as normal before growing increasingly evil. They were exceptionally cruel and disrespectful towards the prisoners and their elders.

The Khmer Rouge authorities kept remarkably detailed records of the number of prisoners and of how they were treated, many of which have survived. These indicate that about 10,500 persons were detained in Tuol Sleng between 1975 and 1978, although recently this estimate has been significantly increased. In addition, it is estimated that around two thousand children were systematically killed during this period. On arrival prisoners were photographed and personal details were recorded. They were then stripped to their underwear and all possessions taken away. They were shackled by the ankles onto a long communal rail with a lock at the end known as a *Khnoh*. (As mentioned previously, in 1995 I discovered that these communal shackles were still being used in a number of prisons.) The prisoners sat directly on the concrete floors, day and night. They had to ask permission before doing anything, even altering position. Failure to do so resulted in severe beatings. Prisoners were regularly taken to interrogation rooms, during which torture including beatings and 'water boarding' were commonplace, with death frequently the result. The average life expectancy in S-21 was between two and four months.

It is hard to do justice to the horror which I experienced when visiting the centre less than 20 years after these atrocities had been perpetrated. The Vietnamese who had ousted the Khmer Rouge had left the buildings just as they had found them. Several small bare rooms still held only a rusted iron bed frame on which prisoners had been tortured. On the wall were photographs taken by the Vietnamese showing the mutilated bodies which had been found still chained to these beds. In some rooms leg irons and other instruments of torture were still lying on the floor. In another room was the tilted wooden structure where prisoners had been held down with their heads under water. Elsewhere rooms had wall after wall covered with photographs taken by the authorities when prisoners first arrived. Most disturbing of all was the large board where a map of Cambodia had been constructed using the skulls of murdered prisoners. This was as shocking as the displays of similar skulls at the Choeung Ek Memorial on the site several kilometres to the south of Phnom Penh known as the Killing Fields, where the Khmer Rouge executed over one million men, women and children brought from Tuol Sleng and other detention centres, often in the most primitive and brutal fashion.[4]

My guide around Tuol Sleng in January 1995 was a gentle middle-aged woman who described everything to me in detail in a calm and dispassionate manner. Towards the end of my visit she explained that several members of her family had died in S-21. I asked her as politely as I could how she now found the strength to spend her days showing people like me round this abhorrent place. Quietly, she explained that this was her way of ensuring that the memory of her murdered family members and the horrors inflicted on them would never be forgotten.

Japan: the prison as a reflection of a society

> *Pills and porridge: prisons in crisis as struggling pensioners turn to crime*
> In the years to come, many of Japan's 74 prisons will end up looking like Onomichi, an ageing prison about 400 miles south-west of Tokyo that first started catering to older prisoners 20 years ago. The prison, tucked away on a hill overlooking the Seto inland sea, incarcerates just over 300 offenders, 76 of whom are 65 or over. The average age of the men in the special ward is almost 70; the oldest is 89. Almost all are serving sentences of one to several years for theft – usually of food from supermarkets – small-time fraud and, in a few cases, possession of drugs.
>
> Charts on their cell doors stipulate special dietary requirements and medication regimes. A handrail runs the length of the corridor, and makeshift wheelchair ramps are kept at the entrance to the communal baths. As many as 80% of the inmates here have high blood pressure or diabetes. There is a portable mattress on hand in case anyone feels faint, along with a wheelchair and,

> placed discreetly behind a desk, boxes of incontinence pads. (McCurry, 2008)

The comparative rate of imprisonment in every country is calculated per 100,000 of its total population. There are an estimated 10.74 million prisoners in the world, which gives an overall rate of 145 prisoners per 100,000. The rate for the Americas is 376 (with the United States the highest in the world at 639), for Europe it is 187 and for Asia it is 97 (Walmsley, 2018; Coyle et al, 2016). Historically the use of imprisonment in Japan has been low compared with most other countries. When I first visited in 1996 the country had 53,000 prisoners and by the time of my next visit in 2004 this figure had increased to 76,000. By 2014 the total had fallen to 60,500 and in late 2019 it stood at 48,800. This gave an imprisonment rate of 39 per 100,000 of the population, one of the lowest of all industrial countries and in contrast, for example, to South Korea at 106 and England and Wales at 140.

In general terms social mores in Japan are strictly ordered with a relatively high level of public conformity and local enforcement structures. With respect to criminal justice, a key element of policing is the community-based local police posts (*koban*) which are internationally admired for an approach which is based on community involvement and the prevention of crime. There is also a well-developed probation service, with trained staff who are each responsible for a number of volunteers who provide one-to-one support for the men and women who are on probation or parole. All of these features contribute to a low overall crime rate. Experts with whom I have spoken have expressed the considered opinion that courts are initially reluctant to send convicted offenders to prison, preferring to find a community alternative whenever possible; but once a person has served a prison sentence any future offence is more likely to result in a further prison sentence. One consequence of this is that the age profile of prisoners in Japan has always been higher than in other countries. This situation has been exacerbated in recent years by other factors, including the lack of social support for many older people in the community which has led to numerous documented examples of elderly men and women committing offences in the expectation that they will be sent to what they see as the safety of prison where their basic needs will be satisfied.

The regime in Japanese prisons is extremely disciplined and any infractions are severely punished as I saw for myself when I visited in 1996 and again in 2008. Nagoya Prison in Aichi Prefecture on the east side of the main island of Honshu has a particularly bad record in its treatment of prisoners. In December 2001 prison staff sprayed the bare buttocks of a prisoner with a high-pressure hose, inflicting severe damage to his anus and rectum. The man died the following morning from a bacterial infection. Eventually two members of staff were brought to trial at the local district court and in November 2005 they were found guilty of killing him but were given suspended sentences of three years and 14 months respectively as the judge accepted their unusual defence that they had been trying to clean the prisoner and did not intend to kill him. The judge concluded that the cleaning 'was done in an inadequate way that amounts to assault'. The year after the first incident two more prisoners died after suffocating in a 'restraining device'. The Justice Minister commented that the incidents at Nagoya were 'regrettable' but the problem was maltreatment by individual guards rather than in the prison system as a whole. At a news conference she said that she had 'not heard of any similar cases at other prisons' (Watts, 2002). This assertion was widely disputed by other commentators.

New prison legislation was enacted in 2008 which included provision for penal institution visiting committees and for improvements in prison conditions. Notwithstanding these changes, independent bodies have frequently been critical of the treatment of prisoners in Japan. For example, the United Nations Human Rights Council in its Periodic Reviews of Japan's obligations under the Convention against Torture and Other Cruel Inhuman or Degrading Treatment which Japan ratified in 1999, have listed a variety of instances where it has concluded that Japan has fallen short of its obligations.[5] These include abusive treatment of prisoners by staff especially by the use of physical restraints, lack of independent medical treatment and inadequate training of personnel in human rights, ethics and treatment of prisoners in general. The government of Japan has responded robustly to all of these criticisms. For example, the UN has been particularly critical of Japan's excessive and extended use of solitary confinement, citing in its 2007 review several cases where men have been in isolation for over ten years, with one case exceeding 42 years. The government's response was curt and dismissive: 'Incidentally, regarding putting a ceiling on the period of isolation by law, we consider it inappropriate as continued isolation is unavoidable as long as the necessity for isolation continues to exist.'[6]

Fuchu Prison

In February 1996 I was invited to address the Japan Federation of Bar Associations in Tokyo and I took the opportunity to learn more at first hand about the country's penal system, beginning with a visit to Fuchu Prison. Located in the town of the same name on the outskirts of Tokyo it is the largest prison in the country, with a capacity for 2,600 prisoners and on the day of my visit it was holding 2,200, all of them convicted with sentences up to eight years and having served previous terms of imprisonment. When he met me the warden of the prison was armed with an impressive array of statistics. On average prisoners had served more than five previous sentences and 12 per cent had served more than ten. One 60-year-old had been in prison 30 times and was notorious as an 'eat and run' specialist; that is, he would order and consume a meal in a restaurant and then walk out without paying. I learned that the average age of Japanese prisoners was 45 years; 13 per cent were over 60 and a further 21 per cent were in their 50s. This was quite a different age profile from most other countries. Seventeen per cent of prisoners suffered from some form of mental handicap and 34 per cent from some physical ailment, frequently as the result of drug abuse. The prison had 488 foreign prisoners from 45 countries including 13 from the United Kingdom. The average length of sentence for Japanese prisoners was three years and for foreigners it was five years. The latter were invariably deported on release.

The prison, which is set in generous grounds, was built on its present site in 1935. I visited a three-storied block which accommodated 425 prisoners in rooms for up to six prisoners. The rooms were relatively spacious and the large windows provided generous light. The men slept on traditional tatami mats and their personal belongings were laid out on the mat with mathematical precision or in a small storage area above the bed. There was an adjoining toilet area. Foreign prisoners were held in a separate block, also three storeys high but with individual cells opening off both sides of a long corridor. Each contained a western-style bed and a small table and a television set. There was also a toilet in each cell, placed facing the door and unscreened. There was no heating in any accommodation block which meant that they were intensely cold for much of the year. When prisoners were in their cells they were required to sit unmoving on the tatami mat. They took breakfast and the evening meal in their cells. Lunch boxes were taken to them in the work sheds.

Prisoners worked during the day in the extensive industrial complex which had a series of large workshops on two levels. They included shoe-making, woodwork, book-binding, printing and textiles. Each workshop had upwards of 50 prisoners with an average of two instructors and two guards. A very disturbing aspect of the whole operation was the studied concentration of the prisoners. Each stood or sat at his place with his head bowed over his work. Not one eye was raised as our party passed through, neither did the prisoners look at each other. There was a deathly hush throughout the whole place except for noise from the machines. It would only have been possible to enforce such a degree of conformity with an inflexible discipline. As we entered each work shop the guard ran towards the warden at the double, snapped to attention and shouted out the number in the party. We were told that prisoners were allowed to talk during the morning and afternoon breaks and at lunch time but not otherwise. In the course of later discussion at the Japan Federation of Bar Associations we learned that most of the work was being done for private companies and there was considerable concern that in effect this amounted to slave labour.

There were five small visiting boxes for the 2,200 prisoners, which indicated that very few received visits from family or friends. The room was divided into two by a large double skin of plastic glass, and a small circle was pierced with holes to allow the prisoners to talk with their visitors. Up to three visitors could sit on one side of the glass. On the prison side there were two chairs set closely together, one for the prisoner and one for the guard.

The physical conditions in the prison were relatively good; the cells were airy, bright and clean although the unscreened toilet in each cell was objectionable. However, the lack of any heating in the living accommodation resulted in severe cold and we were given to understand that this was deliberate policy as it was felt that prisoners did not deserve the extra comfort that heating would provide. The main point of criticism was the complete lack of any human rapport between staff and prisoners. The level of regimentation both for individuals and for the population as a whole was intense. It was clear that the penalties for any breach of discipline were severe and on the day of our visit there were over 40 prisoners in the solitary confinement unit. A further example of the extreme level of discipline was that prisoners were obliged to face the wall when any staff or visitors walked by.

Tokyo Detention House

The following day I visited the Tokyo Detention House. Built in 1879 it is the largest pre-trial prison in Japan with a capacity for 2,500 prisoners and is situated in a built-up area of the city, surrounded on three sides by motorways. There were 326 foreign prisoners at the time of my visit and I learned that two weeks previously seven Iranian prisoners, who were awaiting trial, had escaped by sawing through bars and using makeshift ladders to scale the prison wall. They were quickly recaptured but this escape, the first in living memory, had caused a great public scandal. When we met the warden he began our discussions by explaining that this was his last week in office as he was to be transferred to an administrative job in the central office and it was obvious that the shame of this was weighing heavily on his mind. It did not seem appropriate to comment that this was a common fate for governors in England when something went wrong in a prison. Our tour of the prison was formal as the Head of Security, the archetype of a chief officer, accompanied us round, making sure that the way ahead was clear and that none of us strayed. As in Fuchu, whenever we passed any prisoners they immediately turned their faces to the wall until we had moved on. The prison showed signs of wear but was spotlessly clean in a highly regimented manner.

The prisoners were held in individual cells, each of which had a large window giving ample natural light. Prisoners spent over 23 hours each day in their cells and were required to sit unmoving on their tatami mat in front of a small table. Again, there was no heating in the prison and given the time of year it was bitterly cold. Some prisoners, all of whom wore their own clothes, were clearly shivering. Beside each living unit there were a number of single exercise pens where prisoners walked on their own for a maximum of 30 minutes each day. They were not allowed to talk to each other and although side by side in cells they were in effect in isolation.

The Chief Medical Officer showed us round the small hospital which was well equipped with what appeared to be sophisticated medical equipment and had a complement of 12 doctors. We were shown a gruesome exhibition of a variety of everyday items which prisoners had swallowed and a series of X-ray plates confirming the fact. The doctor told us in a very matter-of-fact manner that the main work of his medical colleagues was performing surgery to recover these items which the prisoners had swallowed 'in order to get out of prison'. This macabre performance was a clear demonstration of the lack of humanity in this and other prisons.

I visited Japan on two subsequent occasions and learned more about its prisons and the wider justice system; a number of issues are worthy of specific comment.

The high proportion of elderly prisoners

In 1996 the warden of Fuchu Prison had drawn my attention to the fact that the age profile of the prisoners he was holding was much higher than one would find in most other countries, and I learned subsequently that this was true across the prison system as a whole. This statistic needs to be understood alongside the fact that Japan overall has an increasingly ageing population but even when this is taken into account the prison statistics are quite staggering. When I visited again in 2008 I learned that while the total number of police arrests had fallen in the previous year the arrest of senior citizens had risen by more than ten per cent, with many of them repeat offenders who were subsequently convicted of crimes such as theft or fraud. Lawyers with whom I spoke pointed to the fact that many older prisoners lived isolated lives on release and that some would commit minor offences in an attempt to return to prison.

As the proportion of older prisoners increased the prison service has had to develop dedicated facilities to help them cope with daily living:

> The number of Japanese prisoners aged 60 or older has doubled over the past decade to more than 10,000. That outpaces a 30 percent increase in the general population for that age group. The elderly now represent 16 percent of the nation's inmates. Though Japan's crime rate remains relatively low, the spike in elderly crime is another sign of the social and economic strains on the once-confident country.
>
> An entire floor has been converted into a pilot geriatric ward at Onomichi Prison, near the city of Hiroshima. 'The number of senior inmates has been surging, and there is no sign of decrease', said Koki Maezawa, a Justice Ministry official in charge of prison services. 'It's a serious problem that the entire society must tackle so that offenders don't keep coming back to prison once they get out.'
>
> Here at Onomichi Prison, the hallways use ramps, not steps, and prisoners are allowed to use walkers if they need them. 'We have to provide the kind of attention like ordinary nursing homes,' said Yoshihiro Kurahashi, the chief guard at the prison. Everywhere there are signs that this is not a normal prison. In one cell, a gray plastic tarpaulin protects the straw 'tatami' mat floor from bed-wetting. Mattresses cover the walls of another cell, now empty, to protect a former inmate with dementia who repeatedly banged his head against them. More than half the inmates have some form of dementia. (Yamaguchi, 2010)

This issue is no respecter of gender. On the contrary, the increase in the number of older women being sent to prison has been greater than that of males. By 2018 almost one in five women in prison was over the age of 60 years and virtually all of them had been convicted of minor offences, with nine out of ten convictions being for shoplifting. What is the explanation for such an unusual increase in offending by previously law-abiding elderly women? Social commentators point to the changing structures in family life with families being increasingly unable or unwilling to care for older relatives. The number of over-60s living alone increased by a factor of six between 1980 and 2015 and a survey of the figures in Tokyo in 2017 showed that more than half of the seniors who had been convicted of shoplifting lived alone. When questioned many of these elderly prisoners pointed to the fact that they had no one to turn to when they needed assistance (Fukada, 2018).

Increasingly the prison service is being sucked into the world of care for the elderly and has to provide its staff with new skills. By 2018 the Ministry of Justice was developing plans for a simple test for dementia to be administered to all elderly prisoners in the hope that an early identification of such symptoms might make it easier to provide treatment which could reduce the likelihood of future offending. This would include preparing release plans which ensured that the men and women concerned were able to access benefits and other welfare facilities on release from prison.

Prisoners under sentence of death

The number of prisoners awaiting execution in Japan is not officially available but in 1996 it was estimated to be about 55. On the day that I visited the Tokyo Detention House I was advised that there were 28 prisoners on death row, one of whom was aged 79 and had been there for 20 years. The latest estimate is that in 2020 there were 134 prisoners awaiting execution, the highest number ever. Commentators report that on average a prisoner might wait for eight to ten years before execution. The annual number of executions in recent years has been around three, although there was a spike of 18 in 2018.

Prisoners on death row are isolated in single cells and their conditions of detention are even harsher than those for other convicted prisoners. They have no contact with any other prisoner and are not eligible for visits. Death is by hanging and executions are carried out in secrecy. Prisoners are given no prior warning when their time has come and family members are only informed after the event. In its Second Periodic Review of the country the United Nations criticised the failure to give death row prisoners and their families reasonable advance notice of the scheduled date and time of their execution. Again the government was dismissive in its response, offering what can only be described as a Kafkaesque justification:

> Regarding notification on the execution of the death penalty, inmates sentenced to death are to be notified of their execution on the day it is to be performed. This is because, if inmates sentenced to death are notified of their execution before the day it will occur, their peace of mind may be negatively affected and the notification could inflict excessive pain on them. In addition, if the families of inmates sentenced to death are notified in advance of the execution, it would cause unnecessary psychological suffering to those who have received the notification. If the family, etc. of an inmate sentenced to death who has received such a notification visits the inmate and the inmate comes to know the schedule of his/her execution, similar harmful effects may occur. Therefore, we consider that the current method of addressing the situation is unavoidable. (United Nations Committee Against Torture, 2013)

Prison privatisation

The government first mooted proposals to construct a number of new prisons by means of a private finance initiative at the turn of the century when the number of prisoners was increasing significantly, and in 2003 it announced its intention to construct the first such prison near Mine, a small town at the south-west tip of Honshu, the main island in Japan. Mine Rehabilitation Centre received its first prisoners in April 2007.

I was invited to take part in a symposium on prison privatisation in Kyoto in March 2008. The gathering was attended by Ministry of Justice officials, academics and lawyers and the discussion was lively and impassioned. Officials explained that they had studied developments in prison privatisation in the United States, the United Kingdom and other jurisdictions and that the model they proposed to adopt was based largely on what they had observed in France. This would mean that the prisons would be constructed and managed under a private finance initiative (PFI). In simple terms, personnel employed by the Ministry of Justice would be responsible for security and control matters while all other activities would be undertaken by employees of the contracting private consortium. The arguments put forward by officials in favour of this development were similar to those heard in other countries.

There was a need for new prison accommodation to cope with current overcrowding and the government planned to reduce the initial capital cost to the public purse by transferring this to PFI contractors who would be given a 20-year contract. As in other countries which had gone down this road, there was no acknowledgement that revenue payments over that period would be far in excess of any comparative public sector costs. There was an expectation that prisoners would be given more help to settle back into their communities after release and that this would lead, in the words of the Justice Minister, 'toward realizing safe communities by offering high-quality correctional education making use of private-sector creativity'.[7] A further argument was that, particularly in the case of Mine, the new prison would bring some much-needed employment and business to a region where both were in short supply and which was an economic enterprise zone. This was a justification which I had heard used by politicians in other countries such as New Zealand.

After the symposium I took the opportunity to visit Mine Rehabilitation Centre. This involved a journey by the fast Shinkansen train to Yamaguchi, then on a slow-moving local train and finally a one-carriage train which wended its way gently through the countryside. We were deposited at what seemed a deserted railway stop but fortunately our hosts had ordered a taxi in advance and that took us the final miles to the prison. A similar journey by people coming to visit a family member in the prison would have been a draining and expensive experience.

Once we were through the perimeter security we were each fitted with an electronic tag which had to be worn at all times by everyone in the prison, staff and visitors as well as prisoners. The tag provided real-time monitoring of the user's location. According to the prison's website, this is 'used to determine the inmates, movements and increase the effectiveness of the duties of prison officers while reducing their workload'.[8] We were then taken to meet the warden, a government employee, who explained that the prison had capacity for 1,000 prisoners but at that point held only 551; 290 women and 261 men. There were 123 public sector staff and 150 of the contractor's staff. The former group had been transferred from other prisons and were provided with accommodation. Private staff were recruited by the contractor, some locally and others from elsewhere according to their expertise. Supervisory and disciplinary powers over the prisoners were retained by the state prison staff.

We were given an information leaflet which listed the requirements for a prisoner to be accepted at Mine:

> The inmates to be housed in this institution are those who do not have severe physical or mental problems and who are able to adapt to communal life selected out of those inmates who do not have advanced criminal tendencies and are first-time offenders. Moreover, for male inmates, selection is limited to those who fulfil necessary conditions such as having had a stable job in society and the availability of a supportive environment following release.

On that basis, the men and women detained in Mine were hardly typical prisoners.

Given that the prison was completely new, everything was very fresh and up to date. The three-storied accommodation blocks each held 180 prisoners and almost all of the prisoners were in single cells, each 6.5 square metres. The male and female prisoners had completely separate accommodation and services. The cells were unlocked each morning at 7 am and prisoners were free to move around in the evening until 9 pm. Each wing had association and dining areas. There were separate visiting units for male and female sections, each with five cubicles and glass screens.

One of the attractions for the local authority in this underdeveloped region was that it benefitted from the tax income on the significant expenditure at the prison and also that it could count the prisoners as local residents which increased their per capita grants from central government, although these 'local residents' were not on the electoral roll. (This is also an important side benefit for remote communities in the United States which have large prisons in their neighbourhood.)

The opening of the new prison at Mine has been followed by three more PFI prisons, two of which have places for 2,000 prisoners each and one for 1,000.

Comment

Throughout the greater Asian region I have encountered a wide variation in the use and models of imprisonment. India and Pakistan have the two lowest rates of imprisonment in the region and, at respectively 35 and 38 prisoners per 100,000 of their populations, among the lowest in the world. However, these figures have to be set against the fact that in each of these countries prisoners awaiting trial, often for many years, constitute a disturbingly high percentage (respectively 69 and 62) of the total, almost all of them held in grossly overcrowded and unhealthy conditions. It is challenging, to say the least, to collate complete data for China. Using official reports, World Prison Brief has calculated that in 2018 there were 1.7 million convicted prisoners in the country but it also notes that an official report in 2009 acknowledged that a further 650,000 were held in detention centres, a figure which has undoubtedly increased significantly in recent years. In addition there are an estimated 200,000 men and women in pre-trial detention. In the course of visits to Qingdao in Shandong Province and to Huhhot in Inner Mongolia the most striking feature was the iron discipline which was in evidence at all times, coupled with an extremely complex system of continuous assessment for each prisoner.[9],[10] Prison systems in Central Asia still betray the influence of their years as part of the former Soviet system, although Kazakhstan and Kyrgyzstan have been more open in recent decades in their limited attempts to introduce standards which are more in keeping with international norms.

Rather than provide a detailed overview of the region with its wide variations, this chapter has focussed on two quite different instances. The story of Cambodia is one of how a nation attempts to come to terms with its horrific past and makes use of international assistance to do so. However, events and developments there over succeeding years demonstrate, as was cautioned at the time, that no prison system can be reformed in isolation, nor can it be used as a response to wider social and economic weaknesses. The use of imprisonment in Japan and the national peculiarities of the way its prisons operate can be regarded as a case study of the relationship between prisons and the society in which they exist and are a reflection of public and social attitudes not only to prisoners as a group but also to specific sectors such as, in the case of Japan, many isolated elderly men and women. We will return to this issue in the final chapter.

9

Latin America: the iron fist or the New Model?

Some of the most problematic prisons in the world are to be found in Latin America, typified by:

- rampant overcrowding in dilapidated, unsanitary prisons;
- endemic violence of prisoner on prisoner, prisoner on staff and staff on prisoner which regularly results in fatalities, often at a high level;
- very low ratios of staff per prisoner, with personnel who are inexperienced and poorly trained resulting in non-existent or at best inconsistent supervision;
- extensive corruption at institutional and individual levels;
- an absence of appropriate political oversight and strategic direction.

Over the years I have had discussions in many countries with regional intergovernmental agencies, with government ministers and officials, with non-governmental organisations and civil society groups and with academics, and have pored over countless official reports about the dire situation in prisons in the region by bodies such as the Inter-American Commission on Human Rights (2011) and the United Nations Latin American Institute for the Prevention of Crime and the Treatment of Offenders (ILANUD). I have also observed these realities at first hand in several countries in Central America and in South America, from Venezuela and Colombia in the north to Argentina, Chile and Uruguay in the south as well as in Brazil, which has the third-highest prison population in the world after the United States and China. A special edition of the *Prison Service Journal* (Darke and Garces, 2017) presents a unique panorama of the daily reality of life inside several prisons across the region with a number of articles written by men who have experienced this at first hand. The editors comment that:

> Much like the impoverished *barrios* and *favelas* on the outside, socio-political relations in Latin American prison spaces are,

> at the first instance, grounded in everyday interpersonal and collective struggles for order and wellbeing, or ad hoc institutional accommodations conditioned by state abandonment and the normalisation of inhumane living conditions.

Rather than make this chapter a repetitive penal travelogue, I shall again focus on a small number of countries to provide examples of the generic situation in the region and will end with the positive story of how one country is feeling its way towards a different model of imprisonment.

Two vignettes from contemporaneous notes

Villahermosa Prison, Cali, Colombia, May 1995

It is described as a 'small' district prison. In this case 'small' is a relative term; with a stated capacity for 700, the prison holds 1,600 men on the day of our visit. Inside the gate of the prison there is a security area where prison staff check any bags which visitors are taking into the prison. This is not a day for the families of prisoners to visit so the only people coming in are those who are on official business, most of them lawyers coming for a consultation with their clients. As we wait in line for the search we observe that the man in front of us, dressed in a business suit with collar and tie, is carrying a large leather bag. The guard asks him to open it and we can see that it holds a substantial plastic bag filled to the brim with money. The guard nods and waves the man through. I look incredulously at my companion and ask, "Did I just see what I thought I saw?" She nods. "Yes, you did."

Later in the evening we have a meeting with local defence lawyers and I tell them what we witnessed. They shrug and tell us that this is not an uncommon occurrence. The cash would either be delivered to a senior member of staff for favours which had been rendered or it would be taken directly to an important prisoner to be distributed among his gang members. The lawyers go on to explain that all the buildings immediately surrounding the prison are owned by members of the local drugs cartel. This means that observers in the cafes and bars can listen to everything that passers-by are saying and can watch everyone going into and out of the prison. The *capos de carteles*, the drug barons, continue to run their businesses from inside the prison. This money which we saw being taken in so brazenly would be part of that business.

La Planta Prison, Caracas, Venezuela, February 2000

There are very few staff inside the prison and none inside the prisoners' accommodation which consists primarily of large, high-ceilinged rooms, little altered from the time that the building was an electricity plant. The prisoners have their own gangs. Most of them belonged to these in Caracas before they came to the prison and those who had no previous gang allegiance very quickly join one for their own safety. The prisoners are allocated to a living unit according to their gang affiliation. Each unit holds about 150 prisoners who have free movement at all times within the unit. Prisoners have nothing to do. The atmosphere is very clammy and many men are wearing only a towel around their waist.

The fronts of the blocks are large open grilles facing onto a central area which means that each gang can see into the other's living accommodation. Each grille is padlocked with two chains. One is controlled by staff from the outside, the other by the prisoners from the inside. This is to prevent any attempt by prisoners from another gang to enter the unit. Prisoners are appointed in turn throughout the night to sit on guard on a small stool at the inside of each grille in three-hour shifts. Any prisoner who is discovered to have fallen asleep during this guard duty will be killed by his peers.

I am taken round the prison by the director. He has told the prisoners in advance who I am and they have agreed that I can be shown round. The prisoners have no personal privacy; most sleep in hammocks either slung from the ceiling or in small niches along the wall. I am shown the toilet area which is as filthy and foetid as any that I have seen in a prison. The toilets themselves consist of a row of open holes with no screening. Each is stinking, with flies everywhere and large rats are running around without any fear. Behind the toilet area is an equally dirty set of shower heads. At the end of the toilet area rubbish is lying about a metre deep. The director tells me that the prisoners deliberately keep the area dirty so that they can hide guns and other weapons under the mess. He points to wires sticking out of the filth at irregular intervals and explains without any embarrassment that there will be guns and knives concealed in the ordure at the end of the wire to be pulled out immediately if there is any attack from another gang. He then shows me bricks in the wall from which the surrounding mortar has been removed and tells me calmly that weapons and mobile phones will be concealed there. Throughout all of these exchanges we are surrounded by groups of interested prisoners who nod throughout the conversation. He tells me that on average there are about 80 killings each year in the prison.

Colombia

In April 1995 the Permanent Secretary in the Colombian Ministry of Justice and the Director General of the Prison Service (INPEC) visited Brixton Prison as part of an official visit to the United Kingdom as guests of the Foreign Office. The following month I was invited to Colombia by the Public Defender for Cali Region to learn about the human rights situation in general and prison conditions in particular.

My visit began in Bogotá where once again I met the Director General of INPEC. Having recently shown him around Brixton, he was probably more open than he might otherwise have been about the problems he faced in administering the 176 prisons in the country which at that time ranged in size from the largest, La Modelo in Bogotá, to rural prisons with no more than a handful of prisoners. In a very matter-of-fact tone he described the major issues which he had to deal with:

- The physical conditions in many prisons were appalling, with inhuman and overcrowded living accommodation for prisoners and very poor infrastructure.
- Recruitment of staff was a major problem. In Colombia all men from the age of 18 had to complete one year's military service, which could be served as a prison guard. In many prisons a high proportion of the guards fell into this category. That is, they were 18 years of age; they were given very little training; and they would leave the job after 12 months. In some prisons the staff were required to sleep in the prison and in effect were treated very much like the prisoners. The pay was minimal which left them open to corruption, as was to be demonstrated to me very graphically when I went to Villahermosa prison.
- There was little political will for change or improvement. All of the most senior staff in INPEC were political appointees and changed with each new government, as had happened recently.

I was to see for myself what all of this meant on the ground as I visited prisons in Bogotá and in the Cali region. My first visit was to La Modelo. Built in the 1970s, it is situated in a run-down suburb of the city. In 1995 it had a capacity for 1,500 prisoners but was holding 3,450, of whom 80 per cent were awaiting trial. We were told that there were about 150 guards on duty at any one time, a ridiculously small number to supervise so many prisoners, and that they worked 24 hours on and 24 hours off duty. Most of those whom we saw looked as though they were teenagers, and indeed they were. As we passed through the internal security gates we were joined by our escort of about 20 baton carrying guards, some of whom were also carrying guns and tear gas canisters. The escort surrounded us as we walked around the prison. This degree of close supervision may well have been necessary – the director had clearly been instructed that nothing untoward must be allowed to happen to us – but it did nothing to alleviate our sense of unease.

The prisoners were held in five large accommodation units which consisted of blocks of cells four storeys high overlooking an internal patio. Each block, which held about 150 men, had a nominated prisoner described as the 'monitor', who was in effect in control. The open patio had the appearance of a village square with a cafe where food and drink could be purchased, a shop and washing area, and all prisoners had free movement within their patio between 7 am and 4 pm each day. The guards did not enter the patio in the normal course of their duty.

Although the law required segregation of convicted and unconvicted and young from old in practice this did not happen. In theory prisoners were allocated to a patio according to type of offence or status or background but in reality much depended on their affiliation, with one section holding left-wing rebels while another held right-wing government supporters and paramilitaries. The area between these two wings was where much of the inter faction violence took place. External sources informed us that prisoners had easy access to guns and other arms. One patio which was obviously much better equipped than the others was reserved for former officials and for those who could afford to pay for better conditions.

A limited amount of education was available for six hours each day and work for eight hours. There was work for approximately 500 prisoners and this included a shoe-making shop which was managed by a private company as well as workshops where prisoners made bags, furniture and craft items. For every two days of education or work prisoners had one day of their sentence reduced.

Each Saturday male visitors were allowed between 8 am and 1 pm and on Sundays women visitors were allowed, with children able to visit one Sunday each month. The system was very simple with the visitors allowed into the patios where they moved around freely with the prisoners.

The director assured us that there was very little violence in the prison and over the previous year only one prisoner had died by his own hand. This statement went against a large body of external evidence which documented significant violence, including murders. It also begged the question as to why there had been a need for us to be surrounded by a substantial group of armed guards as we walked around the prison.

La Modelo has continued to be beset by murderous violence over successive years. In February 2016 prosecutors began an investigation into more than 100 cases of persons who had 'disappeared' inside the prison between 1999 and 2001; they included visitors to the prison as well as prisoners. This led to the gruesome discovery of the dismembered remains of more than 100 bodies in drains under the prison (Bocanegra, 2016). In March 2020 a riot led to the death of at least 23 prisoners and the injury of a further 87. The Minister of Justice announced that the prison had been virtually destroyed in the subsequent fire.[1]

Over the next several days I travelled to a number of other prisons. In each of them the situation was the same, only the degree of awfulness varied marginally. In Judicial Unit 40, a detention centre in Bogotá, the cells were so full that prisoners were forced to lie on top of each other. In Picota Penitentiary also in Bogotá the security at the entrance was much stricter than at La Modelo since the prison had a high-security unit with 48 spaces which had been built by a North American company and was broadly similar to the special housing units found in the United States. As we approached Palmira Penitentiary in Cali my companion, who was a Public Defender in Cali, told me that there was strong evidence that the prison director had recently been involved in torturing prisoners. In the course of our visit a guard came to the director and handed over two home-made knives which apparently had been retrieved by staff as a result of a tip-off. One of the knives was quite rusty and both looked as though they might have been lying around for some time. The find may have been genuine but it was more probable that it had been laid on for our benefit. In Villahermosa, again in Cali, where I had observed the bagful of cash being taken in, we came across one prisoner in the sick bay who was receiving treatment for nasty-looking bruises to his body. He told us that he had had a verbal exchange with a guard who had later returned with ten other guards and had given him a severe beating. The Public Defender, who was with us, expressed grave concern at what had happened and the director undertook to have a full investigation and to report back. I did not learn the outcome of this.

I later had a meeting with the Public Defender for Cali Region who presented me with some startling statistics. According to official figures there were approximately 30,000 homicides in the country in 1994. Between July 1993 and June 1994 it was reported that 4,000 people had been killed for political or ideological reasons. Between January 1993 and March 1994 it was reported that almost 70 per cent of the extrajudicial, summary or arbitrary executions were carried out by members of the State security forces or paramilitary groups, while guerrilla groups were said to have been responsible for almost 25 per cent. The remainder were carried out by militia. During the same period there were 436 recorded cases of torture. One person was said to disappear each day. The UN Special Rapporteurs on Torture and on Extrajudicial, Summary or Arbitrary Executions had visited Colombia in October 1994 when they had found large-scale and grave abuses by armed insurgents and armed groups at the service of drug traffickers or large landowners as well as extremely high levels of common criminality. They concluded that the absence of a functioning justice system not only prevented the punishment of those responsible for abuses but was in itself an important source of violence. A report by Amnesty International for 1994 commented that the majority of victims of extrajudicial executions were people with no known political connections. Members of indigenous communities were targeted by both government forces and some guerrilla organisations. The killing of so-called 'disposables', the indigent young and the poor, was a major problem.

There were about 200 paramilitary groups active in the country. They were well-armed and tended to have strong links with the military, police and other government forces. They were responsible for a great number of assassinations and for forced emigration and particularly targeted indigent youth and poor people. In the years since then drug cartels have continued to terrorise rural communities with one major group especially active in the Cali region and another in Medellin. Officially the cartels are criticised but unofficially the economy depends on them. In the course of my visit the Public Defender took me on a tour of the city and its *barrios*, commenting that the prices of ordinary houses in the area there were unusually low because of the economic benefits of the drug trade.

One evening in Cali I had a meeting with members of the Association of the Families of the Detained and the Disappeared which had been founded in 1982 after the disappearance of 12 university students. They told me that they had 80 groups across the country. They faced persecution for their work and knew that they were in considerable physical danger. They were regularly photographed by the police, allegedly 'for their own protection'.

What was I to make in conclusion of all of this? It is a truism to say that the prison system in every country reflects the political reality, culture and mores of society and for that reason one cannot talk of reforming a prison system in isolation from the country's criminal justice system nor indeed from the values of the society itself. This was particularly the case in Colombia where the legal framework on which the system was based was sound but was virtually ignored in practice.

On a personal level I was filled with admiration at the selflessness and courage of some of the public servants, such as the regional human rights defender in Cali, and the members of non-governmental organisations whom I met. They were under regular physical threat because of the work which they did yet they continued in a quiet but persistent manner to demand that human rights should be recognised in accordance with the constitution of the country.

Venezuela

In December 1999 I was approached by the Director of the British Council in Venezuela with a request that I should come to Caracas for discussions with the government about prison reform. In February of that year Hugo Chavez had been elected as President and he had made clear to his Minister of Justice that he wished to give a priority to prison reform. Chavez himself had been in prison between 1992 and 1994 after his failed coup attempt. The director explained that the prison system was 'in a parlous state', with the prisons almost entirely under the control of the prisoners. The recently elected government wanted to introduce a number of measures to take back control of the prisons and had indicated that a high priority should be given to training personnel, particularly the prison directors. The Ministry of Justice had approached the UK Embassy for assistance in this work and that led to the request that I should make a preliminary assessment of the situation to make recommendations about what might be done.

I travelled to Caracas in January and after an initial meeting at the British Embassy I was taken immediately to meet the Minister of Justice who was a serving military general. Just as his opposite number in Colombia had done, he painted a graphic and brutally honest picture of the problems which had bedevilled the prison system for years. In my notes of the meeting I summarised the story he told:

- For many years no government interest. No resources, not even enough money to feed prisoners. Deterioration of infrastructure. Shortage of resources, absence of staff training, poor pay and therefore poor academic standing and little community respect.

- Twenty-two thousand prisoners; 66 per cent not sentenced. Prisons are schools of crime. Everyone agrees what needs to be done; the problem is that no one knows how to implement it. Endemic violence. Prisoners leave worse than when they entered.
- In some cases 1,500 prisoners are looked after by five guards. The result is, in the words of the Minister, that 'the prisons are in the hands of the prisoners'. It is impossible to have any discipline, let alone rehabilitation. In several prisons the National Guard has been introduced but still there are problems: force is not the answer.
- Corruption is a major problem. Because of poor pay, guards allow anything to pass.

Following my meeting with the Minister I travelled to the *Centro de Reeducación Artesanal*, more commonly known as La Planta prison, close to the centre of Caracas. Whoever designated the prison as a 'centre for re-education in traditional skills' had a very black sense of humour. It had been converted 25 years previously from its original role as an electricity plant and was still known to all and sundry as 'The Plant'. Any 'traditional skills' learned by its inhabitants were certainly not of a lawful nature. The buildings were crammed into a very tight envelope, bordered on one side by a motorway flyover which soared above the prison walls and on the other by a busy main road. There had been very little change to the original industrial construction, with insecure brick and plaster buildings and very poor perimeter security. Not surprisingly, there were continuous problems with people throwing drugs and weapons over the wall into the exercise areas. With a capacity for 400 men it was holding twice that number on the day of my visit, and the brief description at the beginning of this chapter summarises what I saw on that day.

Given its location La Planta had a very high profile in Venezuela but its problems were similar to those in virtually every other prison in the country as the Minister had acknowledged to me when he stated simply that the prisoners ran the prisons. Violence was endemic in every prison and there were regular outbursts of homicidal violence. In 1994 over 100 prisoners were killed in Sabaneta prison in the city of Maracaibo and in 1996 25 prisoners had been killed in a fire caused by members of the National Guard in La Planta. In the mid-1990s the government had called in the National Guard to ensure the internal security of seven prisons but their brutal treatment of prisoners had led to even more violence. On average 200 prisoners were killed and over 1,000 seriously injured each year.

The immediate cause of the prisoner-on-prisoner violence was the gang warfare which existed within prisons and which had its origin in street culture. I had encountered this in prisons in a number of other countries in Latin America and elsewhere, but the difference in Venezuela was that there was virtually no immediate staff supervision of prisoner areas and the administration appeared to take a fatalistic approach to its inability to control the activities of the prisoners. This was epitomised by the director of La Planta who had no embarrassment at pointing out hiding places for mobile telephones, guns and other weapons even though prisoners were within hearing. As in some other countries there was also an absence of continuity at ministerial level. As I had waited in the Minister's outer office his officials were at pains to point to the double row of photographs of Ministers of Justice; many of them had been in office for a few months at most.

Following the election of President Chavez in February 1999 there was a new political will to tackle the prison crisis and a degree of optimism that something could be done. The Ministry had recognised the pressing need to recruit and train a professional cadre of personnel and I was told that they had set the ambitious target of training approximately 1,800 prison staff within the succeeding 12 months. There were plans to run a series of three-month courses for up to 200 staff on each course; some of these courses would be run in Caracas and others would be delivered in other major cities around the country. More immediately there was a need to provide training and orientation for present and possible future prison directors, very few of whom were adequately prepared for their roles and responsibilities. The Ministry was keen to have the support of the ICPS with this latter initiative.

At the end of my visit I had a final meeting at the UK Embassy. It appeared that the new Venezuelan government was genuine in its wish to improve the terrible situation in the country's prisons and the Ambassador was keen to take advantage of what he saw as a window of opportunity to assist. Given what I had seen in the prisons and my discussions with the Minister I was not sanguine about the likelihood of any radical change within the prison system without similar advances in the criminal justice system as a whole. For example, a high proportion of prisoners were awaiting trial or sentence which underlined the need for reform within the prosecution and courts systems. The very low level of staff salaries made it virtually impossible to recruit personnel of a high enough quality and also to eliminate the real danger of corruption. It also had to be recognised that much of the violence within prisons was a reflection of the violence within civil society: one could not be eradicated without the other.

Allowing for all of these caveats, I acknowledged that it would be important to offer some encouragement to those who were striving for change and I proposed that the best way to do that would be by providing assistance in the proposed professional training for prison directors. This offer was accepted by the Venezuelan government and over the course of the following year two of my colleagues in ICPS developed a training course in consultation with the Ministry of Justice. Their input in Caracas was welcomed but at the end of the exercise they also had little expectation of any long-term improvement in the prisons. And so it transpired.

As time went on, the government struggled increasingly to deliver progress on many fronts, not least within the justice system. This was reflected in consistent increases in the prison population. When I first visited at the start of 2000 this stood at 14,000; by 2010 it had reached 41,000 and by 2017 it had soared to 57,000. The increase of violence in civil society was mirrored by even more violence inside prisons, which continues today.

And what of La Planta which I had visited in January 2000? By 2012 it was holding an astounding 2,500 prisoners and was even more lawless than when I had been there. On 30 April of that year the government announced its intention to close the prison and this sparked off several weeks of violent confrontation between the National Guard and prisoners who were armed with weapons, presumably retrieved from under the morass in the toilets which had been pointed out to me. Almost three weeks later a ceasefire was negotiated and the prisoners agreed to be transferred to other prisons. By the end of May the so-called 'centre for re-education in traditional skills' was finally closed.

Guatemala

I have lost count of the number of prisons which I have visited over many years but I can remember only two when the director of the prison had to ask permission from prisoners before I could go round the prison. The first was in the late 1970s when I went to what was then Long Kesh, later the Maze Prison, in Northern Ireland. I had come over from the Scottish Prison Service to observe the treatment of Irish Republican prisoners and wanted to see at first hand the living accommodation. The Governor of the prison made me welcome when I arrived and went on to explain that he had to get the approval of a senior prisoner before I could go into the compound where the prisoners lived. This was duly given and when a prison officer unlocked the gate of the compound we found the lead prisoner waiting for us on the other side. He swung in beside us and as we walked round it seemed as though he, rather than the Governor, was showing me round.

The only other time I had such an experience was in 2006 when I visited Pavon Prison in Guatemala. The prison, officially Granja Penal de Pavón (Pavon Penal Farm), is on the outskirts of the town of Fraijanes some 30 kilometres from Guatemala City. Opened in 1976, it initially held 800 prisoners who were regarded as low security risk. But 20 years later in the wake of the country's brutal civil war it had changed from being a penal farm and had become a lawless institution holding over 1,000 young men, most of whom had been hardened by their violent experiences. In 1996 the authorities conceded defeat and withdrew staff from inside the prison, leaving it in control of the prisoners. From that point the staff presence was limited to the exterior of the prison. Unbelievably, the authorities signed a formal agreement which transferred internal control to an 'Order Committee' of prisoners. In return the committee undertook to impose order in the prison and to prevent escapes.

When I visited Guatemala in early June 2006 along with a colleague Pavon was holding 1,627 prisoners, all of whom were serving sentences of ten years or more including several sentenced to 50 years' imprisonment. There were 40 security staff who were concerned solely with security *outside* the prison perimeter and there was virtually no interaction between prisoners and staff. In the course of a meeting with the Head of the Prison Service I asked if we could visit the prison. He replied that he had no objection but that he would have to seek the permission of the head of the prisoners' committee. Prison staff would take us as far as the gate of the prison. After that we would be under direction of the prisoners and we would have to take responsibility for our own safety. This was a very unusual and surprising response from the person in overall charge of the country's prisons but after a moment's hesitation we confirmed that we did wish to make the visit.

Our journey south from Guatemala City was a tense affair as we discussed quietly whether on this occasion we were taking a step too far. Over the years I had been in a number of situations in prisons where my safety had been at risk and I had an inbuilt confidence that my 'prison craft' would enable me to sense if we were in immediate danger. We drove off the motorway, up a winding hillside road and onto a track. Before us stood the prison which at first glance had the appearance of a large country estate surrounded by a high wire fence. Inside the fence we could see evidence of vegetable cultivation and some livestock.

We walked towards the main gate which was unlocked by one of the prison officers who were standing outside. Inside we were met by a small group of men who greeted us pleasantly and invited us to follow them. Rounding a corner we were faced by a luxurious two-storey house standing in its own compound. This was the home of Jorge Pinto, known as *El Loco* (The Madman), whom we had been told about prior to our visit. A major Colombian drug overlord, he was one of the two most influential and feared men in the prison. That much was confirmed as we approached the fence which surrounded his compound. Not only did it have its own security entrance, it was also monitored by closed-circuit television and there were five guard dogs in the yard, all provided by Pinto rather than by the authorities. The outside of the wooden house was finished to a very high quality and inside the furnishings were beautifully crafted. Pinto gave us a tour of his accommodation: a large living area with a widescreen television, a bedroom with a king-sized bed, a jacuzzi room and a bar-style kitchen-cum-dining-area. The entire house had broadband internet connection. Coffee was brought to us as we talked.

Pinto then took us on a tour of the prison. He explained that since most of the prisoners had nothing to keep them occupied he had set up a wood workshop where all the materials for his house had been completed. Prisoners, he told us, could order and purchase well-designed wooden items from the workshop. He had also established art classes for the younger prisoners. The prisoners had constructed two well-appointed churches, one for evangelicals and one for Catholics. A small number of prisoners lived in houses which they had built themselves, some of them quite extensive. The vast majority lived in one of the 12 accommodation blocks which were dark, overcrowded and poorly equipped, with private, small, curtained bed spaces off corridors.

It took us quite some time to walk round the prison estate. A small number of prisoners were working making hammocks or cutting back vegetation. The majority were simply hanging around, watching television, playing cards or reading. Pinto repeated his assertion that he had set up his woodwork shop because the authorities did nothing for the prisoners so they had to look after themselves. In the passageways between the blocks there were numerous stalls selling a wide range of food and drink, clothing and other goods and also a barber shop. We were told that these were all run as businesses by prisoners who paid 'rent' to the Order Committee.

Prisoners were able to invite family and friends to visit them, usually from 8 am until 4 pm. Speaking 'in confidence' one prisoner told us quietly that it was possible for visitors to stay overnight if an appropriate tariff was paid.

We visited the segregation unit, an area known by the prisoners as the 'North Pole'. It was a corridor of dirty, stinking concrete cells, where prisoners had no possessions and no bedding that we could see. We were able to speak privately to the dozen or so young men who were being held there. They told us that the Order Committee would decide whether any local regulations had been breached and how long an individual should stay in the segregation unit. An alternative to a spell in the North Pole might be a severe beating. Often this would be punishment for an unpaid debt or failure to pay a bribe. Several of the men had been in segregation for lengthy periods and some said that they felt safer there than they would have done elsewhere in the prison. They told us that weapons were easily available inside the prison and that some well-off prisoners employed maids to clean for them. They claimed that about 20 prostitutes would regularly be in the prison for three or four days at a time. This information was confirmed to us later by the Head of the Prison Service who told us quite openly that the lifestyle of the richest prisoners was funded by their external organised crime activities.

We were then taken to meet Luis Alfonso Zepeda who had been 'elected' as head of the Order Committee two or so years previously. His well-appointed compound also had extensive external security and the whole environment had a surreal atmosphere. At one level it was somewhat akin to a small country house, with chickens running free around the bushes in the yard. At a different level there was an unspoken sense of danger, with several threatening armed guards in evidence. In his sleeping quarters Zepeda had a pistol lying openly by the large bed. He was accompanied by his teenage son, Samuel, who was living with his father in the prison despite the fact that there was no legal authority for his being there. It appeared that the son was there as a trusted assistant in managing his father's 'business' interests.

Zepeda was courteous and happy to discuss arrangements but there was an undoubted underlying sense of menace about him. To listen to him one might have been impressed by the democratic internal management structure which had been developed. He confirmed that the general running of the prison was organised by the Order Committee which had 15 members, all 'elected' by the prisoners, one from each of the 12 sections plus three senior prisoners. They were responsible for agreeing the rules in the prison, for allocating living space to prisoners, for punishing infractions, if need be by segregation. (Others told us that beatings were a common punishment.) Each prisoner was required to pay the committee a sum of money for their living space. As we had observed, there were a variety of private enterprises which provided for all the prisoners' needs. Zepeda said that the director of the prison received a proportion of all the money collected, usually about US $2,000 a month, with other senior members of staff receiving smaller payments.

At the end of our discussion Zepeda asked if we wished to see anything else in the prison. We said that we had seen everything we wanted to. He wished us goodbye and we were escorted to the prison's external gate, where our prison service escorts were waiting to take us back to Guatemala City.

On our return journey we tried to make sense of what we had just witnessed and we related it to our previous discussion with the Head of the Prison Service, Alejandro Giammattei. He had painted a graphic picture of the reality in Pavon. He acknowledged that a decade before the government of the day had decided that it could not impose order in the prison and had formally ceded control to the prisoners but he was at pains to emphasise that the problems in prisons in general and Pavon in particular had to be placed within the wider context of the decades of violence in Guatemalan society and more recently the influx of young men who had been deported to the country from the United States after completing prison sentences there. Many of them had been born to Guatemalan parents but had never themselves lived in the country or else had been taken to the United States at a very young age. In the US they been sucked into the violent Mara gangs formed by young men of Central American extraction, principally from El Salvador but also Guatemala. A vicious circle had been closed when they arrived back in Guatemala. Giammattei estimated that there were up to 40,000 gang members in the country. Any young man entering prison who was not already a member soon joined one of the gangs as a means of protection. The gang leaders, said Giammattei, ran the prisons and could bribe guards to allow any item, including firearms, into the prison.

Alejandro Giammattei had been in post since the previous October and was clearly determined to make a mark. He had formerly stood unsuccessfully for election as Mayor of Guatemala City and made no secret of the fact that he still harboured political aspirations. The fact that he told us several times that he had been in office '218 days and counting' indicated to us that he did not intend to be in his current post for any length of time. He emphasised his determination to regain control of prisons, with Pavon at the top of his list. He indicated that he expected soon to obtain Presidential approval to send in the military and calmly told us that he estimated this might well result in around one hundred prisoner deaths: 'a necessary price'. Giammattei then took us to meet the Interior Minister, Carlos Vielmann, who confirmed that he supported the intentions of the Head of the Prison Service.

Less than four months after our visit the government made its move. On Monday 25 September 2006 the Vice President called international diplomats including the British Ambassador to his office to inform them that 3,000 police officers and military personnel had entered Pavon at 5 am that morning and had forcibly re-established authority in the prison. Seven prisoners had been killed in the process, including Luis Zepeda and Jorge Pinto. All remaining prisoners were being transferred to other prisons. Speaking to the press, Minister Carlos Vielmann said, 'It was a surgical operation to end a centre of drug trafficking, kidnapping and all kinds of illicit activities.' Some of the surviving prisoners claimed that the dead men had offered no resistance and were summarily killed, some apparently in their beds. However, Minister Vielmann waved away the claim as an irritant: 'You can't believe a word, they're criminals' (Carroll, 2006). By the end of the day Pavon stood empty and partly ruined.

The events of 25 September were not the end of the story. In December 2006 the government signed an agreement with the United Nations to establish an International Commission against Impunity in Guatemala to assist state institutions in the investigation of possible abuses of state power. In 2010 the prosecuting authorities ordered the arrest of 18 former senior officials and policemen over the killing of the seven prisoners in Pavon in 2006. They included the former Interior Minister Carlos Vielmann, the former head of the civil police Edwin Sperisen who had led the forces which had re-taken Pavon, and Alejandro Giammattei, who had by 2010 achieved the political ambition he had stated to us and was leader of the opposition party in Guatemala. Vielmann had taken out Spanish citizenship in 2009 and jurisdiction of the charges against him was transferred to the Spanish judicial system, where he was acquitted in 2018. Sperisen had dual Swiss citizenship and his charges were transferred to that jurisdiction. He was sentenced to 15 years' imprisonment in 2018, to be served under house arrest. Giammattei was held in pre-trial detention for ten months in Guatemala before the case against him was dismissed for lack of evidence. Alejandro Giammattei continued his political career and, succeeding at the fourth attempt, on 14 January 2020 he was sworn in as the elected President of the Republic of Guatemala.

And what of Pavon Prison? In the years after 2006 it was brought back into use and it would appear that little has changed. In 2016 a riot broke out between rival gangs who had access to guns and grenades and 14 prisoners died before order was restored. In May 2019 there was a further shoot-out between prisoners in which seven were killed. Fifteen hundred soldiers and police were called in to quell the riot. At the time the prison, with a stated capacity for 800, was holding 4,000 prisoners.[2]

El Salvador

Other countries in the region have problems in their prison systems which are every bit as dire as those in Guatemala. Honduras, for example, has just over 10,000 prison spaces while the actual number of prisoners is over 21,000. With this level of overcrowding combined with poor infrastructure, gross underfunding and very low staffing levels which in effect leave prisoners in charge of the prisons, it is no surprise that tragedies are an all too regular occurrence. In 2003 a fire in Le Caiba prison resulted in the death of 61 prisoners. A year later 107 prisoners died in a fire in San Pedro Sula prison and yet another fire in Comayagua prison led to a shocking 360 deaths. These problems continue. Speaking in January 2020, Eric Olson, of the Seattle International Foundation, said:

> I have seen these problems first hand on visits to jails in Honduras in the past two years. Each prison population functions within a precarious power structure that can erupt with the slightest provocation and unleash horrific violence. In most cases, there are no prison guards to maintain order. That is why it is correct to say that gangs effectively control the prisons. These may not be commonly known gangs like MS-13, but gangs inevitably form within the prison as a survival tactic. Guards are merely there to ensure the prisoners do not escape, and to control the entry and exit of prisoners.[3]

One other country in the region which I know from personal experience is El Salvador. I first visited San Salvador in October 1999 to take part in a seminar on prison reform organised by the Ministry of Justice. Most of those attending that event were senior prison staff and I recollect that we had lively discussions on the problems of prison overcrowding, the best use of scarce resources and the management of high-security prisoners. The atmosphere at the conclusion of the seminar was enthusiastic and the government representatives who were present were optimistic about the possibility of future positive change.

We soon learned that the optimism was badly misplaced. In succeeding years there was a constant stream of serious incidents. For example, in February 2002 in a prison in Santa Ana prisoners attacked guards who were searching for drugs and weapons. They grabbed a collection of guns which had just been confiscated and opened fire on authorities and fellow prisoners. Staff returned fire and killed three prisoners. Another 30 prisoners were injured in the fighting that ensued. As in a number of countries in the region the government's response to continuing violence in the prisons and in wider society was heavy-handed, meeting force with greater force in a policy which was known as *mano dura*, the iron fist. In February 2007 the Director of Prisons announced his intention to appoint military officers to run prisons. The country's Human Rights Ombudswoman was outspoken in her criticism of this development, claiming, 'There is a catastrophic situation in the prisons in the country and we are confronting it with a barbaric, repressive and anti-democratic phenomenon in prison management'.[4]

As in Guatemala a significant factor in the destabilisation of civil society had been the influence of the gangs which had originally been formed by Salvadoreans living in the United States in the 1980s and which had subsequently spread throughout a number of countries in Central America, fuelled by the US government's policy of deportation. Many of these young men ended up in the prison system and within a relatively short period they had in effect taken over the running of the prisons, just as was happening in Guatemala and Honduras. The two main groupings, the *Mara Salvatrucha (MS13)* and the *Diez y Ocho (18)*, were sworn enemies and in August 2004 a confrontation between rival factions resulted in the murder of 31 prisoners in La Esperanza Prison, usually known as Mariona, the largest prison in the country. Following that event the government decided to identify four prisons for gang members, two for each of the major groups, with a view to preventing future violence. In practice this resulted in handing over control of these prisons to the gangs and, some commentators have argued, allowing them to develop their criminal and economic networks not only inside the prisons but also in civil society.

In 2016 I was invited to return to El Salvador as part of a programme to assist the government to improve prison conditions and I found that the scale of the problems had changed dramatically for the worse in the intervening years. The number of prisoners had increased from 7,500 in 1999 to over 35,000, giving an imprisonment rate of 590 per 100,000 of the total population, the seventh highest rate in the world.

I saw for myself what this meant in reality when I visited Mariona Prison on the outskirts of San Salvador. With a stated capacity for 800 prisoners, it was holding around 5,000 on the day of my visit. Resources had not kept pace with the increase in numbers and that was clear from the moment we entered the prison. There were shortages on every front. The low ratio of staff to prisoners meant that the latter were unsupervised for most of the time. The kitchen struggled to provide adequate food. In one large yard we saw men queuing with buckets and empty water bottles in front of the only available water tap. There were three public telephones for the whole prison, although we were told that many prisoners had access to illicit cell phones. A local non-governmental organisation provided work for about 400 men but the vast majority of prisoners lounged about all day with nothing to do. Most of the prisoners were accommodated in large factory-like buildings with minimal facilities. There were very few beds provided and large numbers of prisoners slept on makeshift bedding on the floor. The roof struts and upper-level fencing were festooned with rudimentary hammocks where prisoners perched perilously, watching us as we walked round beneath them. The staff presence in the accommodation units was minimal, meaning that once again the gang leaders in each unit exercised their own authority over other prisoners. Prisoners had to pay for many of the basic necessities of life, including space to sleep.

The prison also held about 200 prisoners who had been identified as gang members, often solely on the basis of their extensive face and body tattoos. For a number of years the government had been imposing what it termed 'exceptional measures' in prisons as part of the official *mano dura* policy. These 200 men were being held in particularly repressive conditions in a small, dark, dirty and grossly overcrowded section. A minimal amount of natural light reached through the grilled gates onto the corridor which fronted the cells. Each small cell held up to 20 prisoners who were obliged to stand or crouch most of the day because of shortage of space. Pieces of cloth and rope were strung from the low ceiling to provide makeshift hammocks. According to the prisoners they were allowed out of the cells for a short period once every one or two weeks to walk in a tiny yard area abutting the living accommodation. Visits from family or friends were not allowed.

Inevitably, conditions such as these carried serious dangers to health, and one of the greatest of these risks was the contagion of infectious diseases. Only belatedly was this danger being acknowledged. Under pressure from the International Committee of the Red Cross the authorities had reluctantly agreed to a tuberculosis screening scheme in prisons under the 'exceptional measures' which had unsurprisingly identified a dramatic increase in the prevalence of tuberculosis.

At the end of his mission to El Salvador in November 2017 the UN High Commissioner for Human Rights issued a formal statement which included the following paragraph:

> We are informed of the State's efforts to fully control the country's prisons through the Extraordinary Security Measures which since April 2016 have placed thousands of people in prolonged and isolated detention under truly inhumane conditions, and with prolonged suspension of family visits. The vulnerability of these inmates is highlighted by an outbreak of tuberculosis, affecting more than a thousand inmates, with several hundred also said to be suffering from malnutrition. I call on the President to end the extraordinary measures and grant international independent organisations, including my Office, access to these detention centres. (Office of the High Commissioner for Human Rights, 2017)

The High Commissioner's request fell on deaf ears and in August 2018 the El Salvador Congress passed a bill which made the 'extraordinary measures' permanent. It also empowered the Justice and Public Security Ministry to take 'all necessary and indispensable measures' to cut off telecommunications to and from detention facilities and gave prison directors the authority to suspend visiting privileges for up to 30 days. A change of government in June 2019 has not brought any change to the '*mano dura*' approach.

Violence unbounded

One of the most striking features of many prison systems in Latin America is the absence of professionally trained personnel which means that prisoners have untrammelled control of their own areas and, as I experienced, staff only enter the prisoner areas in large numbers and suitably armed. The consequence of this lack of official control, other than by means of matched violence, is that the prisoners themselves largely have control. But prisons are not democratic institutions and control by prisoners does not mean control by *all* prisoners equally; rather, the contrary is true. Prison societies are always hierarchical in structure. In some countries the hierarchy is based on the crime of which a person has been convicted; in others it may be based on the locality from which a person comes; in others it may be based on the access which a person has to outside resources; it may be based on the strength of a small group who can dominate the others; and so on. Whatever the basis of the hierarchy, there will usually be three broad strata. There will be a small number who are at the top, who lead and direct. Very often they may not be obvious to the outside observer; they will keep a low profile and may even be considered by senior management of the prison to be model prisoners. Alternatively, management may know who they are but will collude with them so as to ensure an appearance of peace and order in the prison. The second level in the hierarchy consists of the lieutenants and enforcers on behalf of the first group, willing and able to inflict violence as and when so ordered. The third and largest group will include the majority of prisoners who will be under the thumbs of the enforcers and who have to make the best living they can in an unforgiving and unequal society.

These very broad parameters are subject to a variety of nuances in different countries and cultures. They may well be influenced by affiliations and groupings in the non-prison world and this is likely to be most obvious where prisoners live together cheek by jowl in large accommodations units such as dormitories. This was the case in the Gulag camps of the Soviet Union and some of the tradition remains in their successor prison systems in Russia and elsewhere in the region (Oleinik, 2003). In South America, including the countries described in this chapter, the hierarchy mirrors that of the gangs in the community, very often built around the drug cartels, and the walls of the prison are no barrier to the continuance of the violent business on the street as I observed for myself in Villahermosa Prison in Cali. The murderous animosity between the various groups brings an added dimension to what can only be described as a form of internecine warfare such as existed in La Planta in Caracas. A further variation of this is to be found in the prisons of Central America which are filled with first and second generations of young men deported from cities in the United States who brought with them the gang affiliations of Los Angeles, New York and other cities. Yet another variation of these networks is to be found in Brazil where the gangs, such as the First Command of the Capital (PCP) in São Paolo and the Red Command in Rio de Janeiro, which had their genesis within prisons, have now spread to control much of everyday life in the *favelas* of these cities.

In all of these countries there can be no pretence of prison as a place of personal reform, although in a small number of them there are isolated examples of positive practice. In some of them, as we have seen, staff simply withdraw to the perimeter in an attempt to contain violence inside the prison walls and prevent escapes, and when they come into direct contact with the prisoners in the prison, they do so with *la mano dura*, the iron fist.

Dominican Republic

The prison reform work which ICPS carried out in countries around the world was invariably in response to requests for assistance from a variety of sources. Sometimes these came from intergovernmental organisations, such as the United Nations and the Council of Europe. There were also approaches from national governments or from non-governmental organisations working within a particular country; on other occasions the requests came from embassies and other diplomatic sources. An example of the latter came in December 2002 from the newly appointed UK Ambassador to the Dominican Republic. Soon after taking up post he had visited one of country's prisons and had been shocked at the conditions which he had encountered. The Ambassador raised the issue in one of his bilateral meetings and learned that the government would welcome independent advice about how to reform its prison system. It was subsequently agreed that ICPS would visit the Dominican Republic in June 2003 to carry out an initial assessment.

While it is geographically part of the Caribbean the Dominican Republic also has strong economic, social and cultural links with the Spanish-speaking countries of Central America and like them its justice system owes much to the country's historical links with Spain. We were aware that the situation in its prison system had many similarities to those in Guatemala, El Salvador and their neighbours, with the important distinction that it had not been infiltrated by Mara gangs to the same extent as the others.

Our first visit was to the prison of La Victoria, the largest in the country, in the northern outskirts of Santo Domingo. Originally built at the beginning of the 20th century with a stated capacity for 1,200 prisoners it held around 4,500 prisoners in 2003. (By mid-2020 this number had doubled to an unbelievable 9,000.) As we approached the imposing front entrance we were confronted by a depressing sight common to so many large inner-city prisons around the world: a long line of elderly, middle-aged and young women, weighed down by bags of food and other supplies, waiting patiently to be admitted to visit a partner, brother or son. We learned later that the women had to pay for entry to the prison.

Once we were through the internal security gates we found ourselves in what at first glance could best be described as an overcrowded inner-city *barrio*. Large inner courtyards were surrounded by two- and three-storey buildings in which the prisoners lived. The window grilles and barriers were festooned with drying washing. Hundreds of prisoners milled around with no sign of any guards or prison personnel other than the director and his senior staff who were escorting us. There was little overt tension and the prisoners crowded round us in an unthreatening fashion, asking where we were from and why we had come. Some offered to show us round but we explained that the director would do that 'without payment'. The whole ground area was covered by stalls selling all sorts of goods, including fresh food and drink, cooked food, clothes and providing services such as hairdressing. There was even a pawn shop. One of the saddest and most surreal sights was of a blind prisoner who stood silently at a 'crossroads' shaking a begging bowl into which some prisoners dropped a coin or two.

A comment which we heard repeatedly during our week in the country was that 'prison is a business'. Open corruption was endemic at every level. As in many prisons in the region, everything that was needed to survive had to be paid for, from the moment of entry to the moment of release. The first payment was for some personal space to sleep. For those with sufficient funds that might mean a private cell or even a small suite of rooms. Others might be able to afford a corner of an overcrowded room with the option of a bed, a mattress or simply a space on the floor according to the level of payment. Those with no money could be provided with a loan at an extortionate level of interest. There were charges for food and drink to supplement the meagre official diet, for medicines or for families to visit. When it was time for a court appearance the prisoner had to pay for transport to court or to hospital. The fact that many prisoners could not afford this went some way to explaining the abnormally high number of prisoners who were awaiting trial. All of these payments were for goods and services which should have been provided automatically. In addition a variety of services which were illegal in the prison setting could also be obtained at a cost; these included protection, access to drugs, to weapons and to prostitution. We were told that in some cases these payments were made directly to prison staff and sometimes to other prisoners. At the beginning of 2002 an article had been published in a legal publication, the *Judicial Gazette*, which provided price lists for many of these items. The article referred to an 'all-in package' for foreign prisoners which offered everything they were likely to need for an inclusive price, which at that time was over 75,000 pesos (approximately £1,000) per month. We later commented that while the operators of the scheme might well have learned this style of payment from the tour companies managing the country's international holiday resorts, they did not yet require participating prisoners to wear identifying coloured wristbands! All of these activities were taking place under prominently displayed official notices indicating that no prisoner should pay for anything.

During our visit we went to several prisons in different parts of the country. None of them had the complexity of problems which we saw in La Victoria but all had specific difficulties. In a number of rural areas the prisons were small but the relative overcrowding was intense, and this brought its own problems. In one, for example, we found that the unit holding women prisoners was in the same compound as the male prisoners, which left the women open to verbal and physical abuse. There were specific issues about the treatment of younger prisoners and children. The European Union had provided funding for new prison buildings for juveniles in Najayo but had given no thought as to how the young persons were to be treated. We heard clear evidence that the institution was being badly run, with at best ill-treatment and at worst torture, and just three weeks before our visit there had been a riot which had left much of the new juvenile institution uninhabitable. Most of the young people had been transferred to the male prison nearby, where they had previously been held and where there were reports that they had been regularly abused. A small number were still in the ruined part of the new institution, held in shocking conditions. What we witnessed in Najayo was a salutary lesson of the futility of international reform initiatives which focus on new prison building while paying little or no attention to weaknesses and abuses in the personal and social dynamics inside the prisons. Ironically a plaque remained on the ruined wall of the destroyed juvenile institution proudly announcing to the world that it had been built with funding from the European Union.

Our invitation to the Dominican Republic had come directly from President Hipólito Mejía, who had been elected in 2000 representing the centre left Dominican Revolutionary Party. We met with him on the first day of our visit and our meeting began with an exchange of business cards, which was the first and only time I received a business card from a head of state. His read simply 'Hipólito Mejía, Presidente'. As we sat talking in his office a video of his small grandchildren at play was running on a continuous loop on a large television screen on the wall and he took great pride in telling us about each of them. He told us that he was very conscious of the need for radical reform of the prisons and he was looking to us to provide an honest appraisal of what could be done. We went from the President to a working meeting with the Attorney General, who had governmental responsibility for the justice system including the prisons. He reinforced the President's message and said that he expected our report to be a cornerstone of the reforms which he wished to introduce. We subsequently met with a number of other senior figures, including government ministers, several senior parliamentarians, the President of the Supreme Court and the Chief of Police. It was clear that not all of them shared the desire of the President and the Attorney General for radical change.

Shortly after our visit we submitted our report to the Attorney General:

- It began by commenting on some of the strengths which we had identified, which included an overall lack of tension inside most prisons and the considerable involvement of civil society and religious groups.
- It then pointed out that the solution to many of the problems inside prisons would have to be resolved elsewhere in the justice system. Most noticeable was the fact that some 80 per cent of all prisoners were awaiting trial, some of them having been in prison for longer than any sentence they might receive if found guilty. If that issue were dealt with, overcrowding would be all but eliminated.
- The report identified several organisational issues. The most important of these was the fact that there was no recognised prison system. The majority of prisons, particularly the larger ones, were administered by the police while the remainder were managed by the military. Both of these services had made clear to us that they did not welcome this responsibility, that their personnel were not trained to carry out such duties and that they would gladly pass them over to a civilian prison service. We did not formally mention the fact that we had found that the prisons which were run by the military were in general better organised and provided superior care to the prisoners than those managed by the police.
- Linked to the previous point was the fact that there was no specific financial allocation or revenue budget for prisons. The salary and other costs of the police and military who worked in prisons were paid for respectively from the National Police and the National Army budgets.
- Our report recommended that the proposals which had already been discussed for the creation of a professional civilian prison system should be implemented and that its personnel should be specially recruited, be paid at appropriate levels and be given specific training.

- It also made specific recommendations about other matters including the treatment of women and juveniles, the need for proper health provision and the abolition of illegal payments.

In our concluding discussions with the Attorney General we strongly recommended the need to appoint a respected public figure to drive forward the change process and that a priority should be the establishment of a training school for new prison staff. The Attorney General told us that he had a person in mind for this appointment and asked us to meet him. This was Roberto Santana who was to become a key player from then on. A former Rector of the Autonomous University of Santo Domingo and a nationally known media personality, he had been imprisoned on several occasions during the dictatorship for his activities as a student leader. We met him first over tea in our hotel and after a few moments of general conversation we launched into an animated discussion about the dire situation in the country's prisons. He was at pains to stress that he did not profess to be an expert in the intricacies of the world of prisons – although we might have argued in reply that his own personal experience gave him a unique qualification in that respect. However, having been approached by the Attorney General, he had recently visited some of the country's major prisons and said that the main impression which he had come away with was the absolute waste of time and potential which was the daily life of the prisoner. He stressed that he was primarily an educator and that he was convinced that much could be done to provide prisoners with education in its broadest sense, starting at a very basic level to deal with the rampant illiteracy – emphasising the meaning of the evocative Spanish word *analfabetismo*, illiteracy.

We described some of the findings from our report on what we had witnessed in prisons and as our exchange continued we reached an agreement that rather than focussing on a process of gradual reform it might be necessary to develop a completely new model of imprisonment, '*un nuevo modelo*'. I emphasised the principle that the key to a well-managed prison was the relationship between prisoners and staff and that the latter needed to be recruited carefully and then be well trained. Santana responded warmly to this approach, indicating that he would give immediate priority to setting up a training academy and would seek support from former colleagues from the world of education. He also added that he would insist that no member of the police or the military should be recruited. We further agreed that it would be essential on a number of counts for him to have support from someone who had operational prison experience and he told us that he had already identified a senior prison director who had the qualities which would be needed. We ended by proposing that we might arrange for Santana to come to the United Kingdom for further discussions. We emphasised that this was not to suggest that he would find there a perfect model, far from it, but it would allow him to further develop his ideas and exchange opinions.

Before leaving Santo Domingo we had a final discussion with Ambassador Andrew Ashcroft who had arranged and financed our visit. The UK Foreign Office had a special adviser on prison matters in the Caribbean region. He was a former prison governor from England whom I knew and we agreed that it should be proposed to the Attorney General he should be invited to the country to add his support to the new initiatives. Events then happened at some speed. In January 2004 the UK prison adviser visited to offer additional support and in March Roberto Santana and his new deputy, Ysmael Paniagua, visited the United Kingdom and spent some time at the Prison Service Training College as well as visiting several prisons.

By the middle of 2004 it was possible to identify a number of points of substantial progress:

- A temporary prison staff training school had been set up in Puerto Plata under the full-time supervision of Ysmael Paniagua.
- The first cohort of students, who all had previous academic qualifications and who had no previous links with prisons, had been recruited and a number of experienced academics had agreed to provide tuition on a variety of relevant subjects.
- The Attorney General had offered full support for the programme of change.
- A strategy for raising consciousness of the state of the prisons was underway, not only in government but also in academia and among the population more widely.

The Presidential election in May 2004 was won by Leonel Fernandez who took office in August of that year. In conversation with the UK Ambassador before his election Fernandez had indicated that he had read our report of the previous year. He said that he accepted its recommendations and indicated that he looked forward to supporting the work for prison reform. After his election President Fernandez gave his unequivocal backing to the reforms, describing them as an integral part of his three-pronged initiative on judicial, prisons and police reform.

By March 2005 two further prisons, one for women in Najayo and another in Dajabon, were inaugurated as New Model prisons. The difference between the New Model prisons and the combination of overcrowding, corruption, lack of control, widespread abuse of prisoners and inhuman conditions in the old prisons was highlighted by a major riot and fire at a prison in Higuey in that month, in which 136 men were killed in a pitched battle between rival groups of prisoners.

A few months later Attorney General Francisco Brito announced the creation of a separate New Model civilian prison service to be led by Roberto Santana with responsibility for the New Model prisons and the staff training school. It was intended that this would gradually expand throughout the country and in the meantime the other existing prisons would remain under the management of the military and police. This was a far from ideal arrangement but it was a pragmatic resolution to a political dilemma and it placed the New Model on firmer ground with a strong leader who had a high public profile. The long-term expectation was that as the New Model developed and expanded it would gradually replace the existing discredited and corrupt system.

From the outset one of the founding principles of the New Model had been the need for suitable properly trained personnel, and Santana had been determined to establish a dedicated training school which would underline this priority. Limited new funding was always going to be a major issue, particularly for any capital projects; but in addition to being a respected educator and academic Santana was a lateral thinker and entrepreneur. The early New Model prisons were set up in existing public institutions which were converted for their new use at minimal cost. In his search for a location for a staff training school for the new prison service he identified an abandoned government hotel near the city of San Cristobal which could be converted at relatively little expense and in a fairly short time. There was a delicious irony in this choice given the building's previous history. The dictator Rafael Trujillo, who ruled the Dominican Republic with an iron grip between 1930 and 1961, was a native of San Cristobal and had a grand ornate concrete and glass six-floor mansion constructed for his own use in 1947 on a hill overlooking the city, although he never actually lived there. Known as El Cerro, the house had been used for a short period as a hotel, but by 2005 it had lain empty and abandoned for several years. This building, standing in its own grounds, was identified as the new National Penitentiary School and within a matter of months had been renovated and brought into use. It was opened in February 2006 with some style and I was asked to give the inaugural lecture by teleconference from King's College. The basic textbook for the students was to be the ICPS handbook *A Human Rights Approach to Prison Management*.

In June 2006 I visited a number of countries in the region, including Guatemala as described earlier, and I took the opportunity to return to the Dominican Republic and to visit El Cerro. What I found was most impressive. The buildings had been extensively restored and offered a three-month residential course for new recruits to the New Model Prison Service. A course was underway during my visit and I was able to observe various aspects of the programme. As he had promised, Santana had been able to recruit several of his former university colleagues to lead a number of relevant academic modules on the course. Ysmael Paniagua had similarly identified a number of personnel with operational prison experience to lecture on technical subjects.

By this point nine of the 35 prisons in the Dominican Republic were being managed under the New Model and had been renamed as Centres for Correction and Rehabilitation. One of them was Najayo Women's Prison, which I had visited in 2003. Three years later the change in the prison was dramatic. All the staff, a mixture of young men and women, had been recruited and trained under the new arrangements. They were smartly dressed in bright sports shirts and dark trousers and spoke very positively about their work and the principles on which the prison was managed. The prisoners whom we met also talked enthusiastically about the changes which had taken place in the prison. The atmosphere in the prison was calm and purposeful with prisoners moving about relatively freely. Everyone was involved in education or work. The visiting room had been transformed and now included an impressive playroom for visiting children.

In August 2011 I was invited to take part in a regional meeting on prison reform organised by the United Nations in Santo Domingo. The fact that the meeting was taking place in the Dominican Republic was testament to the international interest in what was happening in the country. Never one to miss an opportunity, Santana invited me to stay for a further few days to see how the *Nuevo Modelo* was progressing. He wanted to make best use of my time and so, as well as inviting me to give lectures at the training school in San Cristobal, he took me by helicopter on a breathtaking ride over the beautiful central highland area to visit new centres in the north, where once again I was impressed by what I found.

In June 2012 Roberto Santana stood down as head of the New Model prisons and was replaced by his deputy, Ysmael Paniagua, who had been alongside him from the outset in 2003. Santana was appointed as adviser to the Attorney General and later became head of the UN sponsored Regional Penitentiary Academy.

By 2016, 22 of the prisons in the Dominican Republic, holding 10,000 prisoners, were part of the New Model system. The remaining 15 prisons held 16,000, almost all of whom were pre-trial detainees, including a total of 9,000 in La Victoria. That remained largely the situation in 2020.

Comment

In many countries the manner in which prisons have developed has been influenced by the country's political and social history. This is a theme which runs through many of the chapters in this book and which can be seen, for example, in countries where the concept of the prison was introduced by colonial powers primarily to subdue and to control indigenous populations and where that tradition remains till this day in the design of the buildings, in the militaristic style of management and in the way prisoners are treated. It can also be found in countries of the former Soviet Union where the harsh legacy of the Gulag still runs deep. In the United Kingdom a Victorian belief in the virtue of large institutions as places for reform still informs the design and management of modern prisons. Running in parallel with these organisational and structural influences in many countries is the crucial issue of who is sent to prison; who are the individuals and the groups who are most likely to be segregated from the rest of society behind the high walls and fences of the prison.

In respect of prisons in Guatemala, Honduras and particularly El Salvador I have referred to the significant presence of the members of the Mara and similar gangs whose members were originally deported from the United States. Twenty and more years later there is a second generation of these young men, even more dangerous and desperate than their predecessors. They have brought fear and insecurity to their cities and neighbourhoods. (In Guatemala City we had a real sense of personal danger, even greater than we felt in the prison, as we walked through the streets, and in San Salvador we were warned not to stray far from our hotel which had armed guards at the entrance.)

So far, the only response from governments on all sides of the political spectrum has been the immediate and brutal *mano dura*, intended as a demonstration of the government's superior power. (I was reminded of my early days in Peterhead Prison when a prisoner said to me, "You know, Governor, the only difference between you and me is that your gang is bigger than my gang.") There can be no argument that governments have a right and a responsibility to restore peace and safety to embattled communities, and part of that duty will involve ensuring public order. But force cannot be the sole answer to these deep societal problems. The one thing that the Mara gangs understand is force, and they respond to it with evermore brutal force which they employ against their own communities as well as against the forces of the state. That has led to a vicious spiral which has resulted in El Salvador now having a rate of imprisonment which in world terms is second only to the United States.

A further consequence of this stand-off is that the Maras have brought their violence into the prisons and have used these as fertile recruiting grounds since a prisoner has little chance of survival without the fragile protection which comes with being a gang member. Continuing the deadly game of tit for tat, the government's response has been the long-term and continuing use of 'exceptional measures', which is a euphemism for continuous confinement in dark, unsanitary and grossly overcrowded ground floor dungeons. It is now in the process of building a new high-security prison where these conditions are likely to become a permanent phenomenon.

I was invited to go to El Salvador in 2016 to contribute to a programme of prison reform. I discovered one or two tender shoots of hope where a small number of prisoners were engaged in productive work provided by a local businessman, but the reality is that the government makes no pretence that prison is a place of reform. Rather, its use is regarded as a weapon in the battle against what the government regards as the destabilising elements in society. The disastrous situation in El Salvador confirms the adage that no prison system can be reformed in isolation from a country's wider justice system and from the underlying values of a society.

The lesson from the Dominican Republic is a different one. It demonstrates some of the key factors which are necessary for progress to be made:

- In the early 1960s the country emerged from 30 years of a repressive and brutal dictatorship and since then Dominican society has been more cohesive than in some of the other countries in the region. There is a broad political consensus about the need for prisons to be managed in a manner which will make society safer and more secure. While there may be differences in emphasis, the principle is not a matter of political controversy. This was clear after the 2004 election when the new government continued to support the work which had been initiated by its predecessor and this has also happened after succeeding elections.

- The government identified a key champion of change in Roberto Santana. From the outset he had a clear vision of what needed to be done and how it might be achieved. He came from outside the justice system but brought with him a national credibility which allowed him to tap into many external sources of support. He selected an experienced deputy who provided the necessary operational credibility. He did not seek great amounts of financial support for capital projects but instead was very agile in making use of resources which he sourced from unusual quarters. The conversion of one of Trujillo's former mansions into the new training school was a good example of his lateral thinking. Having established a strong foundation for the New Model, he then organised his succession plan.

The New Model prisons have been remarkably successful. They have now been in existence for some 15 years and have long gone past the stage of being experimental. They have attracted considerable attention in the region and elsewhere and the Penitentiary Training School now offers courses to prison staff in neighbouring countries. In the words of Elias Carranza, the highly respected and experienced former Director of the United Nations Latin American Institute for the Prevention of Crime and the Treatment of Offenders (ILANUD), 'Before, when I would go to a government [somewhere in the region] and say, "Look at what they're doing in Switzerland," they'd respond, "That's a different world." But now I can say, "Look at the Dominican Republic," and they listen' (Fieser, 2014).

There are, however, a number of caveats to be registered. Inevitably, not everyone was fully committed to the new developments and there were a number of vested interests. In 2005 the new Attorney General announced what was in effect the creation of two separate prison systems. Robert Santana was to lead the civilian prison service which would consist of the New Model prisons and the staff training school, while the other existing prisons would remain under the management of the police. The newly appointed civilian head of that part of the prison service was replaced once more by a police general, which remains the position today. In pragmatic terms this decision may have been understandable but in the longer term it implied that there would be little change in that original discredited part of the system.

In practice virtually all convicted prisoners in the Dominican Republic are now held in the New Model prisons while all pre-trial detainees are in the traditional prisons. In 2004 when the New Model got underway there were approximately 13,000 prisoners in the country; today this figure has doubled to 26,000. In 2004 some 77 per cent of prisoners were awaiting trial, today that figure has fallen to 61 per cent, which is still unusually high, suggesting a weakness in the Dominican prosecution and judicial systems.[5] As in many other countries there is a stark lesson that prison systems cannot be reformed in isolation from the rest of the justice system.

10

Barbados and the Inter-American Court of Human Rights

Her Majesty's Prison Glendairy

In September 1994 I attended a judicial seminar on sentencing procedures in the Caribbean in Bridgetown, Barbados. Almost all of the countries in the English-speaking Caribbean were represented, mainly by senior members of their judiciary, politicians and academics. There were also several of us from other jurisdictions who had been invited because of a particular interest or expertise; I had been asked to speak on international standards for the treatment of prisoners. I have little recollection of the details of the conference, other than the fact that at one point there was an animated discussion about the judicial imposition of corporal punishment. This debate was not about whether corporal punishment was an appropriate judicial disposal; not at all. It was about whether flogging a person with a cat-o'-nine-tails administered by lashing across the back was a more effective punishment than whipping with a tamarind switch inflicted on the naked buttocks. It was hard to believe that this subject was even being discussed at a major judicial seminar in the last decade of the 20th century.

But what I most remember about that week was the visit we made to Glendairy Prison. In the Caribbean there are a few prisons with a reputation which reaches beyond national boundaries, invariably for negative rather than positive reasons. These would include Golden Grove in Trinidad, St Catherine's in Jamaica and also Glendairy in Barbados. Built in 1855 and officially known as Her Majesty's Prison this was the only prison in the country, with places for 245 prisoners. Throughout its history it had been overcrowded and at times it had held up to 1,000 male and female prisoners. On the day of our visit in September 1994 it was holding 702 men and 22 women. Glendairy was typical of many prisons around the world of the former British Empire, constructed on an imposing scale, externally visible to the community as a constant reminder of colonial power and domination. Inside the high perimeter walls was a sprawling expanse which included a multi-storied Victorian accommodation block for male prisoners, a discrete prison unit for women and an extensive farm. On our way into the prison we passed a sorry-looking line of women waiting to be allowed into the visiting room for their monthly exchange with fathers, sons and partners, conducted on either side of a long table, separated by a glass panel.

During our visit we made a particular point of asking to see the section which held prisoners who had been condemned to death. This was known as the 'back' prison, built at right angles to the 'front' prison, the whole forming a 'T' shape. The 'back' consisted of a two-storied double corridor formed in such a way that the inner cells backed on to each other and so had no natural light. Prisoners in this section were either undergoing punishment and subject to special security restrictions or on death row. On the day of our visit there were 29 prisoners in this section, 14 of whom had been sentenced to death. We were told that one man had been on death row for four years. Men held in the back prison were in single cells, which were grille fronted, dank and dark. The only bedding was a thin dirty mattress on the floor. On first entering the corridor it was not immediately obvious that there was a human being in any of the cells. When we became accustomed to the half dark we were able to see in each of them the light-coloured palm of a hand against the grille. On closer inspection we could also see a light pair of underpants and we realised that a man was standing up against the grille. Each prisoner was allowed 30 minutes' 'exercise' daily in a small adjacent caged area, with eight prisoners at a time placed in this cage. Apart from this and a few other exceptions, the prisoners in the 'back' spent all day every day confined in their unventilated, dingy cage-like cells.

I returned to Bridgetown in late May 2005 to speak at another conference, this time on the abolition of the death penalty. On this occasion I did not visit Her Majesty's Prison, not because I had no time to do so, but because in March of that year it had all but burned down. When fire broke out on the morning of 29 March the prison was holding 942 prisoners, over three times its capacity. The fire had been started deliberately by prisoners and it spread rapidly throughout the accommodation block within a short period. Police and soldiers from the Barbados Defence Force entered the prison to support prison staff. The majority of the prisoners were moved to the open courtyard and by evening it appeared that the situation was under control. However, in the course of the night some prisoners were able to set other fires. Additional security personnel arrived from the neighbouring island states of St Lucia and St Vincent and one prisoner was killed before order was restored. It was clear that Glendairy could no longer be used to house prisoners and within a short period all prisoners were transferred to accommodation in a former United States naval base at a remote area known as Harrison Point.

Harrison Point

At the outset there was little public information about the facilities at the temporary prison but there were press reports of poor conditions, unsanitary cells, inedible food, unclean drinking water and that the prisoners had limited or no opportunity to communicate with their relatives. In a report to the United Nations Human Rights Committee in July 2006[1] the government of Barbados referred to the fact that at Harrison Point '10 buildings used for inmate accommodation have been retrofitted providing in-cell sanitary facilities, internal showers and external exercise cages' but provided no other details. In these circumstances it was almost inevitable that there would be some kind of legal action.

Four prisoners, Lennox Boyce, Jeffrey Joseph, Frederick Atkins and Michael Huggins, who had previously been held in Glendairy had been convicted of murder in 2001 and had received mandatory death sentences. They had appealed their cases through various court stages and in June 2006 these reached the Inter-American Court of Human Rights (IACHR) based in Costa Rica.[2] In addition to an appeal against the mandatory nature of the death penalty, the application also referred to the conditions under which they were being detained and I was asked by lawyers for the four men to write an expert report on these conditions for presentation to the court. I agreed to do so and wrote to the Attorney General of Barbados for permission to visit Harrison Point but this was refused 'as a result of heightened security concerns regarding the security of the temporary prison at this time and until the new prison is completed'. The Minister did not expand on the nature of the 'security concerns'. In May 2007 the President of the IACHR issued an order requiring the State of Barbados to grant me access to the temporary prison so that I could prepare my expert testimony for presentation to the court. The date for hearing the case at the IACHR in Costa Rica had been set for early July and it was not until the middle of June that the State finally agreed to allow access. Accordingly arrangements were made at short notice for me to visit Harrison Point and then to travel directly to Costa Rica to present oral testimony to the court.

The situation in 2007

The journey by road from Bridgetown took me the length of the west side of the island, as far north as was possible, to the extremity of the parish of St. Lucy. The US Navy had controlled the Harrison Point facility from 1957 until 1979 when it was handed back to the Barbados government. By its nature the site was remote and I had already discovered that its very existence was not marked on any publicly available maps of the area.

The prison campus was spread over an extensive area and the buildings retained many aspects of the former military base. The whole complex was surrounded by a single wire fence, some three metres high, topped by razor wire. Each of the living units was enclosed by an additional fence, also topped by razor wire, and additional security was provided by German shepherd dogs and their handlers patrolling in the areas between the various compounds. On the day of my visit the prison held 990 men and 49 women, one of whom had her infant son with her. Three hundred of the men and eight of the women were unconvicted.

The women were held in a separate block which had eight rooms, each holding around six prisoners. The prisoners were locked in the rooms for most of the day. Close by there was a small hut used as a classroom and an adjoining exercise yard.

A further security fence led into the main section of the prison and the six blocks which held the male prisoners. Two blocks held prisoners who were on remand, and three held prisoners who were considered to be a low security risk. Each of these blocks had previously been dormitory accommodation for the US Navy personnel and their security had been reinforced by the simple method of constructing a series of conjoined metal cages with grilled sides and roof inside the frame of the original buildings. Each block had 12 of these cages, referred to by the staff as 'cubicles', holding ten to 12 prisoners. There was a toilet in the corner of each cage partially screened by plastic. There was no privacy, with prisoners being able to see from one cage to the next. There was a corridor for staff around three sides of the block. A limited amount of natural light came through small windows on one wall and the whole area was generally dark and unpleasantly warm. Prisoners spent virtually the entire day in the cages and I found most of them lying on their bunk beds or playing checkers, dressed only in boxer shorts. There were small exercise yards attached to each block but access to them was limited and intermittent due, I was told, to shortage of staff.

The available piped water was not safe for drinking so a water lorry came to the prison each day with drinking water which was transferred to the blocks in large containers. The State School Meals Department delivered food to the prison each morning in insulated containers.

There were no facilities for prisoners to have visits from family and friends. Instead there were videoconferencing links to the remaining administrative offices in Glendairy Prison in Bridgetown where family members could go to access them. I was told that prisoners could have one 15-minute session twice per month, although it was hard to see how this could be managed logistically in the time made available since there were 1,000 prisoners. Telephone conversations were recorded. These arrangements were a matter of considerable complaint by both prisoners and their families, some of whom had had no direct contact since March 2005.

There were three other blocks in a separate secure compound holding men who had been designated as requiring medium to high security. The structure in two of them was similar to that in the other blocks. The third was a maximum security block which had accommodation for up to 40 prisoners. Outside the security compound there were two parallel rows of steel shipping containers, each divided into six small cells. Internally they were bare, with no electricity or other fittings and a small narrow window near the ceiling covered with a steel shutter which effectively blocked out any light. At the time of my inspection they were all unoccupied. I was told that they were used infrequently when a prisoner "needed a cooling-off period, which was never more than 24 hours". On the day of my visit they were unbearably hot inside.

During my inspection I paid particular attention to conditions in the maximum security block as this was where the three prisoners who had taken their case to the Inter-American Court were being held. (The fourth applicant, Frederick Atkins, had been transferred to a hospital in October 2005 where he died seven days later as a result of an unspecified illness.) If conditions in the other blocks were bad, those in this high-security unit were ten times worse. Its construction was different from the other blocks which had previously been dormitories. This one, with a much higher roof, looked as though it had been a storehouse or large work shed. Like the other blocks it had internal cages, 24 to hold one person in each and eight with bunk beds for two men. On the day of my visit the block held 37 prisoners. Five of these, including one of the applicants, were described as being on death row although their conditions of confinement were similar to the others. The cages were lined on each side of an internal corridor. There were five narrow windows set high along one wall, providing minimal natural light, and fluorescent lighting strips were on 24 hours a day. I visited the block at about 1 pm; outside there was bright sun but inside it was very dark and not easy to see into the cages. The air was stale and the atmosphere very warm. At the end of the block there was a small toilet and shower area and there was also a small exercise yard off the block. The prisoners had minimal possessions: papers relating to their case, sometimes a book or two and a few toiletries. Each had a plastic slop bucket. Stated briefly, the atmosphere in the block was depressing and oppressive.

Before speaking to the prisoners, I spent some time in discussion with the sergeant on duty. He said that he had been in charge of the unit for two years. Pointing to his moustache which was flecked with grey, he said, "When I came here, this was completely black." He talked about the stress which he and his staff faced on a daily basis, saying that the prisoners regarded them as the 'enemy'. He said that he had never been able to take a meal break during any of his shifts. No chaplain or counsellor ever came to the block. The superintendent rarely visited and the Chief Officer only occasionally. He said that the prisoners were always handcuffed when taken from their cages to the exercise yard or to the bathroom. He told me that a few days previously in anticipation of my visit his staff had been increased from two to four, which meant that he would now be able to allow the prisoners regular access to exercise and the toilet facilities.

I then individually interviewed the three men who had taken their cases to the IACHR. They painted a vivid picture of what their daily life was like. One explained how he had learned to control his bodily functions as they were only given access to the shower and toilet for a short period each morning. The facility was never cleaned and one of the prisoners had recently slipped on the grimy floor, breaking his wrist. Exercise in the small yard was irregular and infrequent. He told me that on one occasion a prisoner who had refused to come out of his cage was shot in the shoulder with a rubber bullet and then sprayed with mace gas. From time to time staff would conduct anal searches for no obvious reason. The men also complained that correspondence with lawyers was opened and censored as a matter of course. At the Chief Officer's insistence I had agreed that he could sit in on the interviews. His presence did not restrain the critical comments by the prisoners and it was instructive that neither during the interviews nor afterwards did he take any issue with what I was being told.

At the end of my visit I had a short courtesy meeting with the Assistant Superintendent. I told him that I was free the following day and that, if the government thought it would be helpful, I would be willing to go to see the new prison which was under construction at Dodds in St Philip parish. He said this was a matter for the Attorney General but that he suspected it might be difficult to arrange a visit at such short notice since the contractors were working at full speed to get the prison ready. Given the difficulties which I had encountered in obtaining the government's permission to visit Harrison Point, it was no surprise that I heard nothing further about my offer to visit Dodds and so I then travelled to Costa Rica to give evidence before the Inter-American Court.

Inter-American Court of Human Rights

The Court was being asked to rule that the State of Barbados had violated the Inter-American Convention on Human Rights on three counts:

- The mandatory death penalty for a murder conviction.
- The sentence of the death penalty on one of the applicants. (The original death penalty sentences on the other applicants had already been commuted to life imprisonment.)
- The prison conditions in which the applicants were being held constituted cruel, inhuman and degrading treatment.

My task was to make an oral statement to the Court in respect of the third of these issues. I spent the day before the hearing discussing my findings and my conclusions with the applicants' legal team who had originally instructed me. I then crafted my statement ready to present it to the Court.

On the morning of 11 July I listened as arguments were presented in respect of the death penalty issues. When the court turned to the matter of prison conditions it heard first from the Superintendent of Prisons. Lt Colonel John Nurse had been in charge of Glendairy Prison since 2001, then of Harrison Point and was also overseeing the construction of the new prison at Dodds. His case, briefly, was that the conditions previously in Glendairy and at that juncture in Harrison Point did not constitute cruel, inhuman and degrading treatment. He had a shaky foundation for his arguments but he presented them as best he could. I was then called to the witness stand. As I read out my statement the seven judges listened intently. My conclusion was clear:

> It is my opinion that, in respect of some of the above issues singly and all of them conjointly, the state of Barbados has violated

> article 5 (2) of the Inter-American Convention on Human Rights in respect of its treatment of the applicants. I base that opinion on my knowledge of previous findings of this Court and of the European Court of Human Rights in respect of prison conditions in a number of countries and also of the recommendations of the Council of Europe Committee for the Prevention of Torture in respect of its visits to the 47 member states of the Council of Europe.

The applicants' legal team was led by Keir Starmer QC of Doughty Street Chambers, London, assisted by two senior members of the Barbados and Trinidad Bars. Starmer took me through my statement item by item, probing each of my findings, seeking justification for any comment which he thought might be challenged by the government lawyers. As on other occasions when I have been called to provide expert evidence in courts of law, I enjoyed the cut and thrust of question and answer and when the examination ended I felt drained but confident that I had defended my report successfully. Keir had done his job well and the State's legal team had little more than a few points of detail to raise when they cross-examined me. Finally, several of the judges sought clarification on a number of points of detail before I stood down. With that, the hearing had come to an end and judgement was reserved.

The court delivered its judgement on 20 November 2007 and found that the State of Barbados had violated the Inter-American Convention on Human Rights in respect of all the issues before it.[3] In respect of prison conditions it concluded that:

> the conditions in which these three alleged victims have been and continue to be detained, in particular in relation to the lack of privacy, contact with the outside world, and exercise, as well as being kept in cages and forced to use slop buckets in plain view of others, amount to inhuman and degrading treatment and fail to respect the human dignity of the person, in contravention to Article 5(1) and 5(2) of the Convention, to the detriment of Messrs. Boyce, Joseph, Atkins and Huggins.

Comment

In respect of the mandatory death penalty the State of Barbados moved at a glacial pace towards abolition. In May 2009 the Attorney General announced his intention to include abolition as part of wider constitutional changes which he would bring before parliament. This did not happen and in September 2015 the State was summoned before the Inter-American Court to explain its failure to comply with its earlier binding order. Finally, in June 2018 the Caribbean Court of Justice declared that the mandatory death penalty in Barbados was unconstitutional. This meant in effect that it was abolished as a sentence.

The new prison at Dodds in St Philip was officially opened in October 2007 and the following month the transfer of prisoners from Harrison Point began. Included among their number were Lennox Boyce, Jeffrey Joseph and Michael Huggins, the three remaining prisoners who had taken their case to the Inter-American Court. The site of the former prison lay empty after the last prisoners left until March 2020 when the government of Barbados announced its intention to open the buildings as an isolation and quarantine centre for people infected by COVID-19.

11

Sub-Saharan Africa: an expensive colonial legacy

South Africa

In August 1995 I was invited to South Africa to address the annual conference of the African Society of International and Comparative Law which was being held in the newly democratic Republic of South Africa for the first time, attended by 150 people from all over the continent including the Assistant Secretary General of the United Nations and the Assistant Secretary General of the Organisation of African Unity. The government minister who opened the conference spoke for all when he commented that the fact that the pan-African gathering was taking place in South Africa was the realisation of what until then had been an impossible dream. It was a high honour that I had been invited to speak there.

On arrival at Johannesburg International Airport I was met by a driver, let's call him Jairus, who had spent the previous two days virtually without a break ferrying people to the conference location in Rustenburg, a two-hour drive to the north of Johannesburg. He was clearly exhausted and almost asleep at the wheel so I felt it was in my interest to keep him talking as much as possible. As we drove he pointed out the various White suburbs we passed through coming out of Johannesburg and then on to Alexandra township where, he said, the living conditions "were not fit for pigs". Jairus himself lived in Soweto. He told me that he had a son and a daughter aged 15 and eight years respectively and was able to send them to what had previously been a school exclusively for White children where, he said, they were guaranteed a good education. He had to meet the costs of their schooling and as a consequence had to work every hour possible to raise the necessary finance. Jairus expressed disappointment that general living conditions had not improved at all but hoped that, while his generation would have little benefit, his children would do so. He talked without bitterness about the folly of apartheid and how people had been taught to fear each other, about how White parents would tell their children that the 'Kaffirs' were dangerous people, about how they were kept separate, about how there was still an apartheid based on economics and wealth. He spoke about his hopes for the future and commented that sanctions and boycotts of food had contributed to mass unemployment and even more poverty, although it had to be acknowledged that they had been powerful influences for change. I told Jairus that the rest of the world was full of admiration for South Africa and the manner in which it was dealing with its past history and looking positively to the future. My words sounded inadequate but he accepted them without comment.

In opening my presentation to the conference I said:

> 'It is helpful to remind ourselves that the use of imprisonment as a direct punishment of the court is a relatively modern phenomenon which had its beginnings in Western Europe and North America about 250 years ago. It has now spread to most countries in the world. Let me say at the outset that the prison is not indigenous to many countries and cultures. Most African societies traditionally had other ways of dealing with people who broke their rules and customs. I shall be suggesting to you today that Africa should look closely at the use it makes of imprisonment within its criminal justice systems. I believe that in this respect Western countries have much to learn from Africa and that Africa has little to learn from the West. If that is the case, it is highly appropriate that debate on this subject should be taken forward at a conference such as this.
>
> In many African countries prisons are housed in old buildings, often over 100 years old. The prison systems are a legacy from former colonial times, British, French or Portuguese. It is quite disconcerting to be in a town which is otherwise quite African in character and to turn a corner to be confronted by a grandiose building which is a minor replica of Wormwood Scrubs prison in London. Prisons such as this are totally unsuited to African culture. They were originally built, not to protect local people, but as a means for the colonial power to control local people. Today, especially in countries where resources are scarce it does not make sense to take large numbers of able-bodied young men out of society, to make them unproductive and unable to support their families and to place the burden of their upkeep on the state.
>
> The purpose of a system of criminal justice is to restore the balance between the victim and the offender, a balance which has been disturbed by the commission of a crime. This principle tends to be overlooked in many criminal justice systems, where

> the state has taken on itself the responsibility for representing the victim to such an extent that the victim has largely been pushed to the margins of the process. The principle of balance underlies much of traditional law in Africa. I would like to suggest to you that if you are seriously interested in dealing with the problems of crime in your respective communities, rather than looking to the Western example of locking up more and more people in prison, you would do well to examine your ancient heritage and to look to more traditional forms of community justice.'

As a foreigner, a White person from another culture, I had been uncertain about the wisdom of making a statement like this before such a distinguished African audience. I need not have been concerned. As I spoke there was a whispering of approval and nodding of heads and the ensuing discussion explored what this might mean in practice. It was not being suggested that there should be a return to the traditions of previous centuries, when an individual who had committed murder might be exiled from his village community for seven years, as in Chinua Achebe's classic book *Things Fall Apart* (1958), or when the resolution might involve harsh physical punishment; although there may have been an anticipation of the 'gacaca' courts which were later introduced as a method of dealing with the terrible genocide which at the time of the conference had just taken place in Rwanda.[1]

An aside: prisoner voting

Another speaker at the conference was Albie Sachs, who had lost an arm and the sight in one eye as a result of a car bomb explosion while in exile in Mozambique during the time of apartheid and by 1995 was a judge of the Constitutional Court of South Africa. In the course of a conversation he told me how he had convinced fellow drafters of the new South African Constitution that universal adult suffrage should indeed be universal and that constitutionally prisoners should be allowed to vote. He said that one of the comparisons he had used to advance his argument had been that prisoners in the United Kingdom had the right to take part in elections. I had to tell him that unfortunately that was not the case but that I would be happy henceforth to use the obverse of his argument in the United Kingdom. I have done this, but so far without success.

In December 2014 Justice Albie Sachs delivered the Nelson Mandela and Oliver Tambo Lecture in the University of Strathclyde, Glasgow. On that occasion I took the opportunity to remind him of our conversation about whether prisoners should have the right to vote in elections. Our subsequent exchange was later published in the journal *Scottish Justice Matters* (Sachs and Coyle, 2015), including the following response from Sachs:

> When it came to how South Africa should approach the matter, our Constitutional Court unanimously upheld the right of prisoners to vote. If I can be excused for citing myself, in the case of August [August *v* Electoral Commission and Others (1999)] I wrote for the Court that: 'Universal adult suffrage on a common voters roll is one of the foundational values of our entire constitutional order. The achievement of the franchise has historically been important both for the acquisition of the rights of full and effective citizenship by all South Africans regardless of race, and for the accomplishment of an all-embracing nationhood. The universality of the franchise is important not only for nationhood and democracy. The vote of each and every citizen is a badge of dignity and of personhood. Quite literally, it says that everybody counts. In a country of great disparities of wealth and power, it declares that whoever we are, whether rich or poor, exalted or disgraced, we all belong to the same democratic South African nation; that our destinies are intertwined in a single interactive polity.'

Contrast the view of this eminent jurist with that of UK Prime Minister David Cameron speaking in the House of Commons in November 2010: "I see no reason why prisoners should have the vote. This is not a situation that I want this country to be in. It makes me physically ill even to contemplate having to give the vote to anyone who is in prison."[2]

Department of Corrections

Shortly before I left for South Africa I had been contacted by Brigadier Henk Greef of the Department of Corrections, whom I had met when he had been a member of a parliamentary delegation to London earlier that year. His department had learned of my intended visit and he asked if I would extend my stay after the conference so that I could visit some prisons and give a lecture to staff. I agreed to this and the department prepared a programme for me and Joseph Etima, Commissioner of Prisons in Uganda, who was also attending the conference in Rustenburg.

The programme which had been prepared for us was a full one, starting each day at 6.45 am. We travelled first to Pretoria for a three-hour meeting with the Commissioner and his senior team. The session began with Etima and me being invited to make presentations about the prison systems in our respective countries and then to respond to the extensive questions which followed. At this stage discussion was focussed on issues which were of concern in most prison systems, and the South Africans wished to learn particularly about how Uganda managed the mutual problems of shortage of resources, poor infrastructure and overcrowding. They then questioned me about regimes and activities for prisoners in the United Kingdom as well as recruitment and training of personnel.

After that we moved on to the main issue of the day which was the situation in our host country.

At this juncture, along with all other government departments in the new South Africa, the Department of Corrections had embarked on a programme of radical change at all levels as it continued to shed the excesses and injustices of the apartheid era. This was of particular importance for the prison system which had been a significant tool of repression during the previous regime. Round the table there was much talk about the need to change attitudes and to move from a militaristic structure. We were assured that the racial imbalance within the personnel, notably at senior levels, was being met head on. There had already been two senior appointments from outside the service. One, who was at the table with us, was 34-year-old General Esmeraldo, who had joined the department two months previously as Deputy Commissioner in charge of Personnel Services, having previously been a personnel manager with a large local authority. The other one we were to meet later in our visit. The Commissioner, General H.J. Bruyn, informed us proudly that he had already announced publicly that within the next five years the ratio of senior staff in the service would be 70 per cent Black and 30 per cent White. Events were soon to prove that this was a gross underestimate. Looking around the table, he said that this change would clearly have implications for current senior personnel.

The department had created a 'Full Range Leadership' course for senior personnel which was being rolled out in its three main staff training complexes. This programme had a double purpose. The first was to impress on the existing White senior staff the need for a fundamental change in the way the service carried out its responsibilities and to make clear to all personnel that there would have to be a completely different dynamic in the way they dealt with prisoners on a daily basis. The second purpose was to assist the integration of new Black and what were then described as 'mixed-race' senior staff who had recently been appointed and to bring them up to speed with operational demands. Joseph Etima and I were reminded that the main reason we had been invited to the department was to address two of these Leadership courses which were currently running. There was logic to this double act: he the Commissioner of a neighbouring prison service who was internationally respected as I knew from previous dealings with him and I, an experienced senior prison governor from the United Kingdom.

Later that day we were taken to the Staff Training Centre in Baviaanspoort, about half an hour outside Pretoria, where we both made presentations to 20 or so senior personnel who were taking part in the leadership course. The following day we conducted a similar exercise in the training centre at Kroonstad where the 60 members who were on the final day of the course ranged from the brigadier commanding the area to heads of prisons and warrant officers. The discussion following our presentations on both occasions was animated and in our subsequent exchange of views Joseph Etima and I agreed that, whatever any private feelings, the attitudes expressed confirmed the existence of a general understanding that radical change was essential and that senior staff were behind its implementation.

As I talked with the people on these two courses I harked back to comments I had heard a few years before from the Director General of the Czech Prison Service who had delivered an impressive programme of modernisation of his service within a remarkably short period of time. He described how he had gathered all senior staff together at an early stage in the process and had emphasised to them that radical change was inevitable. He told them that they would all have to learn new methods of working. He understood that many of them would find that very difficult and he promised to give them all the support they needed, but they must be in no doubt that opposing the change was not an option. He told me that, in the event, the staff fell into three main groupings. Approximately one third embraced the changes and thrived on them. One third were very suspicious of the changes and never really internalised them; at the same time, they accepted that they had to be implemented and they got on with them as best they could. The final third simply could or would not cope with what the new model required of them and the Director had steered them gently but firmly towards retirement. I wondered how many of the senior staff I met on that visit to South Africa would fall into that third category.

Kroonstad is a small town in the Free State Province some 220 kilometres south of Pretoria and was the location of the largest of the three staff training centres for the Department of Corrections. We were greeted by the Head of the centre and the Provincial Commissioner of Prisons, General Sitole. The latter had been with the Department for four months and was its first Black general, having previously been headmaster of a school in Soweto. He had worked initially in headquarters and had just been appointed Commissioner with responsibility for the 27 prisons in the Free State. He had a confident but unassuming personality, was small in stature and still becoming accustomed to his military status and his fine khaki uniform with its brass buttons and white lanyard. On at least two occasions after we had sat down to talk and then were in the process of moving on he was pursued by one of his large White deputies calling, "General, General, you have forgotten your hat!"

At the time of our visit the centre was still known as the John Vorster Training Centre, having been opened by the former Premier in 1968. His bust remained in a prominent position at the entry to the complex and his photograph was displayed in the senior staff mess, symbols of the fact that much still needed to change in the new South Africa. The facilities in the centre were of a very high standard, with accommodation for over 500 students, an outdoor Olympic standard swimming pool, small rugby and football stadiums and a well-equipped gym. In June 1998 President Mandela visited the centre, by which time its name had been changed to the Kroonstad Department of Corrections Training College, and Vorster's bust had disappeared. In his address to staff the President made a comment that I have subsequently included in many of my presentations to prison personnel around the world:

> The way that a society treats its prisoners is one of the sharpest reflections of its character. … The full contribution which our prisons can make towards a permanent reduction in the country's crime-rate lies also in the way in which they treat prisoners. We cannot emphasise enough the importance of both professionalism and respect for human rights.[3]

The two Staff Training Centres at which Joseph Etima and I spoke were located in large departmental complexes, both of which included two prisons. The area nearest the Training Centres was laid aside for accommodation for staff working in the centres and the two prisons. As was the case in the United Kingdom until the late 1970s, housing was all allocated according to rank; the more senior the rank, the more generous the size and the better the appointments. The facilities for staff included an impressive sports complex, playgrounds for the children, shops and a petrol station. The whole complex was very much what Goffman (1961) would have recognised as a 'total institution'.

Baviaanspoort had a maximum and a medium security prison for male prisoners, the former holding 960 prisoners and the latter 481. Of a total of 452 staff, 235 were White. We visited the maximum security prison which had been built in 1922 and was in the process of major refurbishment. The prison complex was clean and well laid out with several cultivated garden areas. We were there just before 4 pm and all prisoners were locked in their cells which, so we were told, was because of a staff union meeting. However, one of the prisoners told us that they were locked up each day at 2.30 pm. We were shown one accommodation room which held ten prisoners in bunk beds and other rooms which held up to 25 prisoners. In each there was a large television and a washroom leading off with a shower, toilet and washbasins to which the prisoners had constant access. Prisoners in the medium security prison worked in the large farm which was on the complex. There was extensive dairy and pig farming and large areas under cultivation.

On the Kroonstad complex there was a prison for women and another for men. There were 152 women who were held in four blocks, each of which surrounded an open patio. The accommodation was in ten bedded rooms, each of which had its own toilet and shower area. There was an adequately equipped education unit and a medical facility. The women worked each weekday, with Wednesday and Friday afternoons off. As was the case in many countries, the main work for the women was in textiles, largely making clothing for male prisoners throughout the country. Sentences ranged from 46 days to life. Six of the prisoners had babies. The women slept in the same room with their babies beside them in cots.

The main prison in the complex held 1,365 males serving sentences ranging from 30 days to life; their ages ranged from 17 to 75 years. There was a total of 165 staff, which was an impossibly small number to supervise such a large group of prisoners and it was noticeable that staff carried American-style nightsticks openly as they went around. There was a further unit which held 527 male prisoners in the remaining unit, who were looked after by 108 staff. We were told that allocation to either of the prisons was made simply according to available space. The prison workshops had places for a total of 100 prisoners, which confirmed the fact that the vast majority of prisoners spent most of their day confined to their living accommodation.

Throughout the 1990s the rate of imprisonment in South Africa rose steeply, peaking at around 190,000 in 2004. It reduced considerably over succeeding years although in the last few years it has begun to rise again and in 2020 stood at 154,000. The Republic has one of the highest rates of imprisonment in Africa and overcrowding in prisons stands around 38 per cent. There are regular reports of severe ill-treatment of prisoners, particularly in the 'super maximum' security prisons in Pretoria and Kokstad and also in Pollsmoor in Cape Town which has a stated capacity for 4,000 men but regularly holds around 7,000. Manguang Correctional Centre in Bloemfontein is one of two private prisons in the Republic. It was managed by the UK security company G4S between its opening in 2001 and 2013 when the government took it back into public hands after a series of substantiated allegations of ill-treatment and torture of prisoners. It was returned to G4S in August the following year but it continues to attract regular criticism. In March 2020 following lengthy external pressure the government reluctantly published a highly critical report on the management of the prison up to 2013.

In some respects the manner in which imprisonment has been used over the years in South Africa is a paradigm of the prison as a place for the control or subjugation of the group in society which has been identified as the 'other', the group which threatens or at least is perceived to be a threat to the establishment and which needs to be kept in check. At the beginning of the 20th century in South Africa that group was made up predominately of Boers who opposed British rule. To deal with them the British authorities created a new type of prison, the concentration camp. For most of the 20th century the minority White population regarded the indigenous Black majority population as the 'other' and this was reflected in the composition of the prison population, while those who managed the system were exclusively White. Since the 1990s there has been a dramatic change in the racial make-up of prison personnel particularly at senior levels. The majority of prisoners are still Black but now, it can be argued, their distinguishing feature is not their ethnicity. It is the fact that, as in most countries, they come predominately from the marginalised social and economic groups of society.

Gambia

The physical conditions in many prisons in sub-Saharan Africa are among the worst in the world, especially where there are endemic levels of overcrowding. But there is more to a prison than its physical condition. I cast my mind back to a visit which I made in July 1992 to the Central State Prison in Banjul, known colloquially as Mile 2 Prison. The cooking and hygiene provision was all but non-existent and the degree of overcrowding beggared belief with prisoners sleeping cheek by jowl on wooden pallets on the ground.

I was in Banjul to attend a conference organised by the African Commission on Human and People's Rights and at the end of our visit to the prison we gathered in the prison's large open-air compound for a concert organised by the prisoners. As it drew to a climax, with great cheering and clapping by the assembled prisoners, a group of them performed a traditional dance in our honour. The Commissioner of Prisons was sitting among the guests on a raised platform. He suddenly rose and joined the prisoners in the dance, gyrating in their midst with enthusiasm to great applause from the hundreds of prisoners who were watching. This was done very naturally and with no formality. One could never have imagined such an occurrence in a European prison.

At the same time, it has to be remembered that our visit took place before Mile 2 Prison became notorious for its abuse and torture of the political prisoners who were held there at the behest of Yahya Jammeh, who became President after leading a military coup in 1994 and went on to rule Gambia for more than two murderous decades.

Mozambique

In 2002 ICPS published its handbook *A Human Rights Approach to Prison Management*. The work on this key publication was funded by the Human Rights Policy Department in the UK Foreign & Commonwealth Office (FCO) and it subsequently publicised the handbook widely through many of its Embassies and High Commissions. Andrew Soper was one of the key official FCO officials who supported the preparation of the handbook and we worked with him again when he was appointed as Deputy UK Ambassador to Brazil. In 2007 Andrew became UK High Commissioner in Mozambique and he arranged for me to go to Maputo to discuss the possibility of prison reform with the government.

Traditionally, as in a number of countries, the Ministry of Justice was responsible for prisons holding convicted prisoners in Mozambique while pre-trial prisoners were held in police custody under the control of the Ministry of the Interior. In 2006 the responsibility for all prisons and prisoners was transferred to the Ministry of Justice, although in practice that meant little change in the non-urban areas where the only places of detention were police lock-ups. Many international reports were extremely critical of conditions in both prisons and police cells and of the treatment of those under detention, and there were substantiated reports of extrajudicial killings, physical and other abuses. The Minister of Justice and the Director of Prisons had been very ambivalent when the High Commissioner suggested that I might be invited to the country, but just a week before my intended arrival they finally gave their approval.

Visits to prisons

I landed in Maputo just before noon on 11 November and by 2.30 pm I was visiting prisons. I went first to the Civil Prison which was designated to hold 'non-violent remand prisoners'. According to law prisoners should have been brought before an investigating judge within 24 hours and no later than 72 hours after arrest but since there were only two such judges in the city that was never the case, with most detainees waiting several months for their first court appearance. That was the main reason for the unusually high ratio of pre-trial prisoners in the country.

The small prison was grossly overcrowded and was holding over 300 prisoners that day, 13 of whom were women. The prisoners were kept in cramped rooms, around 18 to each, with no mattresses and only blankets on the floor. They spent all day in the accommodation blocks, although they were able to move around the corridor since the cells had no doors and were screened only by blankets. The women's section consisted of three rooms; two with five prisoners and one with three women and two babies. Each had a thin mattress laid out on the concrete floor. The area was relatively clean and there was an outside washing area. The cooking area was in the open air and staff said that breakfast was served in the morning and lunch around 3 pm. The women, on the other hand, told me that they were provided with food only once a day. In the male prison the kitchen cookers were unusable and meals had to be cooked over an open fire in the yard. The prison did not have its own supply of drinking water but depended on a water lorry which came daily, just as I had observed in Harrison Point prison in Barbados. There was one small medical room for the whole prison and a nurse visited daily. The director said that the main illnesses were HIV/AIDS and malaria, although he was unable to provide any data.

Prisoners were allowed one visit every fortnight in a large, bright room with long bench tables. When the room was full, visits were restricted to 30 minutes but visitors could then go out and rejoin the queue to come back again. There was a large adjoining room where prisoners' families could hand in food parcels and I was told privately that the prisoners were largely dependent on these for their sustenance.

I was then taken to Maputo Central Prison. Its structure was similar to many other prisons in the region which dated from colonial times. It had a high outer wall with a traditional main gate; inside, the gatehouse gave onto an open area leading to the main buildings. Just as in the civil prison the central prison had no private supply of drinking water and as we went in we had to stand aside as the water lorry which delivered fresh water each day was coming out. We later saw the prisoners queuing at various water points in the prison grounds to fill their own plastic containers.

The prison had a stated capacity for 800 prisoners and held over 1,600 on the day of my visit. The youngest prisoners were 16 years old and the majority were 25 years or younger. The living units had about 30 cells on either side of a long, narrow corridor. Each held over 100 prisoners, with around seven prisoners in each relatively small room. Most of the rooms had Asian-style toilets in a corner. The roof of the dining room had collapsed some time previously and so prisoners had to take meals back to their living accommodation. In theory there were two meals a day which were cooked over open fires in the yard but, as with the other prison, it was not clear that in reality two were provided. The relatively new director told me that he had begun a programme with prisoners cultivating vegetables in the extensive grounds of the prison as a way of supplementing food supplies.

As our group came back to the entrance of the prison we were confronted by about 60 of the youngest prisoners who lined up to sing the national anthem in my honour.

Prison staff training course

Prior to 2006 there had been no specific training for prison staff, who were for all practical purposes still police officers. Since then the Ministry of Justice had set up a recruit training course for new prison staff which took place within the police training school. In the course of my visit the first of these courses was coming to an end and I was invited to address the participants. The police training school was situated some distance outside Maputo and the final part of our journey involved a five-mile drive down an unmetalled road. As we approached the school we saw 300 or so young recruits sitting patiently on the ground in the open air under a group of great baobab trees, with a single table and chair placed in front of them. I was introduced to the students and gave them an impromptu lecture on the importance of the career on which they were embarking and what would be required of them in their professional work and ended by handing over copies of the ICPS Handbook in Portuguese to the school for use as textbooks in the training course. The Ministry deserved praise for setting up such a course but one was left questioning the degree of change which would be possible, given the absence of resources for training, evidenced by the fact that the students had to sit on the ground in the open air and the shocking lack of infrastructure which I had just seen in the prisons themselves.

Comment

What I witnessed in the two Mozambican prisons which I visited in 2007 epitomised many of the major issues about the use of imprisonment in many countries in sub-Saharan Africa. The buildings had been constructed in the colonial era and had long passed the time when they should have been demolished, but the government could not, or would not, find the funding to replace them. Nor was there any revenue funding for the most basic infrastructure. We had witnessed clear proof of that when we saw the water lorry which came in each day to provide the only supply of drinking water; in one case for over 300 prisoners and in the other for over 1,600. The other glaring insufficiency was that neither prison had a functioning kitchen or dining area, being dependent instead on cooking over open fires. There was evidence that prisoners relied on their families to supply them with food. When the High Commissioner had first approached the Director of Prisons to ask what help he might provide, the answer which came back was that he would like to have 20 Land Rovers to enable him to deliver remand prisoners to court on their due dates. It was difficult to see how one might begin any discussion about prison reform when the essentials of daily life were so blatantly absent.

When I visited in 2007 there were around ten thousand prisoners in Mozambique. By 2020 this number had almost doubled to 19,800 and the stated prison capacity stood at 8,500, which implied an occupancy rate of 230 per cent. The shocking state of prisons in South Africa, Gambia and Mozambique are by no means unique. Rather, they are replicated to a greater or lesser degree in the majority of countries in the region. Prisons in sub-Saharan Africa remain an expensive colonial legacy.

12

The Jericho Monitoring Mission

In the course of the last 20 years I have been asked to take on a variety of official national and international commitments. For example, between 2005 and 2010 I sat as a member of a three-person panel appointed by the Secretary of State for Northern Ireland to inquire into whether there was evidence of any official collusion in the death of Billy Wright, a loyalist prisoner who was murdered by three republican prisoners in the Maze Prison. The inquiry was one of several established as part of the Belfast (Good Friday) Peace Agreement (*Billy Wright Inquiry Report*, 2010). In 2015 I was invited by the Irish Justice Minister to assist the Inspector of Prisons in a review of the organisation of the Irish Prison Service (Inspector of Prisons, 2015). In earlier chapters I have described some of my work with the European CPT in Russia and elsewhere, with the United Nations in Cambodia and before the IACHR in Costa Rica. One unanticipated and unique piece of international work was the contribution I was asked to make in setting up and overseeing what became known as the Jericho Monitoring Mission.

First request

On the morning of Friday 1 March 2002 while working in my office in King's College London I received an unexpected telephone call from the FCO asking if I would come immediately to King Charles Street for an urgent meeting. When I arrived there an hour later I was told that Foreign Secretary Jack Straw had asked if I would be prepared to travel immediately to Tel Aviv and then on to Ramallah to inspect security arrangements in the prison attached to Yasser Arafat's compound, the Mukataa. I learned that there had been discussions at 'a high governmental level' about providing a small United Kingdom mission to monitor the detention of five prisoners who were being held by the Palestinian Authority in the Ramallah prison. My task would be to assess whether such a proposal might be feasible. I agreed to take on this assignment and flew that night from London Heathrow to Ben Gurion airport, touching down at 7 am to be met at the steps of the plane and driven directly to the Residence of the UK Ambassador to Israel, Sherard Cowper-Coles.

Backstory 1

On Wednesday 17 October 2001 Israeli government Minister Rehavam Ze'evi had been fatally shot outside his room in the Hyatt Hotel in Jerusalem. The Popular Front for the Liberation of Palestine (PFLP) claimed responsibility for the murder.

In response to immense pressure from the Israeli government, Yasser Arafat, Chairman of the Palestine Liberation Organization (PLO), had arrested Ahmed Sa'adat, the PFLP Secretary General, and also demanded that the four men who had been directly involved in the murder should be handed over to the PLO authority in Ramallah. Within a few months this had been done and the four men were summarily convicted and sentenced:

- Hamdi Qur'an, the gunman who had fired the shot which killed Ze'evi, was sentenced to 18 years imprisonment.
- Basel al-Asmar, the backup gunman and lookout, was sentenced to 12 years.
- Majdi Rahima Rimawi, the driver of the getaway car, was sentenced to 8 years.
- Iyad Gholmi, head of the PFLP's military wing on the West Bank and planner of the assassination, was sentenced to one year.

Ahmad Sa'adat continued to be detained without charge.

The Israeli government led by Prime Minister Ariel Sharon was convinced that the detention of the five men was something of a charade, believing that they were largely free to come and go from the Mukataa at will. The Israelis were demanding that the men should be handed over to them to face justice while Yasser Arafat was equally insistent that this was not going to happen. In November 2001 Prime Minister Tony Blair visited Ariel Sharon in Jerusalem. In the course of discussion Blair had suggested to Sharon that one way out of the dispute might be for the United Kingdom to provide a team of expert monitors to confirm that the five prisoners were indeed being held in continuous detention by the Palestinian authorities. Sharon listened to what Blair said but did not directly respond.

By the end of February 2002 the Second Intifada (Palestinian uprising against the Israeli occupation of the West Bank and Gaza Strip) had intensified. The Israel Defence Force (IDF) controlled all movement into and out of the West Bank and had overrun the refugee camp in Jenin. Yasser Arafat was unable to travel even in the sector which was technically under Palestinian control; in reality he and his senior aides were confined to their compound in the Mukataa. As a first step to de-escalation the Israeli government wanted clear evidence that Ze'evi's assassins were being held in continuous and appropriate detention. If that could be confirmed they would consider reducing the restrictions on Arafat's movements. The Israelis would not be satisfied solely by assurances from the Palestinian Authority and indicated to the UK Ambassador that they now wished to explore the earlier offer of UK involvement in the supervision of the detention of the five prisoners. That was the background to the telephone call to me from the FCO on 1 March.

Ramallah: March 2002

I spent the first part of the weekend of 2–3 March in meetings with UK Ambassador Cowper-Coles in Tel Aviv and Consul General Geoffrey Adams in Jerusalem and their senior staff, being given a crash course on the current political situation and about the reality of the Second Intifada which had begun some 18 months previously. They made clear to me that they viewed the proposal to set up an independent monitoring arrangement for the five prisoners in Ramallah as an important element of international plans to de-escalate immediate violence. The US Consul General joined us for discussions in Jerusalem. At that juncture the US had indicated its support for the monitoring proposal but did not wish to be directly involved.

In the course of the weekend I was taken to the Israeli government offices for a meeting with Danny Ayalon who was at that point the Prime Minister's adviser on foreign affairs. (He was later to be Israeli Ambassador to the US and then Deputy Foreign Minister.) Ayalon confirmed that the Israeli government's preference was that the men who had assassinated Minister Ze'evi should be handed over to face a proper judicial process. However, as long as the men were in Palestinian custody the priority was for an assurance that they were subject to continuous detention and not free to come and go in Ramallah as they wished. This message was reinforced during subsequent talks with senior members of Shin Bet, the Israeli Security Agency.

On the morning of Monday 4 March I travelled to Ramallah. During this and subsequent visits I experienced at first hand the tight grip which the IDF had on all movement into and out of the West Bank. Notwithstanding the fact that I travelled at all times in marked diplomatic transport escorted by British Embassy officials we were subjected to rigorous checks by the IDF before being allowed into and out of the Palestinian areas.

The Mukataa in Ramallah, as in many other centres of population in the region, had originally been constructed in the 1920s during the British Mandate in Palestine as a compound which included the military headquarters, a court of law and a prison. In 1996 it became the official West Bank headquarters of the Palestinian National Authority and the residence of Yasser Arafat. In the course of my visit I had discussions with Mohammed Rashid, one of Arafat's senior advisers, who described to me the perspective of the Palestinian Authority (PA) in respect of the five prisoners and then took me to inspect the prison, which turned out to be typical of many such in the region. Surrounded by a solid wall, it had a mixture of single and communal cells on two floors, a small administration block and a medical area. I also met the five prisoners, who were being held in the medical block. One of them, Iyad Gholmi, had three limbs in plaster, having broken them when leaping through a window in an attempt to evade arrest by the PA.

I then returned to the UK Consulate General in Jerusalem to report on what I had found. My conclusion was that the buildings were sound, with physical security appropriate for a prison. The key issue was whether there was political will on the part of the Palestinian authorities to keep the five prisoners in continuous custody. If that was forthcoming, it would be possible for a team of independent individuals to monitor the situation in the prison. The only person on the Palestinian side who could provide the necessary approval for this was Yasser Arafat himself. Clearly he would have received a report from Rashid about my visit together with an assessment of my credibility. I was told that Arafat would typically conduct business and meet visitors during the night hours. We waited patiently through the evening and early night for a call. Around 1 am the Consul General's telephone rang: Arafat wanted to see me at once.

The Consul General and I left immediately and within a short period we had negotiated the various IDF roadblocks which I had passed through earlier in the day. On arrival in the Mukataa we were shown directly into Arafat's quarters and were given a warm welcome by the President. He was keen to emphasise that the prisoners were under Palestinian control and that this was not negotiable. I was able to reassure him that this was not in question and that the international monitors would restrict themselves to providing confirmation that the PA was fulfilling its promise to keep the men in continuous secure detention. Our discussions did not last long. It seemed clear that Arafat knew that he had few options but that, equally, it was important that he should be seen to be retaining what authority he had by agreeing to the new arrangement. He indicated his approval and we quickly said our goodbyes.

By this time it was around 2 am and we returned to the Consulate General for a final debrief on the day's activities. The conclusion was that it would be possible to establish a UK monitoring team in Ramallah. We discussed draft terms of reference for the monitors and I indicated that I would be prepared to oversee the establishment of the team if these were agreed by all sides. The incursions of IDF personnel into the West Bank which had begun the previous week meant that it would not be possible to make any immediate start to the monitoring.

I then retired to my room in the American Colony Hotel in Jerusalem for what remained of the night before taking a return flight to London on 5 March. For the next seven or so weeks I heard no more.

Backstory 2

Throughout March the Second Intifada continued to intensify with no obvious outcome. A spate of Palestinian suicide bombings culminated on 27 March in the deaths of 22 people who were attending a Passover meal in Netanya. This led to Operation Defensive Shield by the IDF which began on 29 March with an incursion into Ramallah which placed Yasser Arafat under siege in the Mukataa and was followed by incursions into the six largest cities in the West Bank and their surrounding localities. A number of Palestinian militia took refuge in the Church of the Nativity in Bethlehem which was surrounded by the IDF.

There was concern on the part of the UK and the US that Sharon was about to order a final assault on the Mukataa to seize the five detainees as well as Fouad Shubaki, Arafat's senior financial adviser, who was thought to have arranged a shipment of Iranian weapons aboard the freighter *Karine A* which had been intercepted by the Israelis. Fearing a bloodbath which might well have also resulted in the death of Arafat, US President Bush made clear to Sharon that such a raid on the compound would not be tolerated. The only option which remained was to revisit Tony Blair's proposal for an international monitoring mission to oversee the detention of the prisoners.

Jericho: April–May 2002

On Monday 29 April I took a further call from the FCO, asking if I would be prepared to travel immediately to the Middle East for a second time to revisit the proposal for monitoring the Palestinian detainees. So, less than two months after my first journey I again took the night flight from Heathrow to Ben Gurion Airport. On arrival I was taken immediately to the UK Consulate General in East Jerusalem and after a shower and shave it was straight into business.

Tuesday 30 April

Consul General Geoffrey Adams brought me up to date on the situation, describing how the barrels of the IDF tanks were literally at the windows of Arafat's quarters and a considerable part of the Mukataa, including the former prison, was in ruins. The Palestinians were restricted to a few rooms, with no electricity or running water. On Sunday 28 April Ariel Sharon's office had unexpectedly called Tony Blair's office to ask whether the previous offer of providing UK monitors for the prisoners was still on the table. It was and the UK government wanted to respond with maximum speed. In collaboration with the United States, the aim of the UK and US governments was to break the impasse in the siege of the church in Bethlehem and that of the Ramallah Mukataa by brokering a deal in respect of the detention of the six prisoners.

The immediate challenge was to achieve a formal agreement with the Israelis and the Palestinians that the deal should proceed and how the logistics were to be implemented. The FCO in London had already begun the process of assembling a team of UK monitors and indications from US diplomats were that, while their government was reluctant to take the lead in the direct monitoring, it would be willing to provide a presence.

Ambassador Sherard Cowper-Coles then arrived, followed shortly by US Ambassador Dan Kurtzer. After some further discussion the three of us travelled to the Israeli government offices in Jerusalem. The Israeli team was led by Dov Weisglass, newly appointed Director General of the Prime Minister's office, and also included Danny Ayalon, who had led their team in the discussions in early March. The meeting took place in the cabinet room. The Israeli demand was that the prisoners should be held 'in the same security conditions as would someone in the UK who had murdered a cabinet minister'. In order to ensure that, the Israelis demanded that they should be held in joint UK/US custody. The Ambassadors made clear that was not on offer. Instead, the monitors would confirm that the prisoners were appropriately held in Palestinian custody.

After several hours of negotiations it was agreed that:

- The prison in Jericho met the requirements of a secure prison. It had been a prison during the British mandate period.
- The transfer of the six prisoners would be in secure armoured vehicles provided by the US with a Palestinian guard escorting each prisoner. Monitors and UK diplomats would also go with the convoy.
- The legal status of the prisoners was a matter for the PA and the monitoring team would not become involved in that.
- No decision needed to be taken about the length of the monitoring process; at the moment it was to be open-ended.
- The chain of command for the UK/US monitoring teams would be through their respective governments.
- The Israeli demands on security conditions would be borne in mind by Andrew Coyle when he inspected Jericho.
- The concern about the possibility of external assault would also be borne in mind.

It was agreed that as the next step I would lead a team to Jericho to inspect the Mukataa prison as well as another possible location and would subsequently report back. Along with FCO officials and diplomats as well as a UK former soldier and OSCE (Organisation for Security and Co-operation in Europe) monitor who was to lead the monitoring team, I then made the short journey from Jerusalem to Jericho. On arrival at the Mukataa we were greeted by Sami Musulman, Mayor of Jericho, and Brigadier Mohammed Abu Bakr, the Palestinian military commander of the Jericho region who had overall authority for the prison. The prison itself had been built about 1936 and stood within the grounds of the military barracks for the Jericho region. It was a standard former colonial prison, capable of holding about a hundred prisoners, and the part where the six prisoners were to be kept was the former military prison, which had been unused for around two years. It was in a state of disrepair although the basic level of physical security was acceptable in the circumstances.

We then moved on to the main Mukataa for detailed discussion on logistics. The principal issue to be agreed was where the two unconvicted prisoners were to be held. The Palestinians wanted them to be accommodated in the administration building, which was not part of the prison proper. There they would be in relatively well-appointed rooms with freedom to move within the administration block. Knowing that this would not be acceptable to the Israelis, I said that they had to be held in the prison proper. The Palestinians were very upset at this because of the senior standing of the two unconvicted men but they finally accepted my position. The four convicted prisoners would be held in one large cell at the end of an open compound, where they would be able to take their daily exercise. The two uncharged prisoners would be held in a small secure suite with an entrance area, two large rooms, a kitchenette/shower area and a separate toilet. I pointed out a number of issues which would have to be dealt with immediately and they were all agreed to by the Palestinians.

I asked Brigadier Abu Bakr if he could provide me with a layout plan of the prison. He said that he did not have one but, with a smile, he suggested that I might find one in the Public Record Office in Kew on the outskirts of London. "After all," he said, "it was your people who built it."

On our return to the Consulate General in Jerusalem we were joined by colleagues from the US Consulate General and later by a US Army Colonel who had just flown in from Washington as the advance US monitor. We discussed detailed logistical arrangements and I insisted that the six prisoners should be moved in individual secure vehicles. It was agreed that the Americans would provide these.

Ambassador Sherard Cowper-Coles then arrived and we prepared to go back for further discussions with the Israeli government. At the same time Consul General Geoffrey Adams was to lead a parallel team to negotiate with the Palestinians. We were joined at the Israeli government offices by US Ambassador Dan Kurtzer and the Israeli team was again led by Dov Weisglass. Discussions began about 8 pm and continued through the night. At one point we were joined by senior Israeli military personnel, who needed to be convinced that the imprisonment of the prisoners would be genuine. Once again we met in the cabinet room. A door from this room led straight into Prime Minster Sharon's private office. As the night wore on Weisglass and later the two Ambassadors shuttled to and from Sharon's office while I remained in the outer room.

At around 1 am Sharon said that he wanted to meet me face to face. It later transpired that this was to be the key confrontation: if he decided that I was 'a serious person' then the arrangements could proceed. He grilled me for about 20 minutes and apparently I was able to satisfy him. He suddenly said, "Right, that's fine." Immediately Cowper-Coles stood up and ushered us all out after we had said goodbye to Sharon. He clearly did not want any further discussion to begin which might cloud Sharon's decision. Now that Sharon had given his approval, all further discussions would be restricted to processes.

By this time it was after 1.30 am on Wednesday and we agreed with Weisglass and Ayalon that I would meet senior Israeli security personnel at 9 am. They had previously pointed out that none of them were prison experts and they did not have a clear picture in their minds about what I meant in practice by secure custody. I agreed to provide them with a set of operating procedures and spent a further 90 minutes or so in my hotel room drafting these.

Wednesday 1 May

Meeting with Israeli security personnel

Our meeting took place in a private suite in the King David Hotel where I led a team consisting of the UK and US lead monitors and the security adviser from the British Embassy. The Israeli team was led by the Head of the central command of Shinbet and included the Head of the IDF for the West Bank, the Head of the IDF for the Ramallah area, who would oversee transfer arrangements, and the deputy judge advocate general. It was made clear that, although Sharon had agreed in principle to the arrangements, if we could not satisfy this meeting on the details, they would report back and the agreement would be cancelled.

We had an intense three-hour discussion, covering a whole variety of issues and in the event I was able to hold to all our agreed positions. The Israeli side asked how we would be able to confirm the identities of the six prisoners. On the face of it, this was not an unreasonable question. Along with the FCO officials I had only had a brief meeting with five of the prisoners in March. I explained that we would require the PA officials in Ramallah to provide us with the relevant documentation for each prisoner. With a straight face I said that I assumed that Shinbet would have the fingerprints of each of the prisoners and if they provided us with copies we could check these against the fingerprints of the men who were presented to us. With equally straight faces our interlocutors suggested that the easiest solution would be for the IDF personnel who were to accompany the convoy to have a private meeting with each of the prisoners and to "have some words with them" in order to verify their identities. I refused to agree to this and no more was said about the matter of identification.

We covered all the transfer arrangements and then went on to discuss conditions in the prison in Jericho.

In due course the Israeli side asked for an adjournment to consider everything and to collect the personal details on the prisoners which they had promised. When we reconvened they pronounced themselves satisfied and produced the promised papers. At the beginning of the morning meeting I had asked if they had an aerial photograph of the prison and they said they would see what they could do. At the beginning of the second meeting they handed over two large photographs. I asked if these were up to date. They looked at me quizzically and explained that, following my request, they had sent an F16 plane into the air over Jericho to take the photographs for us: "Yes, sir, they are up to date."

We agreed that if all the logistics could be arranged, the transfer would take place that evening. The IDF Area Commander promised that there would be no roadblocks or other delays to the convoy. It was agreed that once I was satisfied that the transfer had been completed and that the prisoners were securely located I would telephone Danny Ayalon with my confirmation that this had happened.

Further briefing at the Consulate

We then returned to the Consulate to make final arrangements for the transfer of the prisoners. The Americans and some of the UK Consulate staff understandably thought that the whole process was moving too quickly and wanted to delay the transfer until Thursday. I took the view that we should move as rapidly as possible on the grounds that the longer we delayed the greater the possibility of something going wrong. Fortunately the senior diplomats agreed that the transfer should be carried out with all possible speed and it was decided that it should take place that evening.

By this time two more members of the UK monitoring team had arrived; both of them were former soldiers who had worked as OSCE monitors in the Balkans. There was final agreement that the main convoy should consist of six armoured US vehicles, each containing one prisoner and one unarmed Palestinian escort. In addition to the US driver there would be an armed US escort in the front and a similar person in the rear of each vehicle. Four monitors would be in four of the six vehicles. Additional UK vehicles would convey personnel from the UK Consulate, and IDF vehicles would escort the convoy to the outskirts of Ramallah. By this time the international media were fully aware of what was happening and were likely to be in close attendance. I decided that I would best be deployed by going ahead to Jericho to ensure that everything was prepared for the prisoners' arrival while the senior UK monitor went to Ramallah to see the convoy on its way.

The transfer

The IDF were keen that the transfer should be effected during the hours of darkness in order to reduce publicity and the possibility of public disorder, although by this time it was clear that there would be a great deal of media interest. We decided that for logistical reasons the earliest the transfers could be arranged would be late evening, thus meeting their request. At about 6 pm the escorting team left Jerusalem for Ramallah and I left for Jericho about the same time.

On arrival at the Jericho Mukataa I had my first meeting with Saeb Erekat who introduced himself as the local MP for Jericho. He was also a member of Arafat's cabinet and a key player in the political process. I quickly learned that his appointed task was to ensure that the prisoners, especially the two who had not been charged, were given the best possible conditions of detention. Immediately on my arrival, I was ushered into a formal meeting with him in the administration block. He informed me that, regardless of any decisions made the previous day, the two uncharged prisoners would be located in the offices of the administration block. I told him that this would not be possible and we had an animated discussion for about 30 minutes. In the course of our negotiations he used his mobile phone to call Arafat to discuss what was being talked about. He then called the US Consul General, who clearly supported my stance. Following that telephone call, Erakat suddenly agreed with the arrangements which I had previously made. I then told the military commander, Abu Bakr, that when the six prisoners arrived they should be taken together to his office, where I wanted to explain to them the conditions of their detention and the role of the UK/US monitors. I suggested that he should provide them with drinks and something simple to eat. They would then be taken singly across the corridor for a medical examination before being taken directly to their accommodation in the prison.

While this was going on in Jericho, the other team had arrived in Ramallah. The monitors used the information provided by the Israelis to confirm the identities of the six prisoners. This took some considerable time and it was 9 pm before they were ready to leave for Jericho. National and international television were covering all of these activities in live time. As a result, in Jericho we were able to watch on television the departure of the convoy from Ramallah. A large crowd of local people had gathered outside the Mukataa in Jericho and the compound itself was very busy with local Palestinian military personnel.

The convoy arrived in Jericho at about 10 pm. It did so to great applause from the local populace gathered outside the gates and its arrival was recorded by the international media. We had previously arranged that the escort vehicles would be parked within the compound so as to block the view of the television cameras as the prisoners came out of the vehicles. The vehicles drove into the large compound at high speed, almost knocking down several individuals in the process. Fouad Shubaki was in the first vehicle. He disembarked to an ecstatic welcome from the assembled Palestinian military. It took me a few moments to recognise him as one of the prisoners. Despite the general euphoria we were able to get all six prisoners into the office as arranged, where I was able to tell them what procedure would be followed.

The first major confrontation was when Ahmed Sa'adat attempted to use the office telephone. I said that he should not do so. Saeb Erakat protested strongly that this was against all international prison rules since a prisoner should be able to tell his family when he had been transferred. Not for the first or last time that night I found myself thinking furiously on my feet and I agreed that Sa'adat could telephone his wife if the number was observed by the Palestinian staff in advance. He duly made the call, only for it to be unanswered.

The next development was that Saeb Erakat announced loudly that it was outrageous that the prisoners had not had a proper meal. By this time the four convicted prisoners, who were clearly of no great interest to the assembled Palestinians, had begun to move to medical examination and thence to their agreed accommodation in the prison. Ten or 15 minutes later someone appeared with two large black plastic bags, and numerous tinfoil containers of rice, chicken, falafel and various other breads were emptied onto the table. By this time, Shubaki was sitting at the middle of the table, clearly the centre of attention and enjoying every minute. He insisted that I join the party: "Dr Andrew, you must join us. Come and eat." I demurred but someone took me firmly by the wrist and guided me to the table. I had no choice but to take a mouthful or so of food; by this time I was also very hungry. Within a few moments a feast was in progress. The final touch in the surrealism came when we were joined by 'Chip', the uniformed head of the US security team, who sat in a relaxed manner in the midst of the feast with his 'six guns' buckled around his thighs. The UK diplomats circled around me, asking anxiously, "Have we lost control?

Is this out of control?" I assured them that it was not, sounding much more confident than I felt.

I kept a close watch on Shubaki's consumption of the meal. As he clearly got to the end I leaned over and said to him, via the interpreter, "It is time everyone settled down. We should finish in five minutes." He was talking nineteen to the dozen and gave no sign that he had heard me, although I knew that he had. Five minutes elapsed, then another five. Just as I was wondering what my next move should be, Shubaki rose and, to my great relief, announced that he was ready to see the doctor. He then crossed the corridor into the medical room.

The corridor was full of people: Palestinians in uniform and in civilian dress, the UK/US monitors and diplomats and 'Chip' with his holstered handguns. I had asked 'Chip' to stay behind with a vehicle in case any of the prisoners refused to go into their accommodation and we had to remove them; whither that might be, I had no idea.

The four previous medical examinations had each taken about five minutes. After about ten minutes Shubaki was still in the medical room and I caught sight of Abu Bakr, the military commander, going into the room. I called the interpreter and followed him into the room. Shubaki was sitting in the centre of the room smoking a large cigar. He had his shirt rolled up to expose his expansive stomach; after all, this was meant to be a medical examination. The deputy military commander had obviously also got into the room previously without my noticing. When I told Abu Bakr that he had no right to be there he protested that as Governor of the prison he had the right to go anywhere. I asked him if he had not heard about the rules of medical confidentiality and told him that he and his deputy would have to leave. They did so with some reluctance. As I left the room I reminded Shubaki that he was in the room for a medical examination and pointed out that smoking was bad for his health. It was clear by this time that we both understood the game that was being played, with him pushing everything to the absolute limit but not going beyond the ultimate boundaries. A few moments later Shubaki emerged from the medical room and his escort took him towards the living quarters. I decided that I should accompany his entourage and left the lead monitor to supervise Sa'adat's movements.

At one point the doctor told me that he was concerned about Iyad Gholmi. When we had seen him in March he had both legs and one arm in plaster, having jumped from a first-floor window in an attempt to evade arrest. One of his legs was still in plaster and he was moved around in a wheelchair. The doctor said that he was worried about infection and wished to take him to hospital for an X-ray. I agreed but asked that this should be delayed until the next morning and the doctor agreed. He then told me that he was also concerned about Shubaki who had a lump on his stomach and was showing signs of stress. He also wanted to transfer him to hospital. I said that we should discuss that in the morning as well.

When we arrived at the cell suite Shubaki stood outside and protested loudly that he was being required to go into a security cell. I told him that this was what had been agreed with Yasser Arafat. He eventually stomped into the suite and walked round the rooms, with various others in attendance, demonstrating how inappropriate the accommodation was for someone of his standing. Once he was inside I stood in the middle of the main doorway so that he could not leave the suite. He understood what I was doing and did not attempt to leave. After a few moments someone arrived with his two suitcases of luggage. One of the monitors asked me whether we should search them. I replied that the priority for the night was to get the prisoners locked up and that the luggage could be searched in the morning.

I told Abu Bakr that it was time we left everyone to settle down for the night. Shubaki said that he wanted his dirty laundry to be taken away and proceeded to unpack his cases slowly. This was marginally annoying but it did give us the opportunity to check what was in the cases. Shubaki told me that he wished to complain to me officially about the conditions of his imprisonment. I replied that everyone was too tired but that I would return in the morning for a discussion with him. By this time Ahmad Sa'adat had arrived and I got everyone else to move out of the suite. I watched the Palestinian guard lock the main cell door.

I turned to give a final briefing to the three international monitors who were to take the first shift. Out of the corner of my eye I saw Abu Bakr appear with a tray containing a pot of tea, two cups and packets of biscuits. I asked him what he was doing and he told me that he was taking the two prisoners their final cup of tea of the night. I told him that the door had been locked and could not be opened until morning. He protested that he was being prevented from going somewhere in his own prison. I told him that this was the procedure in every security prison in the world; once a cell had been secured for the night it could not be re-opened until the next morning. The cell door had a hatch in it with a large gauge grille. I said that he could pass the tea and biscuits through the hatch. I left him squashing packets of biscuits through the grille.

I had a final word with the monitors and then went out to the main compound of the prison to make my calls. The first was to Danny

Ayalon and I confirmed to him that the six prisoners were locked in their cells as had been agreed and that I was satisfied that the prison was secure. He thanked me for the information and then asked in a conversational manner when I would be leaving the country. I told him that I planned to do so on Friday. Ayalon expressed great regret that I would not have any opportunity to see the beauties of Israel and I replied that I hoped to return one day under happier circumstances. He thanked me for my efforts. I then called Mohammed Rashid of the PA to advise him that the transfer had been safely effected. I returned to the commander's office and we watched on national television as the Israeli tanks slowly withdrew from Arafat's compound in Ramallah. By this time it was after midnight and we returned in our armoured vehicle to Jerusalem.

Thursday 2 May

Return to Jericho

An additional seven UK monitors had arrived at the American Colony Hotel the previous evening and my first task on Thursday morning was to give them a thorough briefing about the situation and what their role was to be. I then spent some time with the lead monitor developing the operational procedures which were to be implemented by the PA guards and verified by the UK/US monitors. In late morning we returned to Jericho accompanied by the new set of monitors. On arrival we went first to the prison compound to be briefed by the team who had been on duty all night. They said that all had gone reasonably well and there had been no problem from the convicted prisoners. When the cell suite of the unconvicted prisoners had been opened in the morning, the first visitor was the person in civilian clothes who had taken away Shubaki's laundry the night before. He had a completely new set of clothes for Shubaki. As he stayed around the monitors queried why he, as a civilian, was there. He disappeared and returned 15 minutes later in a new military uniform. Next on the scene was Shubaki's barber. In due course Shubaki himself appeared, dressed very smartly, and announced that he was ready to go for his hospital appointment. The monitors said that they had no instructions to that effect and that he could not go. He went back into his cell without argument. He eventually came back into the compound and sat for the rest of the morning drinking coffee, surrounded by a large group of men.

In discussion the previous day Saeb Erekat had asked me what the prisoners were entitled to have in their cells. I explained that the main responsibility of the monitors was to ensure that the prisoners were in continuous secure custody and that a record was being kept of those who came to visit them. As far as the monitors were concerned, the prisoners were entitled to have access to whatever facilities were approved by Palestinian legislation. The monitors reported that early that morning a large refrigerator had been delivered, followed by a satellite television set. This had been linked to a similar set which was installed in the monitors' office, complete with access to 250 channels.

On my arrival I had been told that Saeb Erekat was waiting to see me and I had replied that I wanted to talk first to the monitors. Having spoken to them, I went to see Erekat and I presented him with the set of draft procedures which I had drawn up. We had quite a discussion about them and whether they amounted to an attempt by me to overrule Palestinian legislation on imprisonment. I told him that the procedures took account of the copy of the relevant legislation with which we had been provided. He said that he would take the procedures away and ask his legal advisers to comment. I explained that the set of procedures was not a document for discussion; rather, this was what I would be instructing the monitors to verify. If they saw any breach of these procedures, they would report the fact to the UK and US Consuls General, who would take the matter up with the PA.

By the time this discussion had been completed it was early afternoon and we were keen to get the first set of monitors back to Jerusalem to stand down. Having promised to return to speak to Shubaki, I did not want to leave without doing so. I went back to the compound and into his cell. He was lying on his bed, giving the appearance of being most unwell, which was presumably a reaction to being refused permission to go to hospital for an examination. Despite his allegedly poor state of health, he was in energetic conversation with a couple of staff. He was obviously aware of my presence but continued to talk volubly with the others. After a few moments I gave him a wave of the hand and marched out of the cell. As far as I was concerned, my promise to return to speak to him had been fulfilled.

Press conference

With the transfer safely completed, the Ambassador and Consul General were keen to get some positive media publicity about the UK lead in the operation, and the media in Jerusalem were invited to a press conference at our hotel. It was chaired by the Political Secretary in the Consulate and was attended by around ten international correspondents. He explained the background to what had happened and I talked in general terms about the operation itself and what the monitors would be doing. There was extensive coverage in the following day's press and on BBC television. The Israeli government had also briefed their press, which carried quite hawkish reports about the operation and my involvement, describing me as someone 'whose name arouses fear among all British criminals' and that after meeting me Prime Minister Sharon had concluded that I 'was a serious, responsible and experienced man who will ensure that the prisoners are given the conditions of prisoners and not a rest home'.[1]

Friday 3 May

The morning began with a full briefing in the Consulate General. We reviewed everything that had happened, agreed the report which was to go back to the FCO and confirmed the next steps. I had previously suggested to the FCO that they should invite Duncan McLaughlan, a former governor of the Maze and Maghaberry Prisons and recently retired from the Northern Ireland Prison Service, to come out to oversee the bedding-in of the monitoring teams after I left. He had agreed to this and had arrived on Thursday evening so I spent several hours briefing him on what had happened and what his role would be.

In the early afternoon I left for Tel Aviv to return to London. At the airport I was subjected to the usual intense procedure at emigration with a young security officer interrogating me at length to discover as much as she could about my visit while I made sure that she got as little information as possible. I had a sense of satisfaction that she learned nothing about my activities in Jericho.

Backstory 3

From the outset the Jericho Monitoring Mission (JMM) was one element of a much wider political and military equation. After it was established the Second Intifada continued with suicide bombing by Palestinians and violent response by the Israelis. On 6 June the IDF embarked on a new assault on Arafat's compound in the Ramallah Mukataa, destroying much of what remained of the buildings. The PA pointed to this latter as a breach of the Ramallah Agreement. At the same time the Israeli government complained strongly to the UK government that the JMM was failing to ensure that the PFLP prisoners in Jericho were being appropriately secluded.

Visit in July 2002

The JMM had been established with some haste in response to immediate political imperatives. It was a matter of significant professional pride that the logistics had been put into place successfully and at speed in a manner which was able to achieve the original objectives of the Ramallah Agreement. Within a matter of a week or so a team of eight British and six American monitors had been assembled, with one of the British monitors as Head of Mission and an American as Deputy Head. Most of the British monitors were former military personnel who had previous experience as observers for OSCE or other intergovernmental organisations, while the remainder had been former prison officers in Northern Ireland. All of them were employed directly by the FCO. The United States contracted their monitoring to DynCorp, an international private security company, and many of their monitors also had previous military or correctional experience. The operating procedures which I had drawn up had given the monitors a clear set of standards to work to.

In July the FCO asked me to return to Jericho to make an updated assessment of the situation and the extent to which the monitors were able to fulfil their mission. Specifically, I was charged with passing a clear message to the Palestinians that they were expected to comply fully with the operating procedures which had been set out alongside the Ramallah Agreement. Having done that, my task then was to convince the Israeli government that the Mission was operating effectively.

I travelled to Jerusalem on 22 July. Following a briefing at the UK Consulate General I spent some time with the Head and Deputy Head of JMM, who had a base in the American Colony Hotel in East Jerusalem. I then travelled with them to Jericho, where I spent the rest of the day in the Mukataa, having discussions with the monitors, inspecting the prison compound and talking with the six prisoners. I concluded my visit by meeting representatives of the PA led by Saeb Erekat. The following day I had an intense meeting in Tel Aviv with senior Israeli government officials led by Danny Ayalon. The Shin Bet officials pressed me very hard with demands that the six prisoners, and in particular Shubaki and Sa'adat, should be subjected to more severe conditions of detention. My visit concluded with a meeting with the UK and US Consuls General during which a memorandum was drafted to be sent to Abdel Razaq al-Yehya, PA Minister of Interior, highlighting a number of areas which required urgent attention.

Follow-up visits

In the course of the following three years I received regular updates on the performance of the monitoring mission and at the request of the FCO visited the team in mid-year 2003, 2004 and 2005 to assess the situation. Subsequent visits reinforced my conclusion that, while the JMM continued to fulfil its technical remit, its role in the wider political and diplomatic regional developments was becoming increasingly anomalous. The dynamics of the Second Intifada had changed considerably and in addition key political players on all sides had changed, including those on the diplomatic side. At the outset it had been envisaged that the mission might last for a year or two at the most but that had not been written into the Ramallah Agreement and no serious thought had been given to an exit strategy. By 2004 this was becoming a priority for the FCO and I was asked to explore options as to how this might happen. This was also an issue of concern for the monitors themselves who were very conscious of the heightened tension in the region and the vulnerability of their situation. There had been an increase in the number of prisoners in the main prison and there were indications that a number of these were linked to Islamic Jihad. There was disquiet on the Palestinian side about the continued detention of the prisoners, particularly the three who were not serving sentences, and at some point it was possible that the PA might decide to release them. The Israeli government was unlikely to allow that to happen. The Israeli Defence Force always had the option to take the initiative with a pre-emptive assault on the Mukataa to remove the six prisoners. In any of these scenarios there would be serious concern for the safety and indeed the lives of the UK and US monitors.

By the time of what turned out to be my final visit in July 2005 there had been a number of important developments in the region. The death of Yasser Arafat in November 2004 clearly had implications for the mission since the lifting of the restrictions which the Israelis had placed on him had been one of the main elements of the Ramallah Agreement in 2002. Another was the disengagement of Israel from Gaza which had been under consideration for two years and was to be implemented in August 2005. As time had gone on the varying political interests and priorities had altered considerably. The Israelis had always believed that the prisoners in Jericho were continuing to organise PFLP military activities. Units of the IDF were in position on the high ground around Jericho and were clearly becoming restive. New Palestinian elections had been scheduled for July 2005 (although they were subsequently postponed until January 2006) and the ruling Fatah party was being challenged by the Hamas party. From the perspective of some Palestinians the continued detention of the 'Jericho 6' was a matter of serious political controversy and likely to affect the outcome of the forthcoming elections. All of these issues had had an influence on the way the JMM was operating. It had become more difficult to recruit and retain suitably qualified UK monitors, and the turnover of Heads of Mission had led to weak leadership. At the same time, internal Palestinian politics were affecting attitudes in the prison, where the authorities were increasingly reluctant to enforce restrictions which were written into the Operating Procedures. In the course of that visit I had a further meeting with Shin Bet who, while they were very dismissive of what the JMM was achieving, did not respond at all positively to an indication that it might be brought to an early end.

I reported all of these concerns back to the FCO and once again repeated my conclusion that ultimately the decision about withdrawal of the JMM was likely to be taken on political grounds, rather than on operational or technical ones.

Backstory 4

On 4 January 2006 Ariel Sharon was incapacitated by a massive stroke from which he never recovered. He had been a major force in Israeli politics for many years and it was he who had approved the Ramallah Agreement in May 2002. In August 2005 he had announced his intention to withdraw Israeli forces from the Gaza Strip, causing a rift in the government, which included the defection of Benyamin Netanyahu. After Sharon's stroke Elmut Olmert, who had replaced Netanyahu as finance minister, was appointed as acting Prime Minister. Elections to the Knesset were scheduled for 26 March. Olmert was in a weak political position and under his leadership the Kadima party faced the prospect of losing the election.

In January 2006 Hamas won the first Palestinian legislative elections since 1996. The new Legislative Council met for the first time on 18 February and two days later Ismail Haniya, the leader of Hamas, was nominated to form a new government. He lost no time in announcing his intention to free the PFLP prisoners held in Jericho. On Wednesday 8 March the UK and US Consuls General in Jerusalem wrote to PA President Mahmoud Abbas, stating that the Palestinian Authority had never fully complied with the basic provisions of the 2002 Ramallah Agreement and expressing specific concern that the PA was failing to provide secure conditions for the UK and US monitors. Their letter went on to state that the pending handover of governmental power to Hamas called into question the sustainability of the JMM. The Consuls ended by advising the President that if the situation did not improve with immediate effect the international monitors would be withdrawn. They copied this letter to the Israeli government. These political developments formed the background to the dramatic events which ended the JMM.

14 March 2006: the final act

On the morning of Tuesday 14 March, six days after the Consuls General sent their joint letter to Abbas, the three monitors who were on duty in Jericho left the prison, telling the Palestinian officials that they needed to take their car for repairs. They drove to the IDF checkpoint outside Jericho and onwards to Jerusalem. As soon as the monitors passed the checkpoint IDF forces moved forward and a large body of soldiers, supported by tanks and helicopters, surrounded the Mukataa in what the Israeli government later described as 'Operation Bringing Home the Goods'. They called on all the Palestinians to come out. Many, including a large body of prisoners as well as security personnel, did so and were stripped to their underwear before being taken into custody. Others, including the 'Jericho 6', refused to do so, and in a telephone interview with Al Jazeera television Ahmed Sa'adat announced, "Our choice is to fight or to die. We will not surrender" (Erlanger and Myre, 2006). A brief battle ensued with Israeli artillery bombarding the prison before an armed bulldozer tore down the walls. There could only be one outcome and by nightfall the Chief of the Israeli Central Command announced that the wanted men and several other militants in the prison had surrendered and been taken into Israeli custody.

When the House of Commons sat on the afternoon of 14 March Foreign Secretary Jack Straw issued a Written Ministerial Statement which ended:

> The Palestinian Authority has consistently failed to meet its obligations under the Ramallah Agreement. Ultimately the safety of our personnel has to take precedence. It is with regret that I have to inform the House that these conditions have not been met and we have terminated our involvement with the mission today, 14 March 2006.[2]

The aftermath

The 'Jericho 6' were subsequently convicted and sentenced by Israeli courts:

- In December 2007, Hamdi Quran confessed to assassinating Rehavam Ze'evi together with Basel al-Asmar after being instructed by PFLP member Majdi Rahima Rimawi. He was sentenced to life imprisonment.
- In May 2008, Basel al-Asmar was convicted of murder and was sentenced to 45 years in prison.
- In July 2008, Majdi Rahima Rimawi was convicted of murder for his part in planning the assassination. He was sentenced to life in prison and an additional 80 years.
- In December 2008, Iyad Gholmi, head of the PLFP's military wing at the time of the assassination, was sentenced to 30 years in prison for his role in instigating and planning the assassination.
- In December 2008, an Israeli military court sentenced Ahmad Sa'adat, leader of the Palestinian Front for the Liberation of Palestine, to 30 years in prison for heading an 'illegal terrorist organisation' and for his responsibility for all actions carried out by his organisation.
- In July 2009, Fouad Shubaki was convicted in the Judea Military Court for security offences, including arms smuggling, and financing and organising the *Karine A*, a Gaza-bound weapons ship seized in January 2002. He was sentenced to 20 years' imprisonment.

Comment

Historically the JMM will be a footnote in the history of the Israeli/ Palestinian conflict in the early 21st century.[3] At an immediate level the mission was established as a solution to the need for the PA to respond to the Israeli insistence that action should be taken against the members of the PFLP who had planned and executed the assassination of Minister Rehavam Ze'evi and also Fouad Shubaki who had masterminded the *Karine A* shipment of arms.

It also has to be seen within the wider context of the Second Intifada which had begun in 2000 and which by early 2002 was reaching a high point of violence, even by the terrible standards of the region. The Israeli Defence Force began Operation Defensive Shield on 29 March and within a few days its tanks were at the windows of Arafat's headquarters in Ramallah.

Its forces entered the Jenin refugee camp with resultant devastating loss of lives and at the same time a stand-off had developed at the Church of the Nativity in Bethlehem where Palestinian militants had taken refuge. Against strong opposition from Israel the UN Security Council unanimously agreed to set up an inquiry into what had happened at the Jenin refugee camp.

UK and US diplomats calculated that if they could establish an international monitoring process to demonstrate to the Israelis that the Ze'evi killers and Fouad Shubaki were being held in prison under proper security conditions this might well be the key to unlocking the military and political impasse. This was the task which was entrusted to me in 2002 and which led, among other things, to my late-night meetings with Ariel Sharon and Yasser Arafat. In the former case, to convince Sharon that I was 'a serious person', experienced in managing high-security prisoners and capable of establishing a credible international monitoring structure. In the latter case, to convince Arafat that what was being proposed would leave the prisoners under direct Palestinian control and that the role of the monitors would be limited to ensuring that appropriate custodial standards were being met. I succeeded in both of these aims and the JMM did indeed serve to break the impasse between the Israelis and the Palestinians. Immediately after the mission was set up and the six Palestinian prisoners were transferred to Jericho the IDF units withdrew from Arafat's compound, the siege in Bethlehem was lifted and 13 Palestinian militants were flown under British control to Cyprus. The price for this was that the United Nations, under US pressure, dropped its inquiry into events which had occurred at the Jenin refugee camp.

At the outset little direct thought had been given to what might happen once the immediate purpose of establishing the JMM had been achieved; in due course inevitably the mission slipped down the political agenda and this lack of strategic direction affected the manner in which it operated. It had been clear to me from an early stage that its closure would be subject to political rather than operational considerations and this proved to be the case.

In the event the deciding political factors were a combination of the elections for the Palestinian Legislative Assembly in 2006 which resulted in a victory for Hamas, who made clear their intention to release the six prisoners, and simultaneously on the Israeli side the prospect of elections after the incapacitation of Ariel Sharon. Both of these brought the issue of the 'Jericho 6' back up the political agenda of the UK and the US, resulting in the letter which the respective Consuls General sent to Mahmoud Abbas on 8 March 2006.

The sequence of events which led to the exit of the monitors on the morning of Tuesday 14 March is not entirely clear. Subsequently Israeli officials claimed that the British authorities had informed them on Friday 10 March, two days after the letter to Abbas, that they would be withdrawing the monitoring team but they did not set a precise date for withdrawal. It would appear that UK and US diplomats informed the Israelis and the Palestinians just as the three British monitors on duty departed. The US State Department denied any prior coordination with Israel. Whether that is true or not, the IDF were ready for the withdrawal and lost no time in doing what they had always had the capacity to do by overrunning the prison and capturing the 'Jericho 6', who remain today in Israeli custody.

13

Towards 'a better way'

I began this book with a question that I had asked myself all those years ago when I first walked into Edinburgh Prison: 'What is this place we call the prison?' In the course of the succeeding chapters I have described the daily reality of imprisonment which I have observed over a period of almost 50 years in a variety of countries in different regions of the world. Now I have to attempt to answer my own opening question and also, looking forward, to respond to a further question: 'What is the future of the prison?'

A brief historical review

Prison systems as they exist today in many countries had their genesis particularly in North America and Western Europe at the end of the 18th and beginning of the 19th century. Before that time prisons or jails had existed as places of confinement where the accused awaited trial or the convicted were held until a debt was paid or for execution or transportation, but it was rare that people were sentenced by a court to a term of imprisonment as punishment for an offence or crime (Morris and Rothman, 1995: vii). Over time concerned individuals in Europe and North America, many of them acting out of a sense of religious conviction, began to draw attention to the abysmal conditions in the prisons, most of which were run by local governments and some of which were privately managed, and slowly the conditions in some of these places of detention began to improve (Howard, 1777). One of the unforeseen consequences of these improvements was that courts began to make more use of prison and to sentence offenders directly to prison as punishment for crime.[1]

In many other regions of the world there was little concept of the prison except as a place of short-term detention. In the 19th and early 20th centuries it was colonial powers which brought the practice of imprisonment to many of the nations which they ruled at the time. This legacy persists even today and many prisons in sub-Saharan Africa or South East Asia still have identical layouts which confirm their colonial history. I have witnessed the British architectural influence in prisons in East and West Africa and India alongside the French stamp in

Cambodia and elsewhere in South Asia. As mentioned in the previous chapter, I was forcibly reminded of this several years ago in Jericho when I was advised to go to the Public Record Office in Kew in south west London if I wanted a copy of the plan of the prison in that town.[2]

The increased use of imprisonment in Western Europe as well as in parts of the north east of the United States in the 19th century coincided with and was influenced by a growing social confidence in the benefits of taking problematic groups of individuals out of everyday society and interning them in isolated institutions. This was an era of expansion of large orphanages and reformatories for children, of rambling mental hospitals – and of monolithic prisons.[3] In simple terms the theory underlying these developments was that these groups of 'problem individuals' were taken away from their home and local environments and placed in a so-called 'benign and supportive environment' under the care of trained and experienced professionals in order to be educated or treated or reformed before being allowed to return to society.

As far as prisoners were concerned this meant being separated from all negative influences. They were confined in individual cells and were not permitted to talk to or in some cases even to see other prisoners. They were to be subject only to good influences; to the habit of regular work, study of the Bible and regular visits from the chaplain and the governor. The personal reformation of the prisoner became important.[4] However, the imposition of such a structure bore within it the seeds of its own failure. Technically, this reform of the prisoner was described as rehabilitation. It was based on the assumption that if only the prisoners would do as they were told they could be won away from their lives of crime. The truth is that when properly understood, rehabilitation implies putting on again the garb of citizenship; but this is not a straitjacket into which one can be forced. Certainly an individual can and must be assisted in putting it on but in the final analysis one has to make a personal choice to do so (Bottoms and Preston, 1980; Marshall, 2001).

The theory that individuals could be educated, treated or reformed within large, closed institutions has long since been discredited in most contexts. The orphanages and mental institutions of the last century are relics of the past, remembered today mostly by ongoing public inquiries into the terrible abuse which was perpetrated within many of their walls. It is now generally understood that the necessary services, support and supervision for those who require them can best be delivered within communities, with institutional provision reserved as a last resort. There is one glaring exception. The use of the prison has not only continued; it has expanded exponentially (Cayley, 1998).

In the late 1970s I was appointed Deputy Governor of the new high-security prison in Shotts, Scotland. Less than a mile down the road was Hartwood Psychiatric Hospital, an imposing 19th-century citadel which then held over 1,500 patients and employed a large number of men and women from the surrounding villages. Yet within 20 years Hartwood Hospital was no more. The patients had been removed, the majority to be cared for within their communities, and the empty building stood as an abandoned relic of a bygone social philosophy. Shotts Prison, on the other hand, has not only expanded in size but has been completely rebuilt in the process. It would be inconceivable in the United Kingdom today that we should build a psychiatric hospital to hold 1,500 men and women in conditions of close confinement. Yet we continue to adhere to and expand this concept in our prison systems, attempting to put a 21st-century gloss on 19th-century principles which have been abandoned long since by others.[5]

The veneer of prison as a place of reform has been retained, at least as a concept, in some parts of North America where since the 1970s prisons have been described as 'correctional institutions' staffed by 'correctional officers' and administered by 'correctional services'. Yet in some parts of the United States the dark heritage of the prison is not even below the surface; it is clear for all to see. Located near the border with Mississippi, the Louisiana State Penitentiary is one of the largest maximum security prisons in the United States, holding 6,300 prisoners under the supervision of 1,800 staff. It is commonly known as Angola or by its nicknames 'The Farm' or 'The Plantation'. Its 18,000-acre farm, formerly a cotton plantation, is still worked by predominately Black prisoners supervised by predominately White guards on horseback. It is named after the country in southern Africa from which many of the Louisiana slaves were taken in the 19th century.[6]

With over two million men, women and children in prison the United States has almost 20 per cent of the estimated world total (Herivel and Wright, 2003; Ruth and Reitz, 2003: 92–117). At the end of the 20th century a slogan which went the rounds was '2 million by 2000', an obscene demand from some quarters that the US should be aiming to lock up that number of its citizens by that date. This demand was realised and Timothy Lynch, Director of the Project on Criminal Justice at the right-leaning public policy research organisation the Cato Institute, was driven to comment at that time:

> America's criminal justice system is going to make history this month as the number of incarcerated people surpasses 2 million

> for the first time. But this is a development for which neither political party will attempt to claim credit. Indeed, people across the political spectrum seem to recognize that this is a sad occasion – an occasion that raises a nagging question: Why do so many Americans need to be kept behind iron bars? To appreciate why this is such an extraordinary moment, one needs to put the 2-million-prisoner factoid into context. It took more than 200 years for America to hold 1 million prisoners all at once. And yet we have managed to incarcerate the second million in only the past 10 years. (Lynch, 2000)

Over the last two decades significant increases in prison numbers have also been recorded in many other countries. Kenneth Clarke was the UK government minister with responsibility for prisons in England and Wales in the early 1990s and he was again given that portfolio in 2010. Following his latter appointment he asked an enchantingly disingenuous question: "When I was last responsible for prisons in 1993 there were 45,000 people in prison; I now find that there are 85,000 people in prison. What on earth has happened?"[7] In common with all good lawyers, Clarke was well aware that he should never ask a question to which he did not already know the answer. In this case he did know the answer and, having sown the seed of doubt with his innocent question, he went on in succeeding months to make clear what he thought the answer should be. First, he announced his intention to look at the way in which courts were using short prison sentences and went on to announce his determination to ensure that people with serious mental illness and drug and alcohol addictions would in future be diverted from imprisonment towards hospital and treatment centres in the community. Within a very short time, as frequently happens with government ministers, he was moved from his portfolio before he could actually achieve any change. But in announcing his priorities for action he was identifying some of the drivers in the increase in the number of people being sent to prison.

Who are the prisoners?

In all jurisdictions people who commit serious crimes are sent to prison. There may be variations in the length of sentence which is imposed but courts will invariably imprison those who are convicted of murder or serious personal violence, of serious drug crimes particularly if they involve trafficking, of serious property crimes and of terrorist or organised crimes.[8] These are the prisoners who often make the media headlines, but the reality is that in any prison system they will constitute a relatively small proportion of the total number of prisoners. In respect of this cohort of prisoners there is an added consideration about how they should be treated in prison. They have to be held in secure and safe custody at all times but that does not mean that it should be inhuman and degrading.[9] This was the challenge with which I grappled at Peterhead as described in Chapter 2. There have been a number of high-profile court cases in different countries in recent years which have confirmed that this balance needs to be maintained at all times. Examples are Ilich Ramirez Sanchez (Carlos the Jackal) in France, Abdullah Öcalan in Turkey and Anders Behring Breivik in Norway. As described in previous chapters, there has been an additional complication because of the tendency in a number of countries to classify entire groups of prisoners as requiring maximum security confinement without taking account of individual circumstances. An example of this is the generic treatment of gang members in the United States and in several countries in Latin America, where one of the important identifying characteristics of a gang member is body tattooing which invariably results in detention within a high-security unit, which in California for instance has implied permanent solitary confinement. It is virtually impossible for an individual who has these tattoos to demonstrate that he no longer needs to be held in such restricted confinement.

However, the vast majority of prisoners do not fall into this high-security category. Instead, they are more likely to be individuals who spend their lives at the margins of normal society, involved in offending as one facet of a disorganised lifestyle. Many have varying levels of mental illness and in daily life they exist outside formal institutional systems, unable or unwilling to find regular employment, often homeless and in a tenuous relationship with public health and social services. In many situations these mentally ill men and women exist below the radar of any supportive social or health service. They only come above the radar when they are accused of committing a crime. And the part of the formal system in which they pop up is the criminal justice system; a system which is singularly ill-equipped to deal with their problems. So they find themselves caught up in what is known as the revolving door syndrome. And that revolving door continues to turn. These are the sort of men whom I encountered in F Wing in Brixton Prison in the early 1990s and it was there that one of the less auspicious decisions in my professional past caught up with me.

When I first went to Peterhead Prison I found that in addition to the main population of high-security prisoners there was also a small number of men who were there for historical reasons; prisoners who were serving relatively short sentences but who were unable to function in local prisons for a variety of reasons. When these men completed their sentences they were provided with a travel warrant for the journey back to their home town and ushered out of the gate of the prison. One day a senior officer came to me with an unusual request. One of these men, I will call him Donald, who had served several short sentences in the prison was due for release. The officer explained to me that Donald moved around a great deal and had no real roots. When he had been asked where he wished to go on release he had replied that he would really like to go to London as he had never been there. The senior officer asked for my authority that Donald could be issued with a travel warrant to London. It was clear to me that part of the officer's thinking was that this would take Donald off our hands and we would be unlikely to see him back in Peterhead. After a moment's hesitation and against my better judgement, I agreed and the next day Donald was driven to Aberdeen station and deposited onto a London train. Two years later I was on my first day in charge of Brixton Prison and began my walk around the prison. Staff and prisoners were slightly on edge, wondering how to react to this new Governor. As I entered F Wing there was a momentary hush as everyone looked me up and down. Suddenly the relative silence was broken by a shout from the top landing: "Hey, Mr Coyle. How are you, man?" It was Donald. I called him down and he informed me that he was serving a three-month sentence for shoplifting. With a wry smile he chided me, "I suppose you thought you had got rid of me." Prison, whether in the far north of Scotland or in deepest south London, was the only home that Donald knew.

It is the 'Donalds' of this world and their cousins who are drug and alcohol abusers, persistent petty thieves and those with undiagnosed mental illness who constitute the majority in many of the prisons of the world. Differentials in imprisonment rates between countries are often due to the manner in which each society deals with people who are at its margins.[10] In some it can be argued that imprisonment is used as a form of social control for marginalised groups and for individuals who find it difficult to cope, for whatever reason, in a modern and competitive society.[11]

In many jurisdictions prison is used as a means of dealing with those who are outside the mainstream of society in other ways, often because of their race or their ethnic origin. It is a truism that if one wishes to know which are the marginalised groups in any society, one need only look inside its prisons. In Central Europe it will be the Roma, in

Australia it will be the Aboriginals, in New Zealand it is the Māori, and the situation is little different in the United Kingdom. Most of the prisoners in Brixton in the 1990s were Black – and most of the staff were White. The definition of which groups constitute 'the other' is a dynamic one.[12] In a world of increasing global movement of people it has come to include people who are non-nationals. In 22 jurisdictions in Western Europe over 20 per cent of prisoners are foreign nationals, and in nine of those the rate is over 40 per cent.[13]

There is a great deal of evidence that many societies are becoming increasingly intolerant of those who do not conform to the expected norm, of those who disturb the way of life of the majority, of those whom we might describe as 'the other'. One of the most unusual and unexpected examples of this marginalisation is the treatment of the isolated elderly men and women who are being imprisoned in Japan as described in Chapter 8. This highlights in a dramatic fashion the consequences of what is likely to happen if societies continue down the path of expanding the groups who are to be defined as 'the other' and then proceed to marginalise these groups behind the high walls and fences of the prison.

The purpose of imprisonment

Over the years the reality of imprisonment has remained singularly impervious to change. Charles Dickens visited Pentonville Prison in London in 1850 and found much to criticise in his writings about this and other London prisons.[14] If he were to visit Pentonville today he would be equally disenchanted with what he would find. In 2015 HM Chief Inspector of Prisons for England and Wales reported that he had found prisoners in Pentonville 'located in filthy cells with no eating utensils, toiletries or adequate bedding. … Many men shared very small and cramped cells designed for one and too often the cells had little furniture, extensive graffiti and broken windows' (HM Chief Inspector of Prisons, 2015: 5).

In the Introduction a question was posed as to whether imprisonment has now become 'too convenient a device for dealing with the complexities of human failure'. This resonates with the comment by Vaclav Havel, who was later to become President of the Czech Republic, when writing from his prison cell to his wife about his experiences and those of his fellow prisoners, questioning 'the fact that prisons must exist and that they are as they are, and that mankind has not so far invented a better way of coming to terms with certain things' (Havel, 1990: 270).

Before considering what that 'better way' might be, we should lay down a few markers. In the first place we need to distinguish between the *purpose* of imprisonment, that is, the reason why the court sends a person to prison, and the *objective* of imprisonment, that is, how a person should be treated while in prison. In common with all court sentences this punishment is essentially retrospective in nature; that is to say, it looks back to the crime which has been committed and an individual's responsibility for that crime.[15] The task of the court is to make a judgement as to whether the crime which has been committed and the convicted person's culpability for it are such that the individual should be punished by being deprived of liberty and, if so, for what period of time. That is the main purpose of imprisonment.[16]

Once a person passes through the gates of a prison the prison administration looks to the future, and its task is threefold, focussing on security, on safety and good order inside prisons, and on providing opportunities for persons who are in its care to prepare for their future. In short, prison administrations have an obligation to treat prisoners decently and humanely and to help them to prepare to lead law-abiding lives after release. In international law this is encapsulated in the International Covenant on Civil and Political Rights, Article 10.3: 'The penitentiary system shall comprise treatment of prisoners the essential aim of which shall be their reformation and social rehabilitation' (United Nations, 1976). However, the prison is by definition a place of exile from the community, even allowing for the fact that the degree of exile can be considerably reduced in some instances. This means that prisons are not best placed to prepare people for life after release; in the much quoted phrase of Alexander Paterson, an eminent English Prison Commissioner in the early years of the 20th century: 'It is impossible to train men for freedom in a condition of captivity' (Fox, 1952: 357). This dictum has been borne out by what we have discovered in our tour of prisons of the world. Yet a century after Paterson reached this conclusion politicians and others still find difficulty in accepting its truth.

Efforts in a number of countries to establish in prisoners 'the will to lead law-abiding and self-supporting lives after their release and to fit them to do so', as the UN Standard Minimum Rules for the Treatment of Prisoners: Rule 91 (United Nations, 2015) recommends, have traditionally concentrated on attempting to change people as individuals by reducing the personal weaknesses or failings which have led them to commit crime and by giving them new skills which they can use positively in the future. These are all important initiatives and are to be encouraged but they are not in themselves sufficient.[17] As an example, the Scottish Prison Service of today is light years away from the service which I joined in 1973 in respect of the conditions in its prisons and the way it treats prisoners. However, in terms of its rehabilitative impact the problem is that if what one is doing is inappropriate to begin with, then one merely ends up doing the inappropriate thing better; doing it more effectively and more efficiently perhaps, but still doing an inappropriate thing: attempting to 'train men [and women] for freedom in a condition of captivity'.

That is not to deny instances where there have been positive developments in specific cases and at particular moments in time. In terms of individual prisons one can point to Butner Federal Correctional Institution in North Carolina for its progressive management of difficult prisoners in the early 1980s (Minnis, 1980: 13–16) and to Grendon Prison in England which continues to do similar work at the present time (Genders and Player, 1995); to Boronia Centre for Women in Western Australia where women with small children are prepared for release in a family environment, described by the Inspector of Custodial Services (2018) as 'a shining light in the corrections environment'; and to Bastøy and Halden prisons in Norway. In terms of instigators of far-reaching change within prison systems one thinks of K.J. Lång, one of the key drivers of reform in Finland in the 1980s; of Hans Tulkens who drove through change in the Netherlands prison service in the 1970s and 1980s before becoming founding chairperson of PRI; of Pavel Moczydlowski (1992) who transformed the Polish prison system in the early 1990s from its harsh Soviet tradition to become for a few years a model for the region; and of Roberto Santana, father of the New Model prison system in the Dominican Republic which is described in Chapter 9. Also, over the last two decades there has been an increasing amount of applied academic research into human relationships in prison and what has been described as the quality of prison life. In the UK this has been spearheaded by the Prisons Research Centre in Cambridge University under the direction of Alison Liebling (2004). An excellent example of civil society involvement in prison reform is to be found in New Zealand where the *Rethinking Crime and Punishment* initiative inspired by Sir Kim Workman, one-time Director of the national Corrections Department, has given rise to a new and increasingly influential programme of work by young people driving the *JustSpeak* movement for change in the criminal justice system in New Zealand.[18]

A close study of most of these examples demonstrates that attempts to help people who are in prison to turn their lives around are more likely to be successful when they are linked to a wider aspiration to make communities safer for everyone. One way of achieving this has been by expanding the focus of attention beyond the individual offender to include community and locality. Members of every community want to be safe, to feel safe and to have a greater sense of social inclusion. In terms of responding to these wishes, the criminal justice system has a role to play, but it is a limited one. Rather than concentrating exclusively on the actions of individuals, there is evidence that community safety and security can best be enhanced by initiatives which focus more attention on the location where crime occurs, on the environment and on communities in their entirety (Clear, 2007).

An immediate alternative: justice reinvestment

The intellectual case for a new approach based on community safety and security has been constructed gradually over a number of years. In the United Kingdom one stimulus came from a somewhat unexpected source. Michael Tonry has been Professor of Criminal Law and Policy at the University of Minnesota since 1990. Between 1999 and 2005 he was also Director of the Institute of Criminology at Cambridge University and he used that period to cast a critical eye over criminal justice policy in England and Wales, publishing two major pieces of work in the process. The first (Tonry, 2003) was an edited analysis of the attempts by the New Labour government to deliver on its promise to be 'tough on crime, tough on the causes of crime' and its so-called 'evidence based policy making'. His second book (Tonry, 2004) was a trenchant criticism of the failure of that policy in which he questioned why the UK government had emulated some of the conspicuously unsuccessful policies adopted in the United States. Tonry went on to advocate the need for a radical rethinking of criminal justice policy. This plea was taken up by Bottoms et al (2004) as part of an initiative entitled *Rethinking Crime and Punishment*.

These initiatives built on work which had been carried out earlier in the United States over a number of years by scholars such as Elliott Currie (1998) and Jeremy Travis (2005). Their work and that of others had been picked up at a practical level in a variety of disparate settings and was eventually brought together under the general heading of Justice Reinvestment (Tucker and Cadora, 2003). Very broadly, this has involved assessing the total resources, financial and other, that are expended on the criminal justice system; evaluating what benefit members of the public and taxpayers get from this expenditure; and considering whether there might be other ways of distributing these considerable resources to provide a better return on the investment:

> New research is leading to new strategies for reinvesting the resources that already go toward criminal justice. There is a growing awareness that the criminal justice system cannot effectively restore prisoners to their old neighborhoods without reorganizing resources to make resettlement a primary mission. Moreover, policy makers are beginning to recognize that successful re-entry depends on strong civil institutions, and therefore it cannot be achieved by the criminal justice system alone.[19] From within this crisis of purpose, reconceived measures of performance are spurring innovative experiments in justice reinvestment and attracting diverse, new players. (Cadora, 2007: 9–16)

What became known as the Justice Reinvestment approach had two initial drivers. One was a financial need to control the multibillion-dollar expenditure on prisons at a time of reducing public budgets. The other was a realisation that a significant proportion of people in prison came from quite narrowly defined neighbourhoods. Some of these were described as 'million dollar blocks', meaning that this was the amount it cost each year to imprison a small group of young men from a particular block of housing. Research indicated that the cycle of imprisonment followed by return to the community not only affected the individuals involved but also acted to destabilise the community (Clear, 2009: 26–7).

At the same time urban geographers and other social scientists began to make a link with the fact that these were the same neighbourhoods with the highest rates of deprivation, of unemployment and of poor education provision and of social security support.[20] Similar research in Scotland in 2005 found that half of the prisoner population came from just 155 of the 1,222 local government wards and that one quarter came from 53 wards, most of which were in the deprived areas of Glasgow (Houchin, 2005). The question was then asked, sometimes directly to members of the local communities, as to whether some of the million dollars that was spent annually on imprisonment might be spent more efficiently on local services and infrastructure in a way that might make the whole community safer.

The Oregon experience

Denny Maloney worked for 30 years in the State of Oregon Department of Corrections and in the 1990s he had the responsibility of planning for the number of prison places the State would need in the future.

In addition, as a member of Oregon's Commission on Children and Families, he was involved in developing youth programmes and he was struck by the contrast between these two roles. In conversation he told me, "One day I'd be planning children's services for which there was very little funding and the next I'd be projecting prison spending with very few funding constraints." He went on, "I was driving home one day after a meeting and I thought to myself, 'I have just been planning future jails for some of my daughter's kindergarten classmates'." Policy makers were investing in prisons while funding for education was running short. Denny realised that Oregon would have prison beds but not college classrooms for too many of these children.

As in much of the United States the juvenile court system in Oregon was administered by county authorities. However, if a juvenile county court decided to impose a sentence of custody on a young offender, that person would be sent to a state institution which meant that local governments had no political or economic incentive to keep the young person out of prison; indeed, there was a perverse incentive for the county to transfer responsibility for this young person to the state.

Though communities were eager to prevent crime, they lacked the funds to invest in primary prevention programmes. Maloney had a light-bulb moment. What if he could find a way to transfer the funds that the state was spending on prison places for young people to the county authorities to invest in prevention? He put this idea to local business leaders who enthusiastically championed his notion of a community service programme that would make crime prevention a local rather than a state responsibility, and in 1997 Oregon State introduced a new fiscal arrangement. As an experiment, it awarded a block grant to some counties equal to the amount that the state was spending to incarcerate juveniles from these counties each year. Within certain agreed parameters, the county was free to spend the annual grant as it saw fit. If it continued to send the same number of young offenders to state institutions, it would have to pay back that grant to the state. Alternatively, it could choose to spend some of the grant on other resources which were intended to benefit the community and to provide facilities for the young people. The result was a 72 per cent drop in juvenile incarceration from these counties, redeployment of community supervision in those areas in which the young people lived and leverage of new investments in civic service and neighbourhood revitalisation. This model has since been emulated in a number of other states, which have also seen substantial drops in the use of custody for juveniles and the strengthening of local infrastructure.

The Connecticut experience

In the early 2000s the State of Connecticut in the US was having to cope with rising prison numbers at a time when its budget provision was diminishing. As an alternative to new prison building, state officials chose to experiment with a Justice Reinvestment model that reduced the prison population substantially over two years, while crime rates continued to decline. They began by analysing data about prison growth and the locations where people in prison came from and to which they were returning. The research uncovered a significant fact: half the prison population in the state came from a few neighbourhoods in three cities, including one where a single neighbourhood was costing the state $20 million a year in prison and probation costs. By examining not only criminal justice data but also social services data, the study found that people returning from prison lived in the same neighbourhoods as those where a disproportionate number of people received unemployment insurance and where many families received special welfare payments.

This led to a growing political consensus around proposals to reduce the pressure to provide more prison places and to reinvest anticipated savings in local community projects. The state halted its plans to build additional prisons and reduced the annual prisons budget by $30 million, reinvesting much of the savings in the relevant neighbourhoods. These funds went to support community planning processes, to increase the capacity of the local mental health and addiction services to provide more community outreach and treatment, to new probation programmes that focussed on transition from prison to home, and to providing nearly 100 new probation officers to reduce the size of their caseloads. As a consequence, the State of Connecticut went from having one of the fastest growing prison systems in the country to having one which was significantly reduced in size (Cadora, 2007).

Over the last 20 years there has been a growing interest in the potential of Justice Reinvestment initiatives in a number of countries. Between 2005 and 2007 the ICPS undertook a project in partnership with Gateshead Council in the north of England to examine the extent to which the principles of Justice Reinvestment might be applied in an English setting, and the result of this research was published in 2007 (Allen and Stern, 2007). The issue was taken up by the UK Parliament's Justice Select Committee which published a positive report on its findings (Justice Committee, 2010). The work then attracted the interest of the UK Ministry of Justice which published a number of reports on pilot projects beginning in 2012 (Ministry of Justice, 2012).

In Australia the Law Reform Commission has examined the feasibility of applying the concept, particularly in respect of its Aboriginal communities (Australian Law Reform Commission, 2017: 125–47).

All of these Justice Reinvestment initiatives are gradually building up a powerful case which reinforces the argument for reinvesting some of the resources that currently go exclusively into criminal justice processes, and there is an increasing understanding that the criminal justice system on its own cannot effectively help former offenders to be reintegrated into their communities. As the Justice Reinvestment movement begins to point to the end of an excessive societal dependence on criminal justice, it may also hold the promise of a deeper systemic reform, one which recognises that the resolution of issues of public safety need to engage other institutions in civil society including health and housing, workforce development, family and child welfare (Clear et al, 2011).

It also follows that the principles of Justice Reinvestment should not be limited to the use of imprisonment but should apply across the whole panoply of criminal justice institutions, and there is growing interest in how that might be achieved. One instance of the need for a new approach is the manner in which demands on police services have expanded in recent years. In 2014 the Chief Constable of South Yorkshire in the United Kingdom reported that his officers spent just 25 per cent of their time investigating crime while almost half of their work related to 'things other agencies are increasingly moving away from because of their own budget cuts' (Jeeves, 2014). This assertion was backed up in an analysis by the College of Policing in 2015 which found that non-crime-related incidents accounted for 83 per cent of all calls to police Command and Control Centres, while the Metropolitan Police estimated that 15 to 20 per cent of incidents reported to police in London were linked to mental health (College of Policing, 2015). Some of these will be cases like that of 'Donald' mentioned earlier in this chapter.

The importance of these issues in the United States has been highlighted by scholars such as Alex Vitale (2017). Interviewed in *Jacobin* magazine in 2020, he commented:

> Part of the problem is that for decades now, communities have been told that the only resource they can have to address their community problems is more policing and more incarceration. Communities that have very real crime and public safety problems are desperate for help, and if the only thing on offer is policing, they'll ask for policing.

> Our job is to lay out what the alternatives would look like and give people a sense that they have the power to ask for what they really want. Many people in these communities know that they would be better served by a new youth center with mentoring services or anti-violence programs, but they're told that they can never have those things. People have insecurities, and we have to overcome this idea that the only way to address them is policing. And we can do that in very specific targeted ways. What I often recommend when I travel around the country talking to community organizations is that we should start with a community needs assessment: what are the public safety needs that you're facing that have been turned over to the police to manage? And once we've identified those, we can start to think about what the alternatives might look like. (Uetricht, 2020)

A longer-term alternative: focus on human development

The Justice Reinvestment initiatives which have been developed to date have tended to concentrate on a reallocation of existing funding from criminal justice to social and community programmes. This is an excellent starting point but in the longer term there will have to be a more radical approach. One possible means of achieving this could be through an increased emphasis on what is known as the theory of human development. In the words of the United Nations Development Programme (UNDP), this approach is about 'expanding the richness of human life, rather than simply the richness of the economy in which human beings live'.[21] The theory was first proposed by the economist Mahbub ul Haq (1996) and has been developed since by his colleague the social philosopher Amartya Sen, through his work on economic theories related to indexes of human welfare and well-being (Sen, 2000, 2006, 2009). It is an approach that is focussed on people and their opportunities and choices. In very brief terms, the human development approach is concerned with realising the full potential of people so as to increase their access to opportunity and choice. To put it another way, the human development approach has a positive focus on future improvement in contrast to the criminal justice approach which has a retrospective focus on the reduction of crime. The theory is simply stated but achieving its reality is complex. Since 1990 the UNDP has produced regular progress reports on wide-ranging themes which contribute to this development, largely by means of the Human Development Index which attempts to measure, however incompletely, the basic features of human development across countries in respect, for example, of income, education and life expectancy.[22]

In an attempt to put flesh on the bones of the Development Index in the year 2000 the United Nations agreed eight Millennium Development Goals (MDGs) with the aim of achieving them by 2015.[23] The MDGs did not deliver total success but successive reports indicated that they did result in significant progress. In 2012 the United Nations began the process of establishing the next generation of Sustainable Development Goals (SDGs) for the following 15 years and these were agreed by the General Assembly in late 2015.[24] One criticism of the earlier MDGs had been that they came to be regarded primarily as targets for poor countries to achieve with support from wealthy countries. In contrast every country is expected to achieve the new SDGs and each broad goal includes several detailed targets.

For the purposes of our argument an important feature of the new SDGs is that they include a specific reference to justice. Goal 16 is a commitment to *Promote peaceful and inclusive societies for sustainable development, provide access to justice for all and build effective, accountable and inclusive institutions at all levels*. This recognises that there is a significant interrelation between the rule of law and human development and that their mutual reinforcement is essential for sustainable development at national and international levels. The fundamental importance of Goal 16 is that the issue of justice in its broadest sense now takes its place alongside the other goals which deal with issues such as poverty, hunger, health, education, equality and productive employment. Goal 16 includes ten targets, one of which is a commitment to 'strengthen relevant national institutions, including through international cooperation, for building capacity at all levels, in particular in developing countries, to prevent violence and combat terrorism and crime'.

This approach has crucial implications for the way that criminal justice systems operate and specifically for the way that imprisonment is used. It is important to understand that this will not undermine the core role of the criminal justice system, nor will it deny the use of imprisonment in cases when it is necessary. Instead, it will clarify their purpose and restrict them within their proper parameters. The responsibility of individuals for their own actions will still be acknowledged but the influence of other factors will also be taken into account. Amartya Sen (2000: 12) has drawn attention to this in his writings: 'There is a deep complementarity between individual agency and social arrangements. It is important to give simultaneous recognition to the centrality of individual freedom and to the force of social influences on the extent and reach of individual freedom.' The interrelation between all of these issues and the primacy which should be given to any one of them such as individual agency (that is, personal responsibility) in specific instances is likely to be complex particularly for government and other institutions which are used to operating in silos and are reluctant to read across to other official silos. Sen (2000: 79) hits the nail on the head when he comments that: 'many technocrats are sufficiently disgusted by its messiness to pine for some wonderful formula that would simply give us ready-made weights that are "just right".' These comments have particular resonance for criminal justice systems which focus exclusively on 'individual agency' and which have led governments, politicians and others to seek one simple solution to the challenge of 'reducing re-offending', expecting to find it exclusively within criminal justice processes. Adopting a human development approach may well take politicians and traditional criminal justice experts beyond their comfort zone and into a debate which they and others will find just too 'messy', to use Sen's term. But it is a debate which we should not avoid. The relevance of this approach, particularly through reference to the SDGs, has been emphasised as follows:

> Another strength is that the SDGs address complex and cross-sector problems. They involve much more than technological change. They are problems without straightforward solutions, and so they require a better understanding of how social issues interact with political and technological ones, behavioural changes and critical feedback processes. (Mariana Mazzucato, 2021: 109)

A proper application of the human development approach could provide a way out of the vicious circle of an ever increasing use of criminal justice systems, which are very expensive in fiscal and also in human terms, in a vain attempt to resolve problematic behaviour by individuals and groups; behaviour which should not be ignored but which criminal justice institutions are ill-equipped to alter. Particularly in a time of world economic austerity the argument for a redistribution of the large expenditure on reactive criminal justice solutions to proactive community solutions becomes increasingly relevant.

Final comment

So, where have we got to? In this text we have discussed the reality of imprisonment around the world. We have examined the limits of the extent to which the use of imprisonment can contribute to public safety and security and have put down markers about how the manner in which prisons are organised and prisoners are treated needs to be improved. We then proposed that in the future there should be a better distribution of resources between criminal justice and social justice and have suggested that this might be achieved through an application of the principles of Justice Reinvestment. Finally, we have considered whether many of the issues which have traditionally been dealt with through criminal justice processes might be resolved more appropriately within a more comprehensive Human Development approach. There is a long road yet to travel, and a deeper examination of these issues would lead to a discussion, both legal and philosophical, about the concept of justice itself in its various guises and the difficulty of reaching agreement about how these are to be balanced one against the other. We have at least begun that journey by offering some tentative signposts which might lead us, in Havel's phrase, towards *a better way of coming to terms with certain things.*

Notes

Chapter 1

1 The editors of the textbook *Handbook on Prisons* (Jewkes et al, 2016) invited me to contribute an opening chapter reflecting on how prisons had changed over the course of my professional life. That chapter provided me with an opportunity to describe the reality of prison life in the United Kingdom in the early 1970s and to contrast that, not always favourably, with the reality today in the United Kingdom and in other countries. I also described the situation in prisons in England and Wales in more detail in Coyle (2005).

2 Unless stated otherwise, all prison statistics in the text are taken from World Prison Brief. Available at www.prisonstudies.org

Chapter 2

1 The story of the infamous riot in Attica in 1971 and the violent reaction by the authorities is told in Bell (1985).

2 Traditionally the Chief Officer was the senior uniformed officer in each prison. A good 'Chief' was the eyes and ears of the Governor, respected (and sometimes feared) by everyone in the prison. In 1987 the rank had been abolished and all Chief Officers came out of uniform to become middle-ranking governor grades. In May 1988 in Peterhead the man in question was still referred to universally by staff and prisoners as the 'Chief', despite now wearing civilian clothes – and his former uniform still hung in his office for all to see.

3 Until 1999 the Scottish Office was the department of the United Kingdom government led by the Secretary of State for Scotland which exercised a wide range of government functions, including the administration of prisons.

4 The original intention had been that this statement of policy on the management of long-term prisoners would be followed by similar papers on the management of short-term prisoners, of women prisoners and of young prisoners, but these never materialised.

5 Lord Woolf and his team had visited Shotts Prison and we had discussed the way the prison was operating after the publication of the SPS report *Opportunity and Responsibility*. What he learned in Scotland influenced some of his recommendations.

6 See, for example, 'Brixton Comes Out of Solitary', *The Guardian*, 14 October 1991.

Chapter 3

1 About Our Agency', Federal Bureau of Prisons, accessed 4 May 2020. www.bop.gov/about/agency/

2 Todd Asker et al *v* Governor of the State of California. C 09-05796. CW Settlement Agreement in the US District Court for the Northern District of California.

3 One of the outputs of the conference was an edited book by J. Lobel and P. Scharff Smith (eds) (2020) to which I contributed a chapter on 'The Management of High Security Prisoners: Alternatives to Solitary Confinement'.

4 This is available at www.csc-scc.gc.ca/publications/005007-9009-eng.shtml

5 According to the latest (2018) figures from Prison Policy Initiative, the imprisonment rate for Black males in state and federal prisons is 2,272 per 100,000 compared to 392 per 100,000 for White males: www.prisonpolicy.org/blog/2020/07/27/disparities/

Chapter 4

1 Details of the projects undertaken by ICPS and the research reports which it published can be found on the website: www.prisonstudies.org

Chapter 5

1 There is a wide literature on the particular features of women's imprisonment. Examples are: Carlen, P. (1983, 2002, and Carlen and Worral, 2013) and Owen et al (2017); the authors provide extensive bibliographies. HM Chief Inspector of Prisons (2005) also contains a review of some of the relevant literature at that time, largely in respect of England and Wales.

2 Rodriguez, M.N. (2010) provides a useful perspective on the need to adopt a gender perspective when considering the imprisonment of women while Núñez, D (2010) focusses on the treatment of women in Latin American prisons.

Chapter 6

1 Gulag: Acronym for Glavnoe Upravlenie Lagerei (Main Administration of Labour Camps).

2 Sergei Dovlatov (2011) has written a fictionalised chronicle of his experiences working as a guard in an industrial labour colony in the 1960s which captures the reality of daily life in the Gulag at that time.

3 Sukalo was subsequently appointed Chairman of the Supreme Court of Belarus in 1997, a post which he still held at the end of 2020.

4 See, for example, Melnichuk, T. and Yanutsevich, T. (2020) 'My Brothers on Europe's Last Death Row'. *BBC News* [online] 5 June, available at www.bbc.co.uk/news/stories-52938422

5 Abramkin was a nuclear scientist who had served six years in prisons and in a Siberian colony for anti-Soviet propaganda before being sent into exile to the Tver region in 1985. While in the camps, Abramkin, who had been dismissed in 1976 from the Moscow Institute of Chemical Technology for 'anti-Soviet activity', contracted tuberculosis and its side-effects plagued him for the rest of his life. In 1988, along with fellow dissident Andrei Sakharov, he founded the Prison and Liberty group that later became the Moscow Centre for Prison Reform and then the Centre for Criminal Justice Reform. In the mid-1990s we worked closely with him on a number of penal reform initiatives. He died in January 2013.

6 Among those contributing was Hongda Harry Wu, who had been detained for 19 years in Chinese labour camps. Wu, a gentle unassuming human being, has written a searing description of his own experiences (Wu, 1992) in a dark subworld which continues to exist today.

7 It was during this period that Laura Piacentini, now of Strathclyde University, was given unique permission to undertake her groundbreaking fieldwork in colonies in Siberia and elsewhere, which provided the basis for her excellent analysis of the prison system in post-Soviet Russia (2004).

Chapter 7

1 One of the most quoted aphorisms in prison literature is 'The degree of civilisation in a society can be judged by entering its prisons', invariably attributed to Fyodor Dostoyevsky. I have used it myself on many occasions, referencing it to his *House of the Dead*. I have always been slightly concerned that I could never find the exact reference and recently went so far as to re-read that book carefully and still could

not find the quotation. I then came across an article in the December 2019 issue of the *Los Angeles Review of Books* by Ilya Vinitsky entitled 'Dostoyevsky Misprisioned' which argues quite conclusively that this dictum is not to be found in *House of the Dead* or anywhere else in Dostoyevsky's writing. Still, it's a worthy sentiment although henceforth I should attribute to 'Anonymous'.

2 Varlam Shalamov may well have passed through Zlatoust in the late 1930s en route to the mines of Kolyma where he laboured for 15 years. His classic text, *Kolyma Tales* (1994), recaptures some of the horrors he and others went through as well as describing how they managed to survive.

Chapter 8

1 General Na remained in charge of prisons in Cambodia until late 1999 when he returned to California. He had been progressively marginalised because of his political links to the FUNCINPEC opposition party.

2 See, for example, Vida, T. (2018) 'PM sets Prison Overcrowding Meeting', *Khmer Times* [online] 28 November, available at www.khmertimeskh.com/50553740/pm-sets-prison-overcrowding-meeting/ and Chheng, N. (2020) 'Ministry Tackles Overcrowding in Local Prisons', *The Phnom Penh Post* [online] 8 March, available at www.phnompenhpost.com/national/ministry-tackles-overcrowding-local-prisons

3 The historical details are taken from the information leaflet published by the Tuol Sleng and Documentation Center of Cambodia, 1994.

4 Two informative books on this dark period of Cambodia's history have been written by the French ethnologist, Francois Bizot. In the first (2004) he describes his capture by the Khmer Rouge in 1971 and his interrogation by a young revolutionary named Kaing Guek Eav. In the second (2012) he recounts the discovery that his former jailer had become the infamous 'Comrade Duch' who was in charge of Tuol Sleng and how he gave evidence at Duch's trial for war crimes in 2009.

5 Available at https://undocs.org/pdf?symbol=en/CAT/C/JPN/CO/2

6 Available at https://undocs.org/pdf?symbol=en/CAT/C/JPN/CO/2

7 Private Prison Opens in Yamaguchi.

8 www.mine-center.go.jp

9 Reference has already been made in Chapter 5 to Hongda Harry Wu's description of his 19 years in Chinese labour camps. He expands on these bitter experiences in Wu and Wakeman (1994).

10 Dikotter (2002) describes how Western models of imprisonment came to be superimposed on a traditional Chinese view of society.

Chapter 9

1 La Modelo de Bogotá quedó destruida e internos se niegan a ser identificados: Minjusticia http://zonacero.com/judiciales/la-modelo-de-bogota-quedo-destruida-e-internos-se-niegan-ser-identificados-minjusticia

2 'Guatemala Prison Shooting Kills at Least Seven Inmates', www.bbc.co.uk/news/world-latin-america-48196130

3 'In Honduras, "Gangs Effectively Control the Prisons"', www.worldpoliticsreview.com/trend-lines/28469/how-gangs-effectively-control-honduran-prisons

4 https://upsidedownworld.org/news-briefs/news-briefs-news-briefs/el-salvador

5 See, for example, Jennifer Peirce. 'Overuse of Pretrial Detention in Tension with Judicial and Prison Reforms in the Dominican Republic', *Latin American Law Review*, No. 5 (2020): 45–69. https://doi.org/10.29263/lar05.2020.03

Chapter 10

1 Available at UN CCPR/C/BRB/3 Para 307
2 Application of the Inter-American Commission on Human Rights before the Inter-American Court of Human Rights. Case 12.480. Lennox Boyce, Jeffrey Joseph, Frederick Benjamin Atkins and Michael Huggins (Boyce et al) *v* Barbados.
3 Inter-American Court of Human Rights. Case of Boyce et al *v* Barbados. Judgment of November 20, 2007. www.corteidh.or.cr/docs/casos/articulos/seriec_169_ing.pdf

Chapter 11

1 When mentioning Rwanda, one might recommend Carla Tertsakian's book (2008) on the lives of prisoners in Rwanda. Its title *Le Chateau* refers not to a French-style grand country house but to the name given by prisoners to the one or two planks of wood which constituted the space for a prisoner in grotesquely overcrowded conditions.
2 Hansard. HC Deb 3 November 2010, Vol. 517, col. 921.
3 www.mandela.gov.za/mandela_speeches/1998/980625_dcshr.htm

Chapter 12

1 Yedioth Ahronoh (p5) via *Israel News Today*. 2 May 2002.
2 House of Commons Hansard Written Ministerial Statements for 14 Mar 2006 (pt 2) (parliament.uk).
3 In his book *Elusive Peace* Ahron Bregman (2005: 212–19) places the Jericho Monitoring Mission into the wider context of the Israeli/Palestinian conflict of the time.

Chapter 13

1 Harding, C. et al (1985) is a useful primer on the development of the prison in England and Wales. It includes a helpful review of literature and sources until the time of its publication. McConville (1981) provides a detailed analysis of the interplay between policy and practice in England and Wales up to the centralisation of the system in 1877. David Garland has published extensively on the role of punishment in modern society, most notably in *Punishment and Modern Society* (1990) and *The Culture of Control* (2001).
2 The global dimension of imprisonment in its various historical guises and its culturally specific incarnations is examined by Dikotter and Brown (2007). Shankardass (2000) has edited an informative volume which links punishment theories with prison practices from an Indian as well as an international perspective.
3 Jay (2016) has written a fascinating history of the successive incarnations of the madhouse, onto the asylum, to the mental hospital and beyond. A standard text on the development of the modern model of imprisonment is Foucault (1977). Ignatieff (1978) also provides a concise overview.
4 Gorringe (1996) examines the relationship between penal strategies and theologies of atonement.
5 It has to be remembered that the closure of the former large institutions for the mentally ill was not matched by a provision of adequate community support. As is described later in this chapter, the consequence has been that for a significant number of the men and women in question the only available institutional alternative is the prison. The issue of 'decarceration' is discussed in Scull (1977).

[6] One of the 'Angola 3' mentioned in Chapter 3 has written a compelling account of the 44 years which he spent in Angola (Rideau, 2011).

[7] *Channel 4 News*, 30 June 2010.

[8] One issue which is a matter of contention in some countries is the increasing use of preventive detention; that is, sending a person to prison or detaining them in prison after completion of sentence on the grounds of a continuing risk of future criminal activity or threat to public safety. See, for example, Keyzer (2013).

[9] Principles for the management of prisoners who require to be held in high-security conditions are described in detail in Coyle and Fair (2018: 76–83).

[10] Lappi-Seppälä has provided strong evidence for this in much of his work. See, for instance, Lappi-Seppälä (2011: 303–28).

[11] There is an extensive body of literature on the implications of using imprisonment as a means of social control. A good starting point would be Cohen (1985). Mauer and Chesney-Lind (2002) analyse the social and economic cost of mass imprisonment in the United States and Christie (1993, 2004) has written a number of critical texts.

[12] There is a growing literature on the phenomenon of the increasing number of Muslim prisoners, particularly in European prison systems. Beckford et al (2005) is one example of this.

[13] A comprehensive overview of the treatment of foreign national prisoners in European countries is provided in van Kalmthout et al (2007).

[14] See, for example, *Household Words*, Vol. 1, Magazine No. 5, 27 April 1850. Available at https://prisonvoicesmaria.wordpress.com/2018/01/17/the-separate-silent-system-impact-and-defiance/

[15] The relationship between sentencing theory and the imposition of punishment, including imprisonment, is expertly analysed in Ashworth and Wasik (1998), and the work of Duff (1986) and Lippke (2007) is particularly relevant to the argument in this chapter.

[16] The theory of punishment as a social institution is discussed at length in Duff and Garland (1994), with the introductory chapter by the two editors providing a summary of the relationship between punishment and imprisonment.

[17] Haney (2006: 38) has written in detail and in a convincing manner about failed attempts to realise the rehabilitative ideal in prisons, concluding that 'these beliefs reduced to the core notion that prisoners could and should be remade and reformed through the treatment they received in prison'.

[18] www.justspeak.org.nz/

[19] For several years in the United States it has become increasingly common to use the term 're-entry' in preference to terms such as 'rehabilitation' as a way of placing emphasis on the need for individuals to be assisted to re-enter their communities. This, of course, predicates the need for the existence of a genuine community in the first place.

[20] In the United Kingdom the work of Dorling (for example, 2015, and Dorling and Thomas, 2016) has been particularly important in this field.

[21] United Nations Development Programme. Available at http://hdr.undp.org/en/humandev

[22] http://hdr.undp.org/en/content/human-development-index-hdi#

[23] Reports on the UN Millennium Development Goals are available at www.un.org/millenniumgoals

[24] Available at https://sustainabledevelopment.un.org/

References

Achebe, C. (1958) *Things Fall Apart*, London: William Heinemann Ltd.

Allen, R. and Stern, V. (eds) (2007) *Justice Reinvestment: A New Approach to Crime and Justice*, London: International Centre for Prison Studies.

Angiolini, E. (2012) *Report of the Commission on Women Offenders*, Edinburgh: Scottish Government.

Arbour, L. (1996) *Commission of Inquiry into Certain Events at the Prison for Women in Kingston*, Ottawa: Public Works and Government Services Canada.

Ashworth, A. and Wasik, M. (eds) (1998) *Fundamentals of Sentencing Theory*, Oxford: Clarendon Press.

Australian Law Reform Commission (2017) *Pathways to Justice: An Inquiry into the Incarceration Rate of Aboriginal and Torres Strait Islander Peoples*, Sydney: Australian Government.

Beckford, J., Joly, D. and Khosrokhavar, F. (2005) *Muslims in Prison: Challenge and Change in Britain and France*, Basingstoke: Palgrave Macmillan.

Bell, M. (1985) *The Turkey Shoot: Tracking the Attica Cover-up*, New York: Grove Press Inc.

Billy Wright Inquiry Report (2010), London: The Stationery Office.

Bizot, F. (2004) *The Gate*, London: Vintage Books.

Bizot, F. (2012) *Facing the Torturer: Inside the Mind of a War Criminal*, London: Rider.

Bocanegra, N. (2016) '"Hundreds" of Dismembered Bodies Found in Drain Pipes at Colombian Jail', *Independent* [online], 18 February, available at www.independent.co.uk/news/world/americas/hundreds-dismembered-bodies-found-drain-pipes-colombian-jail-a6881416.html

Bottoms, A. and Preston, R. (1980) *The Coming Penal Crisis*, Edinburgh: Scottish Academic Press.

Bottoms, A., Rex, S. and Robinson, G. (2004) *Alternatives to Prison: Options for an Insecure Society*, Cullompton: Willan Publishing.

Bregman, A. (2005) *Elusive Peace: How the Holy Land Defeated America*, London: Penguin Books.

Cadora, E. (2007) 'Justice Reinvestment in the United States' in R. Allen and V. Stern (eds) *Justice Reinvestment: A New Approach to Crime and Justice*, London: International Centre for Prison Studies.

Carlen, P. (1983) *Women's Imprisonment: A Study in Social Control*, London: Routledge & Kegan Paul.

Carlen, P. (ed) (2002) *Women and Punishment: The Struggle for Justice*, Cullompton: Willan Publishing.

Carlen, P. and Worral, A. (2013) *Analysing Women's Imprisonment*, London: Routledge.

Carroll, R. (2006) 'Bars, Brothels and a Regime of Terror: Inside the Jail Run by Its Inmates', *The Guardian* [online], 30 September, available at www.theguardian.com/world/2006/sep/30/rorycarroll.mainsection

Cassese, A. (1996) *Inhuman States: Imprisonment, Detention and Torture in Europe Today*, Cambridge: Polity Press.

Cayley, D. (1998) *The Expanding Prison: The Crisis in Crime and Punishment and the Search for Alternatives*, Toronto: Anansi Press.

Christie, N. (1993) *Crime Control as Industry: Towards Gulags, Western Style*, London: Routledge.

Christie, N. (2004) *A Suitable Amount of Crime*, London: Routledge.

Clear, T. (2007) *Imprisoning Communities: How Mass Incarceration Makes Disadvantaged Neighborhoods Worse*, New York: Oxford University Press.

Clear, T. (2009) 'Incarceration and Communities', *Criminal Justice Matters*, Vol. 75, No. 1.

Clear, T., Hamilton, J. and Cadora, E. (2011) *Community Justice (2nd edition)*, Abingdon: Routledge.

Cohen, S. (1985) *Visions of Social Control*, Cambridge: Polity Press.

College of Policing (2015) *Estimating Demand on the Police Service*, London: College of Policing.

Corston, J. (2007) *The Corston Report: A Review of Women with Particular Vulnerabilities in the Criminal Justice System*, London: Home Office.

Council of Europe (1991a) CPT/Inf (91)15, *Report to the United Kingdom Government on the Visit to the United Kingdom Carried Out by the European Committee for the Prevention of Torture and Inhuman or Degrading Treatment or Punishment (CPT) from 29 July 1990 to 10 August 1990*, Strasbourg: Council of Europe.

Council of Europe (1991b) CPT/Inf (91)16, *Response of the UK Government to the Report of the European Committee for the Prevention of Torture and Inhuman or Degrading Treatment or Punishment (CPT) from 29 July 1990 to 10 August 1990*, Strasbourg: Council of Europe.

Council of Europe (2013) CPT/Inf (2013)41, *Report to the Russian Government on the Visit to the Russian Federation Carried Out by the European Committee for the Prevention of Torture and Inhuman or Degrading Treatment or Punishment (CPT) from 21 May to 4 June 2012*, Strasbourg: Council of Europe.

Council of Europe (2020) CPT/Inf (2020)18, *Report to the United Kingdom Government on the Visit to the United Kingdom Carried Out by the European Committee for the Prevention of Torture and Inhuman or Degrading Treatment or Punishment (CPT) from 13 to 23 May 2019*, Strasbourg: Council of Europe.

Coyle, A. (1990) 'Chomsky: An Opportunity for Personal Reappraisal', *Scottish Child Magazine*, April–May.

Coyle, A. (1994) *The Prisons We Deserve*, London: Harper Collins.

Coyle, A. (2002) *A Human Rights Approach to Prison Management: Handbook for Prison Staff*, London: International Centre for Prison Studies.

Coyle, A. (2005) *Understanding Prisons*, Maidenhead: Open University Press.

Coyle, A., Fair, H., Jacobson, J. and Walmsley, R. (2016) *Imprisonment Worldwide: The Current Situation and an Alternative Future*, Bristol: Policy Press.

Coyle, A. and Fair, H. (2018) *A Human Rights Approach to Prison Management: Handbook for Prison Staff (3rd edition)*, London: Institute for Criminal Policy Research.

Currie, E. (1998) *Crime and Punishment in America*, New York: Metropolitan Books.

Dallin, D. and Nicolaevsky, B. (1947) *Forced Labour in Soviet Russia*, New Haven: Yale University Press.

Darke, S. and Garces, C. (eds) (2017) 'Informal Dynamics of Survival in Latin American Prisons', *Prison Service Journal*, No. 229, Jan.

Dikotter, F. (2002) *Crime, Punishment and the Prison in Modern China*, New York: Columbia University Press.

Dikotter, F. and Brown, I. (2007) *Cultures of Confinement: A History of the Prison in Africa, Asia and Latin America*, London: Hurst and Co.

Dorling, D. (2015) *Injustice: Why Social Inequality Still Persists*, Bristol: Policy Press.

Dorling, D. and Thomas, B. (2016) *A 21st-Century Atlas of the UK*, Bristol: Policy Press.

Dovlatov, S. (2011) *The Zone: A Prison Guard's Notes*, Richmond: One World Classics.

Drucker, E. (2011) *A Plague of Prisons: The Epidemiology of Mass Incarceration in America*, New York: The New Press.

Duff, A. and Garland, D. (eds) (1994) *A Reader on Punishment*, Oxford: Oxford University Press.

Duff, R. (1986) *Trials and Punishment*, Cambridge: Cambridge University Press.

Erlanger, S. and Myre, G. (2006) 'Israelis Seize 6 in Raid on Prison in the West Bank', *The New York Times*, 15 March, available at www.nytimes.com/2006/03/15/world/middleeast/israelis-seize-6-in-raid-on-prison-in-the-west-bank.html

Evans, M. and Morgan, R. (1998) *Preventing Torture: A Study of the European Convention for the Prevention of Torture and Inhuman or Degrading Treatment or Punishment*, Oxford: Clarendon Press.

Fieser, E. (2014) 'Dominican Republic's More Humane Prison Model', *Reuters* [online], 22 May, available at https://uk.reuters.com/article/uk-dominican-prison-reform/dominican-republics-more-humane-prison-model-idUKKBN0E21IR20140522

Flin, R. and Arbuthnot, K. (eds) (2002) *Incident Command: Tales from the Hot Seat*, Ashgate: Aldershot.

Foucault, M. (1977) *Discipline and Punish: The Birth of the Prison*, London: Allen Lane.

Fox, L. (1952) *The English Prison and Borstal Systems*, London: Routledge & Kegan Paul.

Freeman, J. (1989) 'Air of Hope in the Granite Fortress', *The Glasgow Herald*, 8 July.

Fukada, S. (2018) 'Japan's Prisons are a Haven for Elderly Women', *Bloomberg* [online], 16 March, available at www.bloomberg.com/news/features/2018-03-16/japan-s-prisons-are-a-haven-for-elderly-women

Garland, D. (1990) *Punishment and Modern Society*, Oxford: Clarendon Press.

Garland, D. (2001) *The Culture of Control: Crime and Social Order in Contemporary Society*, Oxford: Oxford University Press.

Genders, E. and Player, E. (1995) *Grendon: A Study of a Therapeutic Prison*, Oxford: Clarendon Press.

General Board of Directors of Prisons in Scotland (1841) *Annual Report*, London: HMSO.

Goffman, E. (1961) *Asylums: Essays on the Social Situation of Mental Patients and Other Inmates*, New York: Anchor Books.

Gorringe, T. (1996) *God's Just Vengeance: Crime, Violence and the Rhetoric of Salvation*, Cambridge: Cambridge University Press.

Haney, C. (2006) *Reforming Punishment: Psychological Limits to the Pains of Imprisonment*, Washington: American Psychological Association.

Harding, C., Hines, B., Ireland, R. and Rawlings, P. (1985) *Imprisonment in England and Wales: A Concise History*, Beckenham: Croom Helm.

Hatton, D. and Fisher, A. (eds) (2009) *Women Prisoners and Health Justice: Perspectives, Issues and Advocacy for an International Hidden Population*, Abingdon: Radcliffe Publishing Ltd.

Havel, V. (1990) *Letters to Olga*, London: Faber & Faber.

Herivel, T. and Wright, P. (eds) (2003) *Prison Nation: The Warehousing of America's Poor*, New York: Routledge.

HM Chief Inspector of Prisons (1990) *Report of an Inspection of HM Prison Brixton*, London: Home Office.

HM Chief Inspector of Prisons (1993) *Report of an Inspection of HM Prison Brixton*, London: Home Office.

HM Chief Inspector of Prisons (2005) *Women in Prison: A Literature Review*, London: HM Inspectorate of Prisons.

HM Chief Inspector of Prisons (2015) *Report of an Unannounced Inspection of HM Prisons Pentonville, 2–13 February 2015*, London: HM Inspectorate of Prisons.

Home Office (1991) *Custody, Care and Justice: The Way Ahead for the Prison Service in England and Wales*, London: HMSO.

Houchin, R. (2005) *Social Exclusion and Imprisonment in Scotland*, Glasgow: Glasgow Caledonian University.

Howard, J. (1777) *The State of the Prisons in England and Wales*, New Jersey: Patterson Smith Reprint Series (1973).

Ignatieff, M. (1978) *A Just Measure of Pain: The Penitentiary in the Industrial Revolution 1750–1850*, New York: Columbia University Press.

Inspector of Custodial Services (2018) *Inspection of Boronia Pre-release Centre for Women*, Perth: Office of the Inspector of Custodial Services.

Inspector of Prisons (2015) *Culture and Organisation in the Irish Prison Service*, Nenagh: Office of the Inspector of Prisons.

Inter-American Commission on Human Rights (2011) *Report on the Human Rights of Persons Derived of Liberty in the Americas*, Washington: Inter-American Commission on Human Rights.

Jay, M. (2016) *This Way Madness Lies: The Asylum and Beyond*, London: Thames & Hudson.

Jeeves, P. (2014) 'Officers Spend Only 25 Per Cent of Their Time Tackling Crime, Says Police Chief', *Daily Express* [online], 5 February, available at www.express.co.uk/news/uk/458045/Officers-spend-only-25-per-cent-of-time-tackling-crime-says-police-chief

Jewkes, Y., Bennett, J. and Crewe, B. (eds) (2016) *Handbook on Prisons (2nd edition)*, Abingdon: Routledge.

Justice Committee (2010) *Cutting Crime: The Case for Justice Reinvestment*, London: The Stationery Office.

Kalinin, Y. (2002) *The Russian Penal System: Past, Present and Future*, London: International Centre for Prison Studies.

Keyzer, P. (ed) (2013) *Preventive Detention: Asking the Fundamental Questions*, Cambridge: Intersentia Publishing Ltd.

Kleinig, J. (1998) 'The Hardness of Hard Treatment' in A. Ashworth and M. Wasik (eds) *Fundamentals of Sentencing Theory*, Oxford: Clarendon Press.

Lappi-Seppälä, T. (2011) 'Explaining Imprisonment in Europe', *European Journal of Criminology*, Vol. 8, No. 4, July.

Lewis, D. (1997) *Hidden Agendas: Politics, Law and Disorder*, London: Hamish Hamilton.

Liebling, A. (2004) *Prisons and Their Moral Performance: A Study of Values, Quality and Prison Life*, Oxford: Oxford University Press.

Lippke, R. (2007) *Rethinking Imprisonment*, Oxford: Oxford University Press.

Lobel, J. and Scharff Smith, P. (eds) (2020) *Solitary Confinement: History, Effects, and Pathways Towards Reform*, Oxford: Oxford University Press.

Lynch, T. (2000) 'All Locked Up', *The Washington Post* [online], 20 February, available at www.washingtonpost.com/archive/opinions/2000/02/20/all-locked-up/5cf3e070-9d9b-45f5-b337-00f2609c1985/

Marshall, C. (2001) *Beyond Retribution*, Cambridge: Eerdmans Publishing.

Mauer, M. and Chesney-Lind, M. (eds) (2002) *Invisible Punishment: The Collateral Consequences of Mass Imprisonment*, New York: The New Press.

Mazzucato, M. (2021) *Mission Economy: A Moonshot Guide to Changing Capitalism*, London: Allen Lane.

McConville, S. (1981) *A History of English Prison Administration*, Vol. 1, 1750–1877, London: Routledge & Kegan Paul.

McCurry, J. (2008) 'Pills and Porridge: Prisons in Crisis as Struggling Pensioners Turn to Crime', *The Guardian* [online] June 19, available at www.theguardian.com/world/2008/jun/19/japan

Mills, H. (1993) '"Remarkable" Improvement at Brixton Jail: Inspector Applauds Transformation at Once-squalid Remand Prison', *The Independent*, [online] 5 August, available at www.independent.co.uk/news/uk/remarkable-improvement-at-brixton-jail-inspector-applauds-transformation-at-oncesqualid-remand-prison-1459270.html

Mills, H. (1996) 'Prison Mothers to Stay in Chains', *The Independent*, 10 January.

Ministry of Justice (2012) *Justice Reinvestment Pilots: First Year Results*, London: The Stationery Office.

Minnis, M. (1980) 'Program Participation of Federal Inmates Involved in the Butner FCI Correctional Experiment', *Journal of Correctional Education*, Vol. 31, No. 2, June.

Moczydlowski, P. (1992) *The Hidden Life of Polish Prisons*, Bloomington: Indiana University Press.

Morris, N. and Rothman, J. (eds) (1995) *Oxford History of the Prison*, Oxford: Oxford University Press.

Moscow Centre for Prison Reform (1996) *In Search of a Solution: Crime, Criminal Policy and Prison Facilities in the Former Soviet Union*, Moscow: Human Rights Publishers.

Narim, K. (2020) 'Prey Sar Prison No Longer Accepts Inmates Due to Overcrowding', *Khmer Times* [online] 21 January, available at www.khmertimeskh.com/50681546/prey-sar-prison-no-longer-accepts-inmates-due-to-overcrowding

Núñez, D. (2010) 'Women, Prison and Human Rights: An Outlook of the Current Situation in Latin America' in E. Carranza (ed) (2010) *Crime, Criminal Justice and Prison in Latin America and the Caribbean*, San José: ILANUD.

Office of the Correctional Investigator (2019) *Office of the Correctional Investigator Annual Report 2018–2019* [online], available at www.oci-bec.gc.ca/cnt/rpt/annrpt/annrpt20182019-eng.aspx

Office of the High Commissioner for Human Rights (2005) *Manual on Human Rights Training for Prison Officials*, Geneva: United Nations.

Office of the High Commissioner for Human Rights (2017) *Statement by UN High Commissioner for Human Rights Zeid Ra'ad Al Hussein at the End of His Mission to El Salvador* [online], available at www.ohchr.org/EN/NewsEvents/Pages/DisplayNews.aspx?NewsID=22412#

Oleinik, A. (2003) *Organized Crime, Prison and Post-Soviet Societies*, Aldershot: Aldgate.

Omaria, W. (1997) *Prison Conditions in Africa: Report of a Pan-African Seminar, Kampala, Uganda, 19–21 September 1996*, London: Penal Reform International.

Owen, B., Wells, J. and Pollock, J. (2017) *In Search of Safety: Confronting Inequality in Women's Imprisonment*, Oakland: University of California Press.

Physicians for Human Rights (1995) *Health Conditions in Cambodia's Prisons*, Boston: Physicians for Human Rights.

Piacentini, L. (2004) *Surviving Russian Prisons: Punishment, Economy and Politics in Transition*, Cullompton: Willan.

Rideau, W. (2011) *In the Place of Justice: A Story of Punishment and Redemption*, London: Profile Books.

Rodriguez, M.N. (2010) 'Women in Prison: An Approach from the Gender Perspective' in E. Carranza (ed) *Crime, Criminal Justice and Prison in Latin America and the Caribbean*, San José: ILANUD.

Ruth, H. and Reitz, K. (2003) *The Challenge of Crime: Rethinking Our Responses*, Cambridge: Harvard University Press.

Rybakov, A. (1988) *Children of the Arbat*, London: Hutchinson.

Sachs, A. and Coyle, A. (2015) 'The Right to Vote', *Scottish Justice Matters*, Vol. 3, No. 1.
Scharff Smith, P. (2014) *When the Innocent Are Punished: The Children of Imprisoned Parents*, Basingstoke: Palgrave Macmillan.
Scottish Prison Service (1989) *Current Issues in Scottish Prisons: Systems of Accountability and Regimes for Difficult Prisoners*, Edinburgh: Scottish Prison Service.
Scottish Prison Service (1990) *Opportunity and Responsibility: Developing New Approaches to the Management of the Long Term Prison System in Scotland*, Edinburgh: HMSO.
Scull, A. (1977) *Decarceration: Community Treatment and the Deviant: A Radical View*, New Jersey: Prentice-Hall Inc.
Sen, A. (2000) *Development as Freedom*, Oxford: Oxford University Press.
Sen, A. (2006) *Identity and Violence*, Oxford: Oxford University Press.
Sen, A. (2009) *The Idea of Justice*, London: Penguin Books.
Shalamov, V. (1994) *Kolyma Tales*, London: Penguin Books.
Shankardass, R. (ed) (2000) *Punishment and the Prison: Indian and International Perspectives*, New Delhi: Sage.
Shifrin, A. (1982) *The First Guidebook to Prisons and Concentration Camps of the Soviet Union*, New York: Bantam Books.
Solzhenitsyn, A. (1973) *The Gulag Archipelago*, Glasgow: Wm Collins.
Stern, V. (ed) (1999) *Sentenced to Die? The Problem of TB in Prisons in Eastern Europe and Central Asia*, London: International Centre for Prison Studies.
Straw, J. (1997) *New Approaches to Crime and Punishment*, London: International Centre for Prison Studies.
Tertsakian, C. (2008) *Le Chateau: The Lives of Prisoners in Rwanda*, London: Arves Books.
Tonry, M. (ed) (2003) *Confronting Crime: Crime Control Policy Under New Labour*, Cullompton: Willan Publishing.
Tonry, M. (2004) *Punishment and Politics: Evidence and Emulation in the Making of Crime Control Policy*, Cullompton: Willan Publishing.
Travis, J. (2005) *But They All Come Back: Facing the Challenges of Prisoner Reentry*, Washington, DC: Urban Institute Press.
Tucker, S. and Cadora, E. (2003) *Ideas for an Open Society: Justice Reinvestment*, Vol. 3, No. 3, Open Society Institute.
Uetricht, M. (2020) '"Policing is Fundamentally a Tool of Social Control to Facilitate Our Exploitation": An interview with Alex Vitale', *Jacobin* [online] 8 June, available at https://jacobinmag.com/2020/06/alex-vitale-police-reform-defund-protests
ul Haq, M. (1996) *Reflections on Human Development*, Oxford: Oxford University Press.

UN Centre for Human Rights (1994) *The State of Cambodian Prisons*, Phnom Penh: UNCHR.

UN Economic and Social Council (1994) *Report of the Special Rapporteur on Torture on his Visit to the Russian Federation*, New York: United Nations.

United Nations (1976) *International Covenant on Civil and Political Rights*, adopted by UN General Assembly resolution 2200A (XXI) of 16 December 1976; entered into force 23 March 1976.

United Nations (2015) *Standard Minimum Rules for the Treatment of Prisoners (The Nelson Mandela Rules)*, adopted by UN General Assembly resolution 70/175 of 17 December 2015.

United Nations Committee Against Torture (UNCAT) (2013) *Concluding Observations on the Second Periodic Report of Japan, Adopted by the Committee at Its Fiftieth Session (6–31 May 2013)* [online], available at https://undocs.org/pdf?symbol=en/CAT/C/JPN/CO/2

van Kalmthout, A., Hofstee-van der Meulen, F. and Dunkel, F. (eds) (2007) *Foreigners in European Prisons*, Nijmegen: Wolf Legal Publishers.

Vantour, J. (1984) *Report of the Study Group on Murder and Assaults in the Ontario Region*, Ottawa: Correctional Service of Canada.

van Zyl Smit, D. and Dunkel, F. (2001) *Imprisonment Today and Tomorrow*, The Hague: Kluwer Law International.

Vitale, A. (2017) *The End of Policing*, Brooklyn: Verso.

Walmsley, R. (2017) *World Female Imprisonment List (4th edition)*, London: Institute for Crime & Justice Policy Research.

Walmsley, R. (2018) *World Prison Population List (12th edition)*, London: Institute for Crime & Justice Policy Research.

Watts, J. (2002) 'Inhumane Behaviour', *The Guardian* [online], 15 November, available at www.theguardian.com/world/2002/nov/15/worlddispatch.japan

Woolf, L. (1991) *Prison Disturbances April 1990 (The Woolf Report)*, London: HMSO.

Wu, H. (1992) *Laogai: The Chinese Gulag*, Boulder: West View Press.

Wu, H. and Wakeman, C. (1994) *Bitter Winds: A Memoir of My Years in China's Gulag*, New York: Wiley.

Yamaguchi, M. (2010) 'Prisons Trying to Cope With Swelling Elderly Population', *The Japan Times* [online], 9 December, available at www.japantimes.co.jp/news/2010/12/09/national/prisons-trying-to-cope-with-swelling-elderly-population/

Index

References to endnotes show both the page number and the note number (231n3).

Q

R